P9-BYA-251

SLEEPING GIANT

Also by Tamara Draut

Strapped: Why America's 20- and 30-Somethings Can't Get Ahead

SLEEPING GIANT

How the New Working Class Will Transform America

TAMARA DRAUT

Doubleday

NEW YORK LONDON TORONTO SYDNEY AUCKLAND

 Published in the United States by Doubleday, a division of Penguin Random House LLC, New York, and distributed in Canada by Random House of Canada, a division of Penguin Random House Limited, Toronto.

www.doubleday.com

DOUBLEDAY and the portrayal of an anchor with a dolphin are registered trademarks of Penguin Random House LLC.

Book design by Maria Carella
Jacket design by John Fontana
Jacket photograph © Victor J. Blue/Bloomberg Via Getty Images

Library of Congress Cataloging-in-Publication Data
Draut, Tamara.
Sleeping giant : how the new working class will transform America / Tamara Draut.—First Edition.
pages cm
ISBN 978-0-385-53977-7 (hardcover)—ISBN 978-0-385-53978-4 (ebook)
1. Working class—United States—History—21st century. 2. Diversity in the workplace—United States—History—21st century. 3. United States—Economic conditions—21st century. I. Title.
HD8072.5.D73 2016
305.5'620973—dc23 2015034385

MANUFACTURED IN THE UNITED STATES OF AMERICA

1 3 5 7 9 10 8 6 4 2

First Edition

FOR MY DAD

Servants, laborers and workmen of different kinds make up the far greater part of every political society. But what improves the circumstances of the greater part can never be regarded as an inconveniency to the whole. No society can surely be flourishing and happy, of which the far greater part of the members are poor and miserable. It is but equity, besides, that they who feed, clothe and lodge the whole body of the people, should have such a share of the produce of their own labor as to be themselves tolerably well fed, clothed and lodged.

—Adam Smith, *The Wealth of Nations*, 1776

Contents

SLEEPING GIANT

Introduction

My father died a few short months after the city of Detroit declared bankruptcy. He was a steelworker, the epitome of the person you likely conjure up when you hear someone described as "working class." White, male, hard hat and lunch pail, steel-toed boots, and a dark blue uniform he'd bring home at the end of every shift and promptly throw in the washing machine. The earthy, sweaty, and metallic smell lingered in the laundry room after he closed the lid. He was America's hero, the brawny backbone of American prosperity and a broad middle class the likes of which the world had never seen. These were the men who soldered, heaved, and secured America's industrial might in the world, and as a result earned the pride and respect of our nation.

That working class is dead, Detroit's bankruptcy a blunt symbol of its ultimate demise.

But *the* working class is not dead.

It's just different. No longer shuttered away in a factory, today's working class is interwoven into nearly every aspect of our lives. It's the black woman in a caretaker's smock wearing special comfort shoes and a name tag above her heart. It's the white man in a uniform (which he had to pay for) who punches in each day and restocks the shelves of your favorite big-box store. It's the Latina home health aide who cares for your mom, the janitor who empties your office wastebasket, the woman who rings up your groceries, and the crew who fix the bumpy freeway you take every day to work.

Yet despite how interwoven this new working class is in our lives, we don't really know enough about it. Its members' concerns don't shape the national agenda or top the headlines in major newspapers. Their stories aren't featured in sitcoms, dramas, or movies. The words "working class" have been scrubbed from our social and political lexicon, rendering invisible the millions of workers who buttress the middle class at best and straddle poverty at worst.

But attention must be paid to the new working class. Our lives—all of our lives—would grind to a halt if the working class waged a general strike. Its sheer scale in size and diverse demographics will shape the future of American politics. And our nation's prosperity will be defined by whether we address its members' declining living standards.

It was in the spring of 2013 that this new working class introduced itself to the world with coordinated walkouts of fast-food workers in major cities across the country. This took place just a few months before the cradle of our once blue-collar nation went bankrupt. But the old blue-collar nation typically paid its workers hourly wages of $17 or more. The fast-food workers—who clock in to one of the largest occupations in America today—were protesting wages that hover around $8 an hour. What began as a movement among fast-food workers has since mushroomed into a major worker justice movement known as the Fight for $15, in which home-care workers, airport workers, adjunct professors, retail workers, and fast-food workers have all come together to fight for better wages and working conditions. It is the tip of the spear of the Sleeping Giant, staking a claim and fertilizing the seeds of a new working-class solidarity.

In just a few short years, the Fight for $15 has been able to claim significant victories, from consciousness-raising to policy changes in red states and blue states. In the 2014 elections, voters in Alaska, Arkansas, Nebraska, and South Dakota passed ballot measures to raise their states' minimum wage.[1] And voters in San Francisco approved a $15 minimum wage increase, matching Seattle's groundbreaking increase. In 2015, Los Angeles joined the list of cities raising the minimum wage to $15 an hour.

For working-class people who aren't engaged directly in the growing chorus of workers taking to the streets, the movement brings attention to their needs and struggles. But as important, the movement emphasizes the dignity and value of their jobs. I've interviewed people all across this country, from the Bible Belt to the East Coast, from the Rust Belt to the Pacific Northwest, and one of the most common grievances they express is the lack of respect they experience in the workplace, and in our society more broadly. Whatever their job, the individuals I talked to described their work as meaningful and embedded with purpose, yet they also told me about the disrespect they get on the job from their bosses and in society from politicians.

For LaShawn* and Michelle, who in many ways typify the new working class, their work is deeply gratifying. The African American couple, both in their late thirties, have been married for twelve years and live on the outskirts of Atlanta. LaShawn is a commercial sanitation driver, emptying Dumpsters at restaurants, apartment complexes, and local businesses for $16.10 an hour. Michelle is a certified nursing assistant (CNA), providing care for the elderly in their homes. She recently switched jobs and now works as a

---

* The names of individuals in this book have been changed. While most people were comfortable using their real names, many of these individuals shared complaints and insights about their workplaces that could make them vulnerable to retaliation by their employer or coworkers. Their race or ethnicity reflects the way they identified their own race or ethnicity during our interview. All names of individuals who work for labor, nonprofit, or other movement-oriented organizations are real.

supervisor, earning $9 an hour for overseeing a staff of CNAs and ensuring that each client receives the best possible care. They both grew up in Atlanta and are now raising their own children there. They love their jobs, deriving true personal satisfaction and pride from their work. Driving a garbage truck is a childhood dream come true for LaShawn, who always had a passion for trucks and sees his job "as getting to play with this big machine and getting paid for it." Yet as we got further into the conversation, it became clear that his pride finds little reciprocation from management. In LaShawn's case, workers are often clocked out by management to avoid paying overtime, even though they're still working—a practice known as wage theft, which is increasingly common in today's working-class jobs. To get close to forty hours, Michelle used to work seven days a week, a pace she maintained for three and a half years before taking her current position. Paying their monthly bills is a challenge, and often credit cards fill in the gap when cash is short. Asked what they'd do if they were paid more, LaShawn said they'd "actually be able to take a check and pay rent and have money set aside to buy groceries. Right now, the way our checks are, you have to make a conscious decision: If I don't pay this bill, I can take that money and put it toward groceries." LaShawn also mentioned that he'd like to have the money to treat his kids and wife to a dinner out or a night at the movies. But he doesn't think our nation's elected officials are much concerned about his family's dreams and struggles. "It feels like the working class are the lepers of society. Needed to carry out the economy, to hold it and make it strong, but disregarded when it comes to our needs," he told me.

As LaShawn and Michelle's story illustrates, gone are the generous pensions, health insurance coverage, and paid vacations that characterized the working-class jobs of the industrial era. Today's service-sector serfs are fighting for the most basic of job perks: a decent paycheck, a stable schedule with enough hours, and paid time off when they or their children are sick. The new working class has jobs, but those jobs no longer provide a livelihood. Let that sink in. A job no longer provides a livelihood for the working class. No matter how you define "working class"—as individuals without bachelor's degrees, as people who get paid by the hour, or as workers who aren't managers or supervisors—its members constitute the majority of American workers and even American adults.

Defining the New Working Class

Social scientists use three common methods to define class—by occupation, income, or education—and there is really no consensus about the "right" way to do it. Michael Zweig, a leading scholar in working-class studies, defines the working class as "people who, when they go to work or when they act as citizens, have comparatively little power or authority. They are the people who do their jobs under more or less close supervision, who have little control over the pace or the content of their work, who aren't the boss of anyone."

Using occupational data as the defining criteria, Zweig estimated that the working class makes up just over 60 percent of the labor force.[2] The weakness of using occupational data to define class is that most political surveys do not capture the occupation of the respondent, making it impossible to ensure consistency in research that draws upon both economic and political data sets, as I do in this book.

The second way of defining class is by income, which has the benefit of being available in both political and economic data sets. Yet defining the working class by income raises complications because of the wide variation in the cost of living in the United States. An annual income of $45,000 results in a very different standard of living in New York City than it does in Omaha, Nebraska. Incomes are also volatile, subject to changes in employment status or the number of hours worked in the household, making it easy for the same household to move in and out of standard income bands in any given year.

The third way to define class is by educational attainment, which is how I've defined the working class in this book. Education level has the benefit of being consistently collected in both economic and political data sets, but, more important, education level is strongly associated with job quality. The reality is that the economic outcomes of individuals who hold bachelor's degrees and those who don't have diverged considerably since the late 1970s. While people with bachelor's degrees experienced real wage growth in the thirty years between 1980 and 2010, incomes among those with only a high school education or some college declined precipitously. Today having a college degree is essential (but no guarantee, of course) to securing a spot among the professional middle class. As unionized manufacturing jobs got sent overseas, the once blurred lines between occupation and class grew quite sharp. The blue-collar middle class is an endangered species, shrunk to a size that makes it no longer identifiable in national surveys. The downside of using education to define the working class is that education is not a perfect proxy for establishing the power or autonomy one has in the workplace or society—the traditional definition of class. There are definitely well-educated workers who hold menial jobs or jobs that pay low wages, just as there are less-well-educated workers who have jobs with great autonomy or power. It is a blunt definition, but in the aggregate it is a reasonably accurate way to distinguish between the working class and the middle class.

In this book, "working class" is defined as individuals in the labor force who do not have bachelor's degrees. This includes high school dropouts, high school graduates, people with some college, and associate's-degree holders. It includes the unemployed, who are counted as still in the labor force as long as they are actively looking for work. Because it is increasingly difficult, and some would argue nearly impossible, to reach the middle class without a bachelor's degree, the middle class is defined in this book as workers with a bachelor's degree or higher. This both distinguishes the type of work performed by the working class and the middle class and reflects a major distinction in how these different classes of workers earn their pay. Nearly six out of ten workers in America are paid hourly wages, as opposed to annual salaries.[3] And the majority (eight out of every ten) of these hourly workers do not hold a bachelor's degree. As a result of the divergence in economic fates experienced by those with and without bachelor's degrees, today's middle class is overwhelmingly a professional class, comprising workers who get paid annual salaries, work in an office setting, and most assuredly do not have to ask permission to take a bathroom break.

The composition of the working class has changed dramatically since 1980:

- The new working class is more racially diverse than it was three decades ago, with more than one-third comprising African Americans (13 percent), Latinos (20 percent), and Asian Americans (4 percent). It's even more diverse if we look at the youngest members of the working class, those aged twenty-five to thirty-four, with people of color making up 47 percent of the younger working class.[4]
- Today, two out of three non-college-educated women are in the labor force, up from just over half in 1980. Meanwhile, non-college-educated men are in the labor force at a lower rate than they were in 1980, down from nine out of ten to eight out of ten.
- Only 13 percent of the working class holds jobs in the manufacturing sector, down from one-quarter in 1980. Today one out of five working-class employees holds a job

in the behemoth retail sector and another one out of five holds a job in the catchall category of professional and related services, a sector that includes the mushrooming health services occupations.[5]

- The median hourly wage of today's working class is $15.61—a full $1.30 less than it was in 1980, after adjusting for inflation.[6] Today more than one-third of full-time workers earn less than $15 an hour, and fully 47 percent of *all* workers earn less than $15 an hour.[7] Close to half of workers making less than $15 per hour are over the age of thirty-five.[8]
- Only five out of the thirty occupations that will add the most jobs to our economy in the next decade will require a bachelor's degree.[9]
- The five occupations that employ the largest number of workers include only one clear middle-class job requiring a bachelor's degree: registered nurse. The rest of America's largest occupations are retail salespeople, cashiers, food service and prep workers, and janitors.[10] Contrary to popular opinion, most of these jobs are not filled by teenagers but by adults who are trying to support themselves and their families with this work.

Despite the elite's fixation on entrepreneurship and knowledge workers, America is powered by wage-earners who punch the clock, wear uniforms, and don't remotely have any power to "lean in" to climb the corporate ladder. For decades now we've been sold the idea that a growing army of knowledge workers, innovating and ideating in amenity-rich office parks, hold the key to our nation's prosperity. Column after column written by the likes of Thomas Friedman and David Brooks argue that the future success of our economy rests on cultivating skills such as creative problem-solving and critical thinking, with a special affinity for fields in science, technology, and engineering. What they fail to acknowledge is that those spots in our labor force are minuscule compared to the scads of new jobs being created in home health care, fast food, and retail. This elite blind spot continues to distort our economic thinking and denigrates the majority of work being done in our country.

The most profound impact of globalization and technology has been the upheaval experienced by workers without college degrees. With so many factories shuttered, typical "men's work" steadily eroded and lower-paying service jobs took its place. As the economic contribution of these former working-class heroes to our nation dwindled, millions of men became zeroes in many people's minds. They seemed to be a dusty anachronism in a sparkling new economy.

Meanwhile, the ranks of women in the workforce grew steadily during the 1980s and 1990s, and waves of immigration began to change the ethnic and racial composition of the workforce. Seeking refuge from the economic dislocation, millions of Americans earned bachelor's and advanced degrees, a process that perversely exacerbated already hardened lines of privilege, with whites earning college degrees at a much greater rate than blacks or Latinos. As a result, today's working class is more black, Latino, and female than it was in the industrial era. And that very fact—the diversity of this new working class—is a major reason that it has been so easy to ignore, dismiss, and marginalize.

When the working class shifted from "making stuff" to "serving people," it brought with it lots of historical baggage. The long-standing "others" in our society—women and people of color—became a much larger share of the non-college-educated workforce. And their marginalized status in our society carried over into the working class, making it easier to overlook and devalue their work.

When working-class women punched the clock in ever greater

numbers in the 1980s and 1990s, it was nearly entirely in the absence of a union. Unlike the hard-hat guys, America's mushrooming "pink collar" workforce lacked the social solidarity that unions had provided for generations of blue-collar workers. And so working-class women toiled on the margins of political and social awareness while preserving their families' dignity by bringing home a paycheck. That's now changing, as women are at the forefront of the new movement for better wages and working conditions and are now almost as likely as men to belong to unions, closing the long-standing gap in unionization. Yet these workers are rarely referred to as working class but rather as "low-wage workers," a designation that negates any whiff of political power or social solidarity.

The new rules of how this globalized, technology-enhanced labor market would be structured—who would win and who would lose—were heavily influenced by the economic interests of America's business elite. Organized labor had long been on its knees, already caught in the downward spiral toward extinction. What's less recognized is how the working class's loss of economic and political power was the inevitable—and often intentional—outcome of an interconnected web of political and business interests. Beginning in the 1970s, the Republican Party realized it could cynically use race to divide the working class and in so doing unravel support for the social contract established in the New Deal. At the same time, big business had set its sights on big labor and big government, killing off the former and buying off the latter.

The Great Power Shift

During the four decades stretching from the New Deal to the early 1970s, when incomes at the bottom grew faster than or as fast as those at the top and union strength reached its apex, it was possible to assume that the peace accord between labor and capital was permanent. Only now are historians and political scientists able to review those years and understand that the accord was never as firm as many believed. We now know that behind the scenes, business leaders were growing weary of pesky regulations concerning safety, clean air, and workers' rights. They were tired of being pushed around by government and by workers. And so, as executives did, someone wrote a memo outlining a plan and shared it widely with the business community. That person was Lewis Powell, a prominent corporate lawyer (who later became a member of the Supreme Court), and the time was 1971.[11]

In the Powell memo, as it's now referred to, the author asserted that the "American economic system is under broad attack" from all corners of society—the media, the pulpit, politicians, and college campuses, to name just a few.[12] Powell argued that this attack required political mobilization by organized business. "Business must learn the lesson . . . that political power is necessary; that such power must be assiduously cultivated; and that when necessary, it must be used aggressively and with determination—without the embarrassment and without the reluctance which has been so characteristic of American business."

He then went on to outline how to achieve this goal, saying that "strength lies in organization, in careful long-range planning and implementation, in consistency of action over an indefinite period of years, in the scale of financing available only through joint effort, and in the political power available only through united action and national organizations."

It didn't take long for Powell's vision to be realized. In 1971, only 175 firms had registered lobbyists in Washington. By 1982, nearly 2,500 did. And the number of corporate PACs increased from under 300 in 1976 to over 1,200 by the mid-1980s.[13] Today, the halls of our nation's Capitol echo with the shoe leather of twenty-four well-heeled business lobbyists for each member of Congress.

As big business was reasserting its right to write the rules of capitalism, it received a major helping hand from the Supreme Court. In 1976 the Court ruled that spending money to influence elections is a form of constitutionally protected free speech, striking down portions of a law aimed at curbing outside influence in elections beyond those involving direct contributions to candidates. The premise that money was tantamount to free speech created a precedent that the Court has used to continue to unravel commonsense limits on how money can be spent in elections. Most recently, in the Citizens United case, the Supreme Court struck down laws limiting the amount corporations could spend in an election, as long as the money is not given directly to candidates or to a party. Corporations and wealthy individuals can now shovel as much money as they like into television ads to support their preferred candidate or lambast their foe. The 2012 presidential election was the first election in which the new "super PACs" were legal. Super PACs can engage in unlimited political spending ("independent" of the campaign) with funds raised from individuals, corporations, unions, and other groups—all of whom can give as much as they like to the super PAC. And give they did. America's wealthy poured $635 million into the cause of distorting our democracy.[14] And the majority of that money came from just 159 individuals who gave $1 million or more.

But Aren't We All Middle Class?

With the weakening of the working class, issues of economic justice were relegated to the back burner at the very time that so many workers found their livelihoods jeopardized by globalization and technological change. Without the countervailing force of a vibrant working class, historically powered by organized labor, the door was propped wide open for the rise of corporate power and politics dominated by big money. It became easier for Congress to deregulate and loosen worker protections. It became easier for leaders to champion free-trade agreements that sold out labor and enriched capital. And it became easier to load up the tax code with benefits for big business and the wealthy.

When once a steelworker and an accountant could live on the same block, drive the same car, vacation at the same place, and eat at the same restaurants, over the course of the 1980s, 1990s, and the first decade of the 2000s, the once blurred boundaries of class crystallized into sharp, distinct lines. As the earnings of non-college-educated workers declined significantly under deregulation and antiworker policies that undermined the minimum wage and degraded working conditions, the trajectories of those with and without bachelor's degrees diverged significantly—and so did the trajectories of their children. Our social circles constricted and our shared experiences evaporated. This tightening of class hierarchies made it hard for those who shape our public debate—journalists, policymakers, public intellectuals—to relate to the lives and struggles of the majority of their fellow citizens: those without college degrees. For those who make policy and shape the news, their social circle has increasingly become more elite, drawn from privileged families and elite private colleges on the two coasts that bracket the nation.

This homogeneity contributed to a very skewed understanding of working life in America. By the late 1990s, these shapers of our collective understanding had drawn a portrait of the workforce in which professional workers were ubiquitous and a new knowledge-based economy triumphant. In this schematic, America's class structure slowly morphed into three broad categories—the poor, the middle class, and the rich—whose makeup resembles the shape of an hourglass. As Jack Metzger brilliantly articulates in

New Working-Class Studies, "The principal problem with this vernacular [of the middle class] is the way it first hides the working class (by including it within the ubiquitous middle) and then forgets it's there by assuming that almost everybody is college educated, professional, and has a reasonably comfortable standard of living."[15]

Today the obsession with the "middle class"—defined as college-degreed professionals—continues to distort and divert attention away from the reality that the majority of workers in this country aren't professionals by any stretch of the definition. They're laborers, working for hourly wages, often with unpredictable and unstable schedules. They outnumber middle-class professionals by three to one, and there is no evidence that future jobs in America will alter this ratio. We are a working-class nation, and in reality always have been.

It's all too common to hear a political pundit say that most Americans identify as middle class. But it isn't true. Part of the problem is that many polls don't even include the option of identifying as "working class," instead offering only upper, middle, and lower class as options. It turns out that when polls offer "working class" as an option, just as many people self-identify as working class as middle class. The General Social Survey, a long-running public opinion survey, found in 2012 that 44 percent of respondents identified themselves as working class; the same percentage who identified themselves as middle class. Interestingly, black and Latino individuals were much more likely than whites to identify as working class.[16] More than two-thirds of Latinos consider themselves working class, compared to 50 percent of blacks and 38 percent of whites. In fact, in every year since the early 1970s, the percentage of Americans who identify as working class has ranged between 44 and 50 percent.

Working-class Americans know they're working class. It's elites who want to pretend everybody is middle class. Why? Because "middle class" and "working class" are terms laden with racial, moral, and cultural symbolism. Since the enormous middle class was created in the decades following World War II and the New Deal, "middle class" has worked as a shortcut to conjure up a very American ideal: upstanding, hardworking, traditional, suburban white families who lived secure and stable lives in tree-lined neighborhoods. On the other hand, "working class" has been imbued with a struggle for power, for recognition, for fair pay. The working class, by nature a notch below the middle class, is vulnerable to judgmental assertions about its economic lot in life. "If only they had gone to college" or "If only they had a stronger work ethic," then they too might have enjoyed the comforts of a middle-class life. Of course, people of color were missing from both these cultural constructs, relegated to the dark and foreboding category of the urban poor. It's much easier to go to battle for "Americans who did all the right things" and got the rug pulled out from under them than it is to stick up for the hardworking, hard-luck, drew-the-short-end-of-the-stick population who too easily remind us that the American dream is more ephemera than enduring reality. And with a working class that is now more black, Latino, and female, it's a battle even harder to wage, let alone win.

The Sleeping Giant Will Rise

But a battle is taking place—a battle of ideas over the fundamental rules of our economy and society. The moneyed and the connected have won the last few rounds. The social contract born of the New Deal is in tatters. Organized labor is limping, and the large majority of Americans are struggling mightily to make ends meet and build better lives for their children. Unless the majority of Americans—a Sleeping Giant if there ever was one—

reclaim their moral and political authority, there is little reason to believe the status quo will change. Thankfully, the Sleeping Giant is beginning to stir.

The Fight for $15 campaign brings together retail, fast-food, home care, and federal contract workers to demand a higher wage and the right to a union. This new labor unrest has rattled some spare change out of the pockets of our most recognizable brands. In 2014 and 2015, Walmart, Gap, Target, and McDonald's all voluntarily announced plans to slowly raise their bottom-rung wage to $9 per hour.[17] (McDonald's limits this modest pay raise only to those stores it directly controls, not to its franchises, where the overwhelming majority of its workers are employed.) While the spokespeople for these companies won't credit the protesters, the voluntary across-the-board raising of their lowest wage is without precedent. In New York, Governor Andrew Cuomo established a wage board to examine wages in the fast-food industry. In 2015 the wage board voted to approve a $15 minimum wage for fast-food workers at chain restaurants, a policy that will boost the pay of roughly 200,000 workers in the state. In the months following the wage board's vote, Governor Cuomo proposed raising the minimum wage to $15 for all workers in New York State. And these are just the wins racked up outside the arena of elections, which, as mentioned earlier, saw voters approve minimum-wage increases in multiple states and big cities in 2014.

As America heads into the 2016 presidential campaign, it remains to be seen whether the working class will finally have a champion. As I argue throughout the book, a working-class agenda is vital for repairing the destruction caused by decades of misguided policies that have fueled inequality at the top and eviscerated living standards at the bottom. But it's also really good politics. *Sleeping Giant* provides the complete analytical framework for understanding the new working class, covering its central role in our economy and its latent political power in our democracy.

The first two chapters of *Sleeping Giant* provide a thorough examination of the jobs of the new working class and how the proliferation of underpaid work has transformed our labor market into a bargain-basement economy, where the largest numbers of people are, and will continue to be, employed in occupations paying less than $12 an hour. The second chapter goes deep into this economy, chronicling the working conditions faced by the new working class under the deregulation of labor rights and protections. You'll hear from truck drivers, home care workers, retail workers, fast-food workers, and general laborers about the pride they feel in their work, but also about the often demeaning and degrading environment of their workplace. Throughout the book I share the stories of many individuals whose identity I've chosen to protect by changing their names. Other than that, all information is factual and based on interviews conducted between August 2014 and August 2015.

In Chapter 3 the book switches from the economic lives of the new working class to their politics, chronicling a surprising and consistent populism even among today's white working class. Throughout the chapter I compare the political beliefs and ideology of the working class and the middle class, revealing divergences that are important for policymakers, activists, and candidates to understand.

The two middle chapters provide a historical analysis of how working-class political power has shifted over the past half century. Chapter 4 tells the story of the great power shift from the working class to corporate interests that occurred during the 1970s and 1980s and how the corporate capture of both political parties fueled the policies that hurt both working- and middle-class Americans. In Chapter 5 I explore how history shows up in the wallets of the new working class by examining the still profound implications of the legacy of marginalization and exclusion of women and people of color in our politics and our policies.

The next chapter delves into the roles inequality and social distance play in how working-class experiences and needs are often overlooked by our nation's elites, particularly the media and Congress. This chapter also discusses the potential for a new alignment of the working class and the middle class and the major barriers to these groups finding common cause. As I argue throughout the book, the Sleeping Giant is beginning to stir, and much of its rumbling is happening at the municipal and state level.

In Chapter 7 I explore burgeoning working-class activism with nonprofit and labor leaders across the country who are pioneering new strategies to build political power and enact policies that are improving the lives of the new working class. Finally, the last chapter articulates the importance of a revived working-class politics and provides a framework for ensuring that the next generation is given a better deal than their parents.

A revived and new working class is critical for repairing our nation's social and economic divides. But there are major challenges to ushering in this countervailing power: Supreme Court decisions that have hamstrung the ability to rein in corporate and individual political spending, as well as a spate of state laws that have aggressively curtailed the ability for workers to form unions. The reality is that the working class has had a boot on its neck for three decades, but while it has shouldered the brunt of the right-wing assault on workers' rights, all of America has suffered as a result. Empowering today's working class, which we depend on more than ever before, is our best chance to revive our commitment to economic opportunity and widely shared prosperity. The future of the American dream depends on it.

CHAPTER ONE

The Bargain-Basement Economy

By the time I arrived at Atrium Medical Center, the relatively new hospital just outside my hometown of Middletown, Ohio, my dad's care was focused on keeping him as comfortable as possible as his body slowly gave out. He wound up in the hospital after falling down the stairs, which resulted in a punctured lung and broken ribs. Lungs are pretty amazing, and if somewhat healthy will actually close holes and heal on their own. But because his lungs were far too damaged owing to asbestos exposure in the factory, along with a pack-a-day cigarette habit that started in his teens, they were stubbornly refusing to heal. And he was much too weak to be a candidate for surgery.

My dad's chances of surviving after that unlucky tumble were determined by the story of his entire working life. Like many men of his time, he graduated from high school and went right to work at Armco Steel (now AK Steel, since being bought by Kawasaki in the 1990s). He started at the bottom, on rotation and on call for any number of dirty, backbreaking jobs in the coke plant. After about a decade, he enrolled in the company's apprenticeship program to become a machinist. After twenty-nine years of service, he retired with a nice pension and a gold tabletop clock. But his body paid the price. While he was "only" seventy-three years old, his body was well worn, especially his lungs, which instead of being plump like pink cotton candy were pockmarked, strained, and a lifeless gray. As he lay in a morphine-induced state of bare consciousness, our family gathered in this sparkling new medical facility, which my hometown was depending on to revive itself in the post-manufacturing world. Just a mile or so down the two-lane highway on which the ten-building medical campus sits are brand-new upscale developments, complete with stainless-steel appliances, granite counters, and sunken bathtubs. In 2015, AK Steel announced plans to build a new $36 million research and innovation center in Middletown, a major recommitment to the town, and one that would have made my dad proud. The area's proximity to Interstate 75, which connects Middletown to Cincinnati to the south and Dayton to the north, makes it appealing for bedroom communities and office developments.

But none of this was on my mind as I sat in my dad's room all day interacting with a cadre of health-care professionals, each of whom was responsible for one aspect of my dad's care. What did manage to break through the haze was the seemingly endless number of health-care workers who played some role in caring for my dad.

There was the young man in scrubs who was the attending physician's assistant and who, unremarkably, was thought to be the doctor until he responded to a medical question by saying, "That's a question for the doctor—I'm just her assistant." There was the respiratory therapist, who was gentle and efficient. There was the nursing assistant who skillfully turned Dad to change his bandages, her body seemingly too small for the task at hand. Then there were the four young men who gingerly yet powerfully managed to move my dad and all the machines tethered to his body into a new bed. And finally there was the nurse who was on duty during what would be Dad's final hours with us. He was young—maybe late twenties—and wonderfully gifted at his job. I remember wondering how many of these young men and women would probably have worked on the factory floor a generation ago. Today health-service occupations are one of the biggest providers of jobs in the economy. And like the small army that cared for my dad, the wages range from poverty-level to solidly middle class.[1]

The need for legions of health-care workers, still mostly women but with a modest and growing percentage of men, will continue to swell as the baby boomers grow old and frail. In fact, it will be the low-paid health-service jobs that will increase the most as more baby boomers retire. This bargain-basement economy will grow the most for the foreseeable future—not the much-touted knowledge economy. Topping the list of occupations that will add the most jobs to our economy are retail salespeople, child-care workers, food preparers and cooks, janitors, bookkeepers, maids, and truck drivers. Of the thirty occupations that will add the most jobs in the coming decade, half pay less than $30,000 a year.[2]

This is the heart of America's working class today. And it will be even more so tomorrow.

Like the hard-hat working-class jobs of previous generations, today's working-class jobs are physically demanding, in somewhat surprising ways. Take, for example, this common job description for home health aides: "Appreciable physical effort or strain. Moderately heavy activity. May include lifting, constant stooping, and walking." Four decades ago, backbreaking work on the factory floor offered hourly wages in the high teens. Being a home health aide, a common example of a manual labor job, entails lifting and moving people, not slabs of ore, and pays an average of $20,000 a year.[3] At its heyday back in 1970, manufacturing accounted for 30 percent of all jobs, making the United States truly a blue-collar nation. No industry today comes close to the sheer dominance manufacturing had in our economy. But taken together, education and health services, along with leisure and hospitality—two big industries where bargain-basement jobs dominate—match the former heft of manufacturing. That's basically what's behind the transformation of working-class jobs in America. As companies shuttered factories in the United States and income inequality began its steady ascent, jobs for home health aides, child-care workers, fast-food workers, janitors, and waiters swelled to accommodate major cultural and social trends, including the growing disposable income of the upper echelon and the time crunch facing all workers, but especially those who have young children or aging parents to care for.

The New Big Jobs: Feeding, Serving, Caring, and Stocking America

The old leviathan of the blue-collar working class, the auto industry, is commonly referred to as the Big Three, meaning GM, Ford, and Chrysler. In their prime, these companies symbolized American ingenuity, prosperity, and industrial hegemony. Despite major setbacks, including bankruptcy filings, the Big Three automakers have rebounded, though employing a fraction of the workers they did at their peak. And in an unprecedented concession, the United Auto Workers (UAW) union agreed in 2007 to a two-tier wage system, with new workers hired at lower wages and with fewer benefits. Today about 134,000 hourly workers are employed by the Big Three, and a full quarter of those workers earn second-tier wages—$15.79 to $19.28 an hour, compared to the first-tier wage of $28.[4] In 2015, the UAW successfully renegotiated contracts with the Big Three automakers, bringing entry-level wages into line with veteran wages. For example, Fiat Chrysler workers approved a new contract that would bump entry-level workers' pay up to $28 an hour after eight years and provide signing bonuses for new hires.[5] Workers at GM and Ford won similar new wage terms. To the tens of millions of individuals working in today's bargain-basement economy taking food orders, bathing the elderly, mopping floors, and stocking warehouses, even the auto workers' second-tier wages would represent a fat raise. One of the reasons even second-tier wages at the Big Three are higher than the average wages in the jobs that form the backbone of the working class today is that those autoworkers still have a union. The same is no longer true for broad swaths of workers toiling in what has become the largest source of jobs in the auto industry, auto parts manufacturing. Today nearly three-quarters of auto jobs are in parts manufacturing, and increasingly those jobs are being filled by temporary staffing agencies. One estimate found that approximately 14 percent of auto-parts workers were hired through a staffing agency, with paychecks 20 percent lower than those of workers who were hired directly.[6]

The degradation of manufacturing jobs, even when they're brought back to the United States, reveals just how challenging it is for today's workers to fight for a decent living. The fact that the once mighty, union-dense manufacturing sector can devolve into a place of low-paid, temporary staffing gigs is indicative of the power that's been lost by our once working-class heroes. And it underscores the obstacles to rebuilding livelihoods for the majority of American workers.

The largest sources of jobs for the new working class fall into four main groups: retail and food jobs, blue-collar jobs, cubicle jobs, and caring jobs (see Table 1). Many of these jobs exist at the bottom of a long line of contracts and subcontracts, or are staffed by temp agencies, or are part of a franchise system—all forms of hiring that no longer align with existing labor laws written almost a century ago, making them vulnerable to wage theft and unsafe working conditions. These jobs are the giant amoeba of the American labor market, swallowing and engulfing more and more of our workers in a huge blob of low-paying work. This reality is not reflected in TED talks, swanky ideas summits, or other intellectu-

Table 1. The Largest Jobs in the Bargain-Basement Economy (2012)

*One of the 10 largest occupations in the United States

+One of the 10 occupations with largest projected growth in new jobs, 2012–2022

OCCUPATION	PERCENT OF ALL JOBS	NUMBER OF WORKERS	MEDIAN HOURLY WAGE	MEDIAN ANNUAL WAGE
Food and Retail Jobs	11.7%	16,956,000	$9.41	$19,574
Retail sales workers*+		4,668,000	10.29	21,410
Cashiers*		3,338,900	9.12	18,970
Combined food preparation and serving workers, including fast food*+		4,438,100	8.84	18,400
Waiters and waitresses*		2,362,200	8.92	18,540
Cooks		2,148,500	9.88	20,550
Blue-Collar Jobs	7.8%	11,400,600	$12.52	$26,032
Hand laborers and material movers*+		3,428,800	11.04	22,970
Janitors and building cleaners (except maids and housekeeping cleaners)*+		2,324,000	10.73	22,320
Truck drivers		1,701,500	18.37	38,200
Maids and housekeepers		1,434,600	9.41	19,570
Landscapers and groundskeeping workers		1,227,100	11.53	23,970
Construction Laborers+		1,284,600	14.02	29,160
Cubicle Jobs	6.4%	9,293,400	$14.97	$31,127
General office clerks*		2,983,500	13.21	27,470
Customer service representatives*+		2,362,800	14.70	30,580
Secretaries and administrative assistants*+		3,947,100	16.99	35,330
The Caring Jobs	3.4%	4,912,800	$10.17	$21,160
Personal care aides+		1,190,600	9.57	19,910
Home health aides+		875,100	10.01	20,820
Nursing assistants+		1,534,400	11.73	24,400
Child-care workers		1,312,700	9.38	19,510

Source: U.S. Department of Labor, U.S. Bureau of Labor Statistics, Table 1.4, Occupations with the Most Job Growth, 2012 and Projected 2022, at http://www.bls.gov/emp/ep_table_104.htm and Occupational Outlook Handbook *at http://www.bls.gov/ooh/.*

ally elite venues where rumination about the knowledge economy, entrepreneurship, and creative destruction are de rigueur. But make no mistake, it is the economy of our present and our future.

Food and Retail Jobs

Topping the list of the largest number of jobs in the bargain-basement economy are food and retail positions, employing nearly 17 million workers. These workers run the gamut from your order-taker at McDonald's to your waitress at Olive Garden to your cashier at CVS to the salesperson at Macy's. Of course, what they all have in common is low pay and a mandate to help satisfy our consumption needs. Back in 1970 the average American family spent most of its money on food to be eaten at home, with just 25 cents of every dollar spent on eating out. By the beginning of the millennium, 42 cents of every dollar spent on food was for take-out or dining out.[7] And that increased demand for food on the go or a family dinner out is one reason that the so-called leisure and hospitality sector has grown from providing just 8 percent of all jobs in 1970 to providing 12 percent in 2013.[8]

There's an enduring image of retail and food workers as being high school or college students who cruise through during summers or work after school year-round but then kiss those jobs goodbye once they've earned better credentials. But like most stereotypes, this image is far from accurate. Among waiters and waitresses who are officially grown-ups—that is, aged twenty-five to sixty-four—a full eight out of ten do not have a college degree. Similarly, most retail salespeople don't have college degrees either: 75 percent. But what about fast-food workers? Aren't they mostly teenagers? Nothing epitomizes teen jobs more than flipping burgers or working the drive-through for any of the big fast-food companies. Well, it turns out that just 30 percent of fast-food workers are teenagers. Another 30 percent are aged twenty to twenty-four. The rest—

40 percent—are twenty-five or older.[9] And just over one-quarter of fast-food workers are parents who must rely on meager pay and unstable schedules to provide for their children.[10]

The reality of retail workers is also quite different from the stereotype. Over half of retail workers are contributing 50 percent or more to their family's income.[11] And as in fast food, most of these jobs are held by adults without college degrees—defying the notion of a teen-centered workplace.

Arlene is a sixty-two-year-old African American woman who talked to me from her hospital bed after being admitted for complications from breast cancer. She recently moved in with her daughter, who is her primary caregiver as she goes through treatment. Arlene has worked in retail for nine years at the Walmart store in Evergreen Park, Illinois. She works the seven a.m. to four p.m. shift at the store, taking an hour-long journey on two buses to make it to work on time. She currently works as a sales associate in the electronics department but has done various jobs at the store, including being a cashier and a door greeter. Her hourly wage is $12.02, but as we'll discuss in the next chapter, a ubiquitous challenge facing workers in food and retail is getting enough hours to earn anything close to a decent living. It's no different for Arlene, whose hours range from twenty-four to thirty-two per week.

I asked Arlene to tell me how she felt treated on the job, and honestly, her answer startled me. She began by saying that Walmart supervisors treat her "very disrespectful, almost like a slave, I can almost relate to slavery because you don't have any rights. I signed on to do this job the way they want it done. On the other hand, you do want to be compensated for what you bring to the table. You want to be able to take care of your basic needs, pay your rent, pay for your utilities, put food on your table. If you are in fact making billions of dollars for this company, then I don't see what the problem could possibly be that you could take care of your basic needs and be compensated fairly. But that's not how it is at Walmart." Arlene, who marched with Martin Luther King Jr. in Chicago at the age of seventeen, today works in a job where she compares the way she's treated to our nation's greatest moral stain.

Arlene isn't alone in her dissatisfaction. Various surveys find that jobs in retail and food service rank very low in terms of job satisfaction.[12]

The Blue-Collar Jobs

In the top-ten list of occupations providing the largest number of jobs in our country, two of the ten (laborers/material movers and janitors) could be described as traditional blue-collar work, that is, physical labor done overwhelmingly by men. But unlike four decades ago, these jobs aren't on the assembly line or factory floor. Today over 2 million people in the new working class are employed as janitors or cleaners, earning an average hourly wage of $10.73.[13] Nearly seven out of ten of these jobs are held by men. About half of them are held by whites, whereas Latinos make up 30 percent, African Americans 16 percent, and Asian Americans 3 percent of the other half.[14] The other big occupation for working-class men today is what's known as hand laborers and material movers, employing 3.4 million people.[15] This is classic manual labor: moving freight or stock to and from cargo containers, warehouses, and docks. It also includes sanitation workers, who pick up commercial and residential garbage and recycling. The job requires a lot of strength, because most of the lifting and moving is done by hand, not by a machine.

When Eric runs errands after work while still wearing his uniform, people regularly come up to him to ask how they can get a job at Coca-Cola, his employer. "People have great respect for Coca-Cola and want to be part of the company," he says. "What they don't realize is that the company doesn't really treat its workers well." Eric is a general laborer at the company's South Metro distribution center on the outskirts of Atlanta, working the night shift. He started with the 4:00 p.m. shift but now does the 8:30 p.m. to 4:30 a.m. shift. He was hired at Coca-Cola (officially known as Coca-Cola Refreshments) in October 2009 and made $11 an hour. Five years later he was at $13.40. Eric confided to me that most of his family doesn't know how little he gets paid; they just assume he's doing well because he works for Coca-Cola. His title, general laborer, covers a lot of different duties, from being a checker (someone who scans the inventory on delivery trucks when they come back to the warehouse to make sure there are no errors) to performing all kinds of tasks in the warehouse, including driving forklifts and unloading trucks. "Anything I'm asked to do, I pretty much do, at a general-labor pay scale." When he started at the company, he worked as a checker, doing data entry of the drivers' sales as they returned to the distribution center. But Eric was transferred to the warehouse, he believes in retaliation for trying to unionize the facility. Eric, an African American, is in good company in the warehouse, which was 100 percent staffed by African Americans when Eric worked there,* while the managers were all white. Damon, one of Eric's former coworkers, explained to me that in the previous year, as a result of the union activity bubbling up, Coca-Cola had brought in new supervisors for the warehouse, all of whom are African American. He told me that during his four years of working in the warehouse, only five white men had been hired for the facility.

When I spoke to Damon, he was out on short-term disability as a result of wear and tear on his back and knees from his job. Despite being just thirty-two years old, his body is worn out. Damon is an

---

* I interviewed Eric in August 2014. He quit the job at Coca-Cola in early 2015. I interviewed Damon to corroborate the allegations Eric made about the working conditions and management composition in the distribution center.

order builder, which means that he puts together the orders to go out for delivery on trucks by manually hoisting cases of beverages and stacking them onto pallets. Damon, like all the "pullers" in the warehouse, is paid by the number of cases he moves during each shift, currently at the rate of 8.4 cents per case. At the start of each shift, the pullers are issued their "pull quota," the number of cases they must move before leaving the warehouse. "I'm the number-one order builder, hands down," Damon explained. "Nobody can outpull me. Because we get paid based on commission, I go out hard. I put my body on the line. In order to make a good living pulling cases, you got to be fast." That fast pace, both Eric and Damon believe, contributed to the death of one of their coworkers, who died of a heart attack while pulling cases. "Every time I go into the warehouse, I see that day all over again," Damon told me. The company offered counseling for the workers but wouldn't approve any time off to deal with the loss of their colleague.

The pressure of the pull quotas is a major issue the workers have tried to get management to address. Pullers are literally running across the warehouse to complete their quota in as few hours as humanly possible, because the longer it takes to meet their quota, the less their hourly rate works out to be. And it's important to note that the workers are not allowed to leave until they've met their quota, no matter how long it takes. Damon says he typically works six or seven hours a day, but most of his coworkers need eleven or twelve hours to complete their quota. The workers get two fifteen-minute breaks plus thirty minutes for lunch, but they don't get paid for these breaks, because they work on commission. "I wouldn't mind taking the break, but I came here to make money. If I'm not getting paid for something, I don't want to do it," Damon said.

The supervisors responded to the workers' complaints about the quotas being too high by shifting some of the orders to another facility. But they also hired more order builders for the South

Metro warehouse, which sounds good until you realize that more workers with fewer overall cases results in a substantial pay cut per worker. Damon explained that his activism has earned him a bad reputation in the warehouse and kept him from being hired for other positions there. He knows his body won't tolerate the demands of hauling cases much longer, so he's applied for several positions in the warehouse and has been passed over for each one. He was particularly excited about a forklift-operating job for the four to eleven a.m. shift, because that schedule would allow him more time with his kids, who are three and nine years old. He was told he didn't get the job because of his attitude. Damon's doctor issued a medical order restricting him from lifting more than fifteen pounds, which he shared with his supervisor. But since he didn't slip and fall at the warehouse, his supervisors won't accommodate the restriction by finding another job for him, even though he has worked there for four years. "Given how long I've worked there, I'd expect for them to say. 'Hey, you got restrictions now, you can do this or that instead,' but they will never let me do nothing else. They won't let me learn nothing else. They just want me to pull cases and pull cases and pull cases and pull cases until there ain't nothing left of me."

Both Damon and Eric described a work environment in which managers play favorites, and only those who "suck up" get promoted to other positions. This is a common refrain among the working-class people I interviewed, in all types of jobs, resulting in arbitrary enforcement of the rules and a climate of intimidation.

Coca-Cola may have an $83 billion brand,[16] but many of its warehouse workers live in poverty despite working full-time jobs. Eric said that one of his coworkers was living in an extended-stay hotel in one of the worst areas of town because he couldn't afford rent. Another was living in the car-wash area of an abandoned gas station. Eric sees it as a basic lack of fairness that a megabrand like

Coca-Cola pays its workers such low wages and treats them with such disrespect. He shared with me stories of workers being denied requests for time off. One of his coworkers had his wisdom teeth pulled and had a doctor's note saying that he should take time off, but his manager denied the request and said he'd get a point on his record if he took the time (a worker with ten points is fired). One of Eric's coworkers described their workplace as a "modern-day plantation-style environment."

The unpaid breaks, the arbitrary enforcement of rules, the refusal to accommodate sick or injured workers, and the dangerous conditions fueled by the per-case payment structure all led Eric to reach out to the local Teamsters about trying to organize the warehouse. Eric is driven to improve the working conditions at the warehouse by his faith and his sense of justice: "God has a purpose in everybody's life. And sometimes he'll take you through a storm in order to get you through the light. So this is just a storm I'm going through right now at Coca-Cola. I love helping people. If I could snap my fingers and make the whole world right, I would do it. Working there at Coke, I fell in love with the people. A lot of men and women working there were walking in fear, and didn't have the courage. In our pursuit of unionship over the last two years, I can see them putting their chins up and squaring their shoulders, ready for it. And that brings me joy, to see them inspired and ready to do better for themselves."

The union drive is an uphill battle, even though Eric estimates that about 70 percent of the warehouse workers are participating at some level in the effort. But that percentage can change dramatically by the time an election is called (if it's ever called), because like most major corporations, Coca-Cola will vigorously fight to keep the union out. The company has already brought in union busters to hold meetings with the workers, which they are required to attend. In an economy where job growth is still too slow and steady full-time jobs are still too elusive, if your front-line manager makes it clear that he expects you to vote against a union, courage can be hard to summon and hard to sustain.

Not everybody has the kind of spirit to demand better treatment, Damon told me. Far too often workers have been convinced that the job at Coca-Cola is the best they can do. But Damon sees it differently, and he tries to convince his fellow workers to demand what they're worth. "You're a human being," he said. "You're not just a piece of machinery to be put on an assembly line. You're a human being. If you're not being treated like a human being and being compensated fairly, then you should speak up."

The Cubicle Jobs

The third largest source of jobs for the working class, coming in at over 9 million, breaks into three large occupational categories: general office clerks, secretaries and administrative assistants, and customer-service representatives. None of these jobs requires more than a high school diploma, though a fair number of college graduates may find themselves doing this kind of work as a way to get their foot in the door. But by and large, these jobs are held by working-class women. They answer phones, file papers, deal with customer complaints, type memos, make copies, order supplies, and basically keep everything in the office running smoothly. These jobs are found in a wide range of settings, from doctors' offices to technology companies to local bank branches. In fact, despite the prevalence of ATMs, over a half million people work as bank tellers, with a median hourly pay of $11.99.[17] And like fast-food and retail workers, one-third of bank tellers must rely on public assistance such as food stamps and health insurance programs.[18] Although bank tellers often must purchase suits to wear to work, their low wage places them squarely in the new working class. As a former bank teller quipped, "You have to dress up, but basically you're working as a cashier at Walmart."[19]

Most bank tellers are paid less than $15 an hour working for an industry in which the top ten banks take in more than $100 billion in profits each year.[20] Erika has worked at a suburban branch of TD Bank in Maryland for five years. The thirty-four-year-old African American woman fell in love with the banking industry while studying business management in college. When she started as a teller she was paid $11 an hour, and in five years she worked her way up to $12.57 and became an assistant head teller. In May 2015, Erika earned a raise to $14. When I talked to her on a Thursday evening, she still did not have her schedule for the following week. TD Bank is open seven days a week, so tellers tend to work both weekdays and weekend shifts, and Erika is no exception. The shifts are long: 7:30 a.m. to 5:30 p.m. or 10:30 a.m. to 8:30 p.m. during the week, and five-hour shifts on weekends. The unpredictable schedule makes it difficult for Erika to get her two teenage children to their various games, especially on the weekend. "I thought I was going into banking to actually provide a service to people. I was inspired by it," she told me. But the reality, she discovered, is pretty much like working in retail.

What most people don't realize is that tellers today are salespeople, with quotas for selling new products each month. TD Bank has strict rules that tellers must follow during every interaction with a customer, which are designed to create consistency and maximize sales. For example, Erika must say each customer's name three times during each transaction, must always offer at least one product, and must be sure to invite the customer back. "It gets a little tricky and a little weird, especially when customers are in a hurry, to say all those things. 'Hey, Mr. Jones, okay, Mr. Jones, thank you, Mr. Jones,' and the customer is looking at you like 'Why do you keep saying my name?' Literally, customers are irritated and they want to go on their way and don't want to hear your speeches and sales pitches." The problem is that if Erika doesn't follow the script, she can be written up. And TD Bank routinely sends out "secret shoppers" to make sure their tellers are following the playbook. Her quota is typically 1,000 points every three months, with each new account (depending on the product) earning 20 to 30 points, which is approximately twenty to thirty new products.

Erika's biggest challenge on the job is the front-line management. As is the case with so many of the people I interviewed, her supervisor has the power to make her life on the job miserable. She's been yelled at by her boss, and despite complaining to human resources, nothing has changed. In addition to challenges with her supervisor, Erika and her coworkers have all tried to get management to provide them with more predictable and stable hours from week to week. So far their complaints about the sales quotas, schedules, and treatment on the job have failed to be remedied by management. While Erika and her colleagues generate revenue for the bank and serve as the face of the brand, their compensation in the most profitable segment of our economy is particularly contentious. TD Bank's top six executives collectively took home over $43 million in compensation in 2014.[21] The way Erika sees it, in addition to being able to pay all her bills, an increase in pay would raise the status of tellers in the industry, who she explained are widely seen as unimportant.

As I discuss more in the next chapter, Erika's experiences are all too common in the bargain-basement economy, where front-line managers call the shots, play favorites, and, most important, have an inordinate amount of power to make the lives of their employees miserable. Like Erika, millions of people in the new working class experience a steady accumulation of indignities on the job, from chaotic scheduling to arbitrary discipline to unpaid sick days. It all adds up to a strong feeling that their work isn't valued and doesn't matter, which is usually in great contrast to how they themselves feel about their work.

The Caring Jobs

At some point in our lives we will all come to rely on the professional care of someone. It may be a personal aide who shops and cooks for an aging parent or a child-care worker who nurtures and educates your toddler. Maybe it'll be a home health aide who bathes, feeds, and clothes a disabled relative. These workers, all of whom earn around $10 an hour, help relieve so many of us from caring burdens that once were familial (and mostly women's) responsibilities.

Historically, when caring work was not provided by a daughter, mother, or other female relative, it was outsourced to the lowest-status women in our society. From black slaves in the South to ethnic immigrants in the North to Chicanas in the Southwest to Japanese immigrants in Hawaii and California, caring for the aged, sick, disabled, and young was poorly paid and highly racialized from the founding of our country to the antebellum period.[22] This legacy continued through the early twentieth century, even under public jobs programs developed after the Great Depression. In both the Works Project Administration (WPA) and the National Youth Administration (NYA), women of color were often directed to take domestic jobs, not public jobs. Similarly, agencies that were set up to help Japanese Americans find work upon their release from internment camps after World War II also directed women to domestic jobs.[23]

Throughout the first half of the twentieth century, it was not uncommon for white middle-class families to employ a woman of color to help clean the house, prepare meals, and care for children or elders. The legacy of this occupational segregation remains today: The majority of these caring jobs are still done by women of color, with a disproportionate share held by black women. Black women make up a full one-third of nursing assistants and home health aides and one-fifth of personal care aides (compared to about 6.5 percent of the population). Latinas make up 14 percent of nursing assistants and home health aides and close to one out of five personal care aides (compared to about 8.5 percent of the population). Taken together, close to 5 million people in our economy are employed as home health aides, personal aides, nursing assistants, and child-care workers, all earning around $9 or $10 an hour.

But it's not uncommon for home care workers to actually earn less than the official minimum wage. How is that possible in America? Back when President Franklin Roosevelt signed into law some of the nation's first labor protections regarding wages and hours, the laws were written to ensure that the majority of jobs worked by African Americans would be exempt—indeed, it was the only way to get the bill passed by a Congress controlled by segregationist southern Democrats.[24] While not explicitly carving out an exception for African American workers, the National Labor Relations Act of 1935, which established the right of workers to collective bargaining, and the Fair Labor Standards Act of 1938, which established the right to a minimum wage and overtime pay, both specifically exempted agricultural and domestic workers from these rights.

Even though caregiving work in the home has become an official part of our economy—and a pretty big one at that, with 2.5 million jobs and fast growth—services provided in the home for pay were essentially not considered "real work" under existing labor law or standards until very recently. Congress attempted to bring more domestic workers under labor protections in 1974 by amending the Fair Labor Standards Act to cover all domestic workers except casual babysitters and individuals who provided "companionship services"—and left it up to the Department of

Labor to define the scope of "companionship services." Something got lost in translation between the Hill and the DOL. Here's how the DOL defined companionship services for the purposes of establishing which kinds of workers would be protected: "fellowship, care, and protection," which included "household work . . . such as meal preparation, bed making, washing of clothes, and other similar services," and general household work not exceeding "20 percent of the total weekly hours worked."[25] Now, I have a lot of companions, but never have I washed their clothes or prepared their meals as part of my companionship. I've certainly never bathed them just because we were companions. But in the early 1970s, the folks at DOL didn't see these kinds of services as work, just as part of good old-fashioned companionship (whose description matches almost perfectly that of an unpaid housewife). This is no accident; for hundreds of years, the work done by women in the home was never viewed as such, and that bias continued to bleed into defining the labor standards for women whose jobs are to care for the elderly, the sick, and the disabled. The no-labor-standards loophole was made even broader by allowing third-party employers such as big home care agencies to claim both the companionship-services exemptions, meaning for-profit agencies could continue to pay workers less than minimum wage and no overtime.

While attempts to update the regulations stalled over the past forty years, home health-care aides and personal care aides are now finally recognized as real workers, not merely "companions," and therefore must be paid minimum wage and overtime. In 2013, President Barack Obama signed an executive order requiring the DOL to amend the regulations. After the order was challenged in the courts, the U.S. Court of Appeals for the District of Columbia Circuit finally ruled that the Labor Department had the power to interpret the law and change the exception. As a result, roughly 2 million domestic workers will finally have the full protection offered to every other worker in America: the right to be paid decently for a day's work and to get paid extra for working overtime.

It's a change that couldn't come soon enough for Myrla, a home care worker in suburban Chicago. She earned $110 per day taking care of elderly patients in their homes. Some were suffering the effects of strokes, others had dementia, and some had chronic, debilitating illnesses like Parkinson's disease. In testimony delivered at the National Domestic Workers Alliance's third National Congress in Washington, D.C., she described her job: "I give them sponge baths twice a day, and once a week I bathe them. I assist them in transferring to the commode and assist in the bathroom. With some clients, I have used a Hoyer lift; others I have lifted manually. I cook their meals and feed them and ensure that their medicine is taken. I do housework, including making beds, doing laundry, washing dishes, and cleaning. Often I am asked to communicate between the family and the medical team. I also log daily activities and make lists of things for the family to buy or order from the pharmacy. I keep track of medications, encourage them to drink liquids, and do range-of-motion exercises. In at least two situations I have also taken care of other family members, including a patient's granddaughter and the husband of a patient. I also train other caregivers and relievers on the routine, and do other work required by the family."[26]

That $110 per day is certainly well earned. But it's important to note that Myrla earns that $110 for sometimes working a twenty-four-hour day when she sleeps over at her client's home. That comes out to an hourly wage of just $4.58—lower than what most people pay their teenage babysitters, but perfectly legal until January 2015. In fact, one out of four care workers earns less than the minimum wage.[27] Myrla joined Latino Union, an organization fighting for greater dignity and rights for home care workers, to use her voice to advocate for better wages and labor protections for the work she loves doing.

Home care work is one of the nation's largest and fastest-growing sources of jobs, fueled in large part by the tidal wave of aging baby boomers. As Myrla's story illustrates, for many of these workers, the job conditions and pay eerily recall the days of domestic servitude. Much of the home care industry is dominated by big for-profit agencies, who recruit and hire out home health aides, personal care assistants, and nursing assistants. The agencies exist thanks to state and federal Medicaid and Medicare contracts, which pay the lion's share (two-thirds) of costs related to home care. But given the profit motive and the right to pay less than minimum wage and no overtime (at least up until January 2015), these agencies could divert most of the money from the contracts for executive compensation and pay the women doing the actual work little more than an allowance (and no benefits, either).

The number of home care industry jobs has more than tripled since the 1970s, and will continue to be one of the largest sources of new jobs for the foreseeable future. The same goes for child-care workers and personal care aides. As structured currently, there are no career advancement opportunities in this field, unless an individual can carve out the time and money needed to rack up a new credential to move up the ladder to licensed practical nurse or medical assistant. There's no universal apprenticeship system in place to provide on-the-job training to move up to better-paid positions. For the new working class, moving up the ladder requires thousands of dollars for community college courses and the time away from work to study and attend classes—an all but closed door for most working-class women.

Ai-jen Poo, director of the National Domestic Workers Alliance, articulated the central role care work plays in our lives by saying, "This is a profession that deserves recognition. It's not like the pipes and railways of old but it is nonetheless infrastructure. It is the work that makes all other work possible."[28]

These Wages Don't a Living Make

When I was growing up, money was tight, especially before my mom went back to work. With four kids to raise and just one breadwinner, my mom became an avid coupon-cutter, hitting the grocery store with an envelope stuffed with savings. Most of my clothes were hand-me-downs, either from my older sister or from our church's rummage sale. But we were never hungry. If I wanted a snack, there was always something to eat. In the winter the house was warm—and it was a house, a two-story, three-bedroom house on half an acre, with a pond, apple trees, and an aboveground pool. This security was all purchased with the earnings from my dad's union job at the steel factory. For the new working class and their children, however, keeping the cupboards and fridge stocked is often a struggle, even with help from food stamps and the local food pantry—and even with two parents punching the clock.

Today the median wage for people in the working class aged twenty-five to sixty-four is $1.30 less per hour than it was in 1980 ($15.61, down from $16.91).[29] Still, looking at the working class as an undifferentiated whole hides very important distinctions by gender, race, and age. Like American society more generally, there's a hierarchy of earnings. Working-class men still outearn all other demographic groups in the working class, despite a nearly $5-per-hour decline in real wages over the past three decades. Today the median hourly wage for working-class men is $17.56, down from $22.04 in 1980. The white working class makes significantly more than any other demographic group, thanks in large part to the higher wages of men. As Table 2 shows, hourly wages for most workers have been stagnant over the past three decades, with modest increases for women and only significant declines for men.

A major challenge facing much of today's working class is getting enough hours on the job. Nearly 15 percent of the working

Table 2. Median Hourly Wages for the Working Class

Median Hourly Wages for the Working Class, 1980–2012 (2013 dollars)

	1980	1990	2000	2012	$ Change 1980–2012
All	$16.91	$16.20	$16.77	$15.61	–$1.30
Men	$22.04	$19.10	$19.51	$17.56	–$4.48
Women	$13.07	$13.50	$14.70	$14.19	$1.12
White	$17.67	$17.14	$18.21	$17.29	–$0.38
Black	$14.14	$13.71	$14.96	$14.32	$0.18
Latino	$14.14	$12.85	$13.01	$13.01	–$1.13
Asian and Pacific Islander	N.A.	$15.42	$15.61	$14.63	–$0.79

Source: Author's analysis of U.S. Department of Labor, Bureau of Labor Statistics, Current Population Survey Annual Social and Economic Supplement.

class today are in part-time jobs, some by choice, but nearly 40 percent of those workers are involuntarily employed part-time—meaning they'd prefer to have a full-time job.[30] In order to cobble together enough income, 5 percent are holding down more than one job.

The declining wages of the new working class are visible in the changing demographics of the food stamp program and the rising ranks of food pantry shoppers. Since 2000, more and more people on food stamps actually have jobs. Many even have full-time jobs. In 2014, for the first-time, working-aged people, not children and seniors, were the majority of food stamp recipients.[31] There's no social program other than welfare that carries a heavier stigma—and to many conservatives, food stamps (now officially called the Supplemental Nutrition Assistance Program/SNAP) are nothing less than a scourge on American society. In 2014, 46 million people—20 percent of all Americans—used food stamps to fill their grocery carts.[32] With the onset of the Great Recession, food stamp enrollment climbed significantly, growing from about 26 million Americans in 2007 to 40 million by 2010. With most new job growth confined to low-paid sectors of the economy, millions of people still struggle to meet their basic needs with a paycheck. According to the Department of Agriculture, about four in ten people who receive food stamp benefits live in households with at least one working adult.[33] Shamefully, many of the working adults receiving food stamps and other government benefits work for some of the most recognizable brands and most profitable companies in the world.

Let's start with fast-food workers—the ones we interact with the most, the so-called front-line workers. According to the UC Berkeley Labor Center, more than half (52 percent) of the families of front-line fast-food workers are enrolled in one or more public programs, compared to 25 percent of the workforce as a whole, with a price tag of over $7 billion per year to taxpayers. About $4 billion of that is for public health-care programs. Another $1 billion is spent on food stamps and another $1 billion comes from the Earned Income Tax Credit.[34] So in order to make ends meet on an hourly wage of just $8.63, most fast-food workers rely on a mix of government benefits, from tax credits to health insurance. Meanwhile, much higher up the hierarchy, fast-food CEOs are living large on earnings 1,200 times that of the average fast-food worker.[35] That's a pay disparity higher than in any other industry, and yet these CEOs are employing millions of people at wages so low they can't make ends meet.

A similar story can be found at America's big-box retailers. Over at Walmart, our nation's largest employer, about $6.2 billion in public assistance programs is spent on employees in the form of public health care, food stamps, and tax credits.[36] A study examining Walmart's cost to taxpayers in Wisconsin found that a single Walmart Supercenter cost taxpayers between $904,542 and $1.75 million per year, or between $3,015 and $5,815, on average, for each of three hundred workers.[37] Let's be clear: Walmart may offer the lowest prices, but it is far from broke. It typically boasts profits of $16 to $17 billion, and it spends billions more buying back its own shares, a move that artificially inflates the stock price, enriching shareholders and CEOs. As in previous years, Walmart spent $6.6 billion in 2013 on share buybacks. Now let's say that instead of buying back its stock, it redirected those profits to its employees in the form of a raise: Walmart could have provided its 825,000 lowest-paid workers a raise of $5.83 an hour, providing them with the dignity of decent pay and at the same time no longer outsourcing the shortfall of their low wages to American taxpayers.[38] Walmart announced in 2015 that it plans $20 billion in stock buybacks over the next two years. "This share repurchase program, combined with our annual dividends, reinforces our continued commitment to delivering increased value to shareholders," said Charles Holley, Walmart's executive vice president and chief financial officer, in a statement on the approved buybacks.[39]

As numerous studies have revealed how often corporations outsource the costs of low wages and benefits to us as taxpayers, conservatives are once again turning up the heat on the issue. But their outrage isn't aimed at the mooching corporations for failing to pay their full and fair share of labor costs. Perversely, they're outraged at the workers (the "takers," in Mitt Romney's callous formulation) who are forced to use food stamps.

These Jobs Aren't Unskilled, They're Underpaid

Labor economists identify occupations as being unskilled, low-skilled, mid-skilled, or high-skilled. This hierarchy can be useful to researchers as a way to cluster occupations to better assess trends in employment based on education and training. These groupings also provide an easy way to analyze the demographics of the jobholders. The problem lies in the fact that these terms have long transcended the academy and are tossed around casually to describe not only the jobs but the workers themselves. From the pages of the *New York Times* to the screeching talking heads on Fox News, it's common to refer to people in many jobs as "unskilled" or "low-skilled" workers. This language is used by conservatives and progressives alike, and I used it myself until I heard a speech given by Barbara Ehrenreich at a conference on inequality sponsored by my organization, Demos. Ehrenreich referred to her time working in low-paid jobs for her best-selling book *Nickel and Dimed*. She worked as a maid, at Walmart, and as a nursing home assistant. Reflecting on the stress and hard work required to do these jobs, she said she learned that "there is no such thing as unskilled labor."[40]

When we categorize work—work that often entails fast thinking, stamina, focus, and often demanding and repeated physical feats—as needing no or little skill, we are stripping these workers of human dignity and rationalizing the proliferation of poverty jobs. If we stop to really think about it, how can any job—labor performed for pay—really take zero or few skills? If that were true, there'd be no need for employers to require applications or in-person interviews for these jobs. After all, if it's unskilled, any person should do. But that's not the case. These jobs do require skills, just not the kind that are attached to academic or vocational credentials. Eric, the Coca-Cola warehouse worker, described to me the grueling pace that he and his fellow workers must maintain in order to meet their shift's quota for wrapping and moving pallets of beverages. He videotaped some of his fellow workers and sent me a clip of one worker running around huge pallet after huge pallet with his wrapping gun, which ensures that the cases of beverage cans are held together when being moved by forklifts to their delivery trucks. This man undeniably has skills—agility, strength, and endurance being just three of them. In addition to employing physical dexterity, these workers must track the inventory using handheld scanners, which inevitably produces occasional errors or incorrectly identifies bar codes. So we can add cognitive skills to the skill set for this job too, namely problem solving and quick thinking.

If you've ever waited on tables—another so-called unskilled job—you know that this is a job that requires a herculean amount of skill, at least if you want to get tips for your work. I always tell people that waiting on tables is one of the hardest jobs I ever had, and to this day, when I am feeling stressed or worried about something in my office job, I have a bad dream about waiting on tables in which I forget the abbreviations for the menu items, forget to put in drink orders, or drop plates full of food. Waiting on tables is a serious juggling act that requires keeping track of where all your diners are in their meal—did Table 10 get their appetizers, is it time to put in the order for Table 2, does Table 4 need a refill, Table 3 is waiting on salads still, Table 1 needs their check, Table 5 is waiting for their change, and on and on. And you have to keep all this information straight while being friendly to people who very often do not return the favor. Doing this job well takes an enormous amount of skill, just not one that comes attached to a certificate or diploma.

Two of the bargain-basement economy's largest occupations are routinely categorized as being unskilled: home health and fast food jobs. If measured by the training required to do these jobs, both require very little. The typical training provided for a home health aide is two weeks. For a fast-food worker, it's on-the-job training, lasting anywhere from two days to two weeks.[41] But for a home health worker charged with preserving the dignity and safety of a disabled or elderly person, an extraordinary number of skills are involved, including, in some ways, the highest of human skills, that of caring for another person who is often quite vulnerable. And if you ask a fast-food worker if his or her job is stressful, you can bet the answer will be yes. Working the floor of a fast-food joint requires serious multitasking skills, often in a hot and unpleasant environment. Fryers need to be cleaned, drinks need to be filled, orders need to be taken, and if one thing goes wrong—something seemingly as small as the syrup on the fountain machine needing replenishment—the whole balancing act collapses. Lines get long. Food gets cold. Fries get burned. And managers and customers get irate.

The ease with which CEOs and elites characterize working-class jobs as either unskilled or low-skilled is an indication of just how far our lived experiences have diverged.

CHAPTER TWO

The New Indignity of Work

"You should be thankful you've got a job." It's an all-too-common sentiment lurking among managers and—let's be honest—many of the talking heads who go on television to argue against raising the minimum wage or to oppose new regulations to protect workers. And in the case of Eric, whom we met in Chapter 1, it's exactly what his supervisor said to him when he dared to challenge the working conditions in the warehouse.

That kind of managerial attitude in response to any complaint about poor working conditions or low wages is not only condescending but the product of a no-holds-barred thirty-year assault on the working class. You see, when workers lack any mechanism to bargain for better wages and treatment, managers—from front-line supervisors all the way up the food chain to CEO—begin operating under a kind of warped sense of noblesse oblige, as if these working-class jobs are a form of charity given to people who would otherwise go begging for food, shelter, and clothing. In my interviews with dozens of wage-earners, I asked what they like most about their job and what they like least. Most people derived real satisfaction from their work and stressed the importance of the role they play in making their employers successful and their customers happy. But their pride in their work and their commitment to doing a good job stood in stark contrast to the way they felt they were treated on the job, especially by management. The most common desire for change in their workplace was simple: more respect. Eric, the general laborer at Coca-Cola, put it this way: "We're making them billions of dollars. Why are we being treated like something you step on in the grass? I don't understand it. I will never understand it."

The lack of respect isn't just reflected in condescending remarks made by managers, although one retail associate spoke at length about how her manager talks down to the salespeople as if they were children. Most home health aides regularly deal with family members who expect them to provide maid service while they're in the house caring for their relatives. Disrespect seems to be baked into today's working-class jobs, and not just in the relations between management and staff. It's also reflected in a slew of common practices based on the very pervasive idea that controlling the cost of labor—workers' hours and wages—is the best way to cut overall costs and boost profits. Low pay, unpaid overtime, unpredictable schedules, and too few hours are all widespread in the bargain-basement economy. These practices strip workers of their humanity, making them feel "invisible" or "disrespected" or "unappreciated"—words frequently used by members of the new working class to describe how they're treated on the job.

Big Brands, Big Lawbreakers

The operating paradigm in the bargain-basement economy is that workers are costs to be minimized rather than assets to be maximized. And companies engage in a number of cost-cutting measures that flagrantly skirt the law, including failing to pay overtime and skimping on basic health and safety precautions.

Stealing Wages from Workers

In the drive to lower labor costs, it has become all too common for employers to cheat their workers out of pay they are legally due. In fact, some of the nation's and the world's most recognizable brands just so happen to be some of the nation's biggest wage criminals. McDonald's, Subway, Domino's, and many other megabrands have repeatedly been found to violate bedrock wage and hour laws by failing to provide overtime, by forcing employees to work off the clock without pay, and by failing to provide meal breaks or regular breaks.[1] Wage theft—the practice of not paying workers for all the time they've worked—is ubiquitous in the restaurant industry. In fact, the restaurant industry has repeatedly had the highest number of legal cases brought for wage theft among all low-paid industries, and owed the largest amount of back wages as a result of investigations by the Wage and Hour Division (WHD) of the Department of Labor.[2] A national poll found that *nine out of ten* fast-food workers experienced some type of wage theft.[3] In 2014 alone, the Department of Labor investigated over five thousand cases of wage theft in restaurants, resulting in nearly $35 million in back pay for workers, trends that have varied little since 2011.[4] In an analysis conducted by CNN Money of the cases brought against fast-food companies between 2000 and 2013, the biggest violators were Subway chains, who were the focus of nearly eleven hundred investigations during that time, mostly for failing to pay overtime.[5] As a result, Subway franchises had to pay over $3.8 million in back pay to its workers. While Subway captured the gold for breaking the law, McDonald's and Dunkin' Donuts rounded out the winners, respectively bringing home the silver and bronze medals. Ripping off the working class isn't confined to the titans of the fast-food industry; some of the bigger full-service restaurant chains are also looting wages from their workers.

Since 2000, the Department of Labor found at least 150 cases of wage theft at IHOP, the syrupy denizen of the family restaurant sector.[6] While IHOP's commercials position it as the place to go for big family breakfasts, its pay practices are anything but wholesome. According to data analyzed by CNN Money, two IHOP locations in Kansas underpaid thirty-five employees, including bus persons, cooks, dishwashers, and servers, resulting in $64,000 in back wages, roughly $1,800 per worker.[7]

There's really no industry in the bargain-basement economy that's innocent of wage and hour violations. Violations are prevalent in day-care facilities, hotels and motels, restaurants, retail businesses, and janitorial services. Unfortunately, there are more lawbreaking companies than the regulators can catch, or than workers will file complaints against. The deck is overwhelmingly stacked in the lawbreakers' favor, because the Wage and Hour Division isn't exactly the kind of operation our business-friendly Congress likes to fund. Back when the Fair Labor Standards Act was signed into law in 1938, there was one WHD investigator for every 11,000 workers; today there is one investigator for every 164,000 covered employees.[8] Despite the needle-in-a-haystack odds, in 2012 alone, $993 million was recovered in stolen wages thanks to the combined efforts of federal investigators, state departments of labor, state attorneys general, and private lawyers.[9] As the Economic Policy Institute points out in a study, that's nearly three times the amount of money stolen during robberies in the same year. But unlike individual robbers, companies and managers that break the law by stealing their workers' wages don't face jail time, just a paltry fine. The maximum civil monetary penalty that a company will be fined for failing to pay the minimum wage or overtime is just $1,100 per violation. Compare that to the substantial savings businesses accumulate by siphoning wages from their workers, and it's obviously a risk worth taking. The $993 million in wages recovered is likely just a small fraction of the amount stolen each year from hourly workers, in part because many of these theft cases go unreported, since it is incumbent on the worker to file a complaint.

A comprehensive survey of hourly workers in three major cities finds that the total loss in wages is at least three times greater than what is officially recovered through investigations and court actions. The survey of 4,300 hourly workers in New York, Chicago, and Los Angeles found that one in four was paid below the minimum wage in a given workweek, three-quarters of those who worked overtime were not paid the required time-and-a-half, and seven out of ten workers who came in early or stayed late were not paid for the time spent working outside of their scheduled shift. As a result of these lawbreaking practices, workers in these three cities alone lost $3 billion in wages in just one year.[10]

There's some important context to consider when judging these wage violations committed by some of the most recognizable brands in the country. By and large, the employees of these establishments are some of the lowest-paid workers in the nation—and that's even if they were appropriately paid for all hours worked. Additionally, today's working class faces a level of flagrant violations of their labor rights that the largely unionized, mostly white blue-collar worker never experienced. In many ways the struggles of these workers to secure better wages and fair treatment more closely resemble the status and frustration of early industrialized wage-earners, who fought for a minimum wage, a forty-hour workweek, and an end to child labor.

Wage theft is disturbingly common in the bargain-basement economy, with companies stealing pay from workers who are usually making just a dollar or two above the minimum wage. It's a key move in the personnel playbook of managers, who are often under intense pressure from corporate higher-ups to lower labor costs.

In 2012 the Department of Labor announced that it had recovered nearly $5 million in back wages for over 4,500 Walmart employees as a result of its investigations into the retailer's violations of laws regarding overtime pay. Walmart had misclassified some of its managers as being exempt from overtime laws, when in fact the scope of their job responsibilities was clearly nonmanagerial, despite their title, and as a result they were eligible for overtime pay. In the department's press release, then secretary of labor Hilda Solis said, "Let this be a signal to other companies that when violations are found, the Labor Department will take appropriate action to ensure that workers receive the wages they have earned."[11] But the same practices continue across the bargain-basement economy, from home health care to janitorial services to warehouse workers to port truckers.

Unfortunately, violating wage and hour laws is not the only kind of lawbreaking committed by companies. Far too many employers of the working class are flagrant violators of health and safety standards designed to protect workers.

Saving Money by Endangering Workers' Lives

At the national level, the employer watchdog is the Occupational Safety and Health Administration, commonly referred to as OSHA. In 2013, 4,405 workers died on the job—an average of 12 people per day. While that represents a substantial decline in worker fatalities from 14,000 in 1970, the year OSHA was created, it is still far too many individuals dying at the workplace, often through no fault of their own. And millions more workers—around 4 million—are injured on the job every year. Of course, not all of these accidents are caused by employers who flagrantly ignore the safety rules. But just about every day OSHA issues a new release citing some of our most recognizable companies for serious or willful violations. A serious violation occurs when there is substantial probability that death or serious physical harm could result from a hazard that the employer knew or should have known about. The most egregious rule-breaking is labeled a willful violation, one that is committed with intentional knowledge of the dangers or voluntary disregard for the law's requirements, or with plain indifference to workers' safety and health—also known as flagrant disregard for the lives and safety of employees. But it's important to keep in mind that OSHA can't file criminal charges against bosses or CEOs who bend or ignore health and safety rules. The most it can do is issue fines, and despite the seriousness of the violations, the fines can often seem skimpy relative to the harm and suffering experienced by workers. The most OSHA can fine a company is $7,000 for each serious violation and $70,000 for a repeated or willful violation.[12] In an unusual showing of bipartisan support, the maximum penalties will increase to $12,500 and $125,000 respectively—the first increase since 1990. The new penalty amounts will take effect by August 2016.

Health and safety violations aren't just restricted to jobs that require physical labor, such as climbing telephone poles, painting bridges, and washing office windows. In fact, in 2014 Dollar Tree, a chain of bargain stores, racked up more OSHA violations than almost any other company in America.[13] All told, OSHA fined Dollar Tree $866,000 between October 2013 and October 2014 for multiple willful violations, with a total of forty-eight violations in its stores across the country. At one store near Dallas, Texas, inspectors found teetering cartons of stock piled twelve to fifteen feet high, gas tanks that weren't properly stored, and electrical panels blocked with merchandise. A *Wall Street Journal* article about the violations quoted a former Dollar Tree employee who said that she quit after a box of cans fell on her head, explaining, "Things are tumbling on you because the space in the storage room is so small. We were always complaining to the manager, but she doesn't do anything." To keep labor costs low, Dollar Tree often has only one or two employees working any given shift in the store—a major reason for boxes of bargain-priced goods to pile up, as no one has the time to shelve the merchandise. The risks of an accident to a customer or an employee caused by falling boxes is apparently one the company is willing to take. This is a company whose CEO was compensated a total of $7.8 million in 2014, and its other top four executives received a total of $10.7 million.[14]

Safety violations are all too common in the telecommunications industry, particularly in the construction and maintenance of cell phone towers. In 2013 thirteen deaths occurred in the communication tower industry, and nine months into 2014, eleven deaths had occurred.[15] Wireless Horizon, a company based in Missouri, apparently provided workers with "safety" equipment in poor condition and failed to conduct an engineering survey and plan—all basic safety measures for a job demolishing a cell phone tower. OSHA fined the company $134,400 for two willful and four serious violations—a pittance considering the intentional disregard for its workers' safety that ultimately led to the deaths of two men.

Companies across all the bargain-basement sectors are all too often cheating workers out of their pay or putting their physical well-being in jeopardy, often deliberately. These are workers who earn wages at the very bottom of the pay scale. They don't have the backing of a union to help ensure a safe workplace and therefore are quite simply at the mercy of their employers, relying on their morality, diligence, and good faith to keep them safe and pay them fairly. Because most workplace investigations are prompted when a worker files a complaint (75 percent of all wage and hour investigations are initiated by worker complaint),[16] it's realistic to assume that most violations go unreported. And with good reason. Workers in restaurant, retail, janitorial, construction, home care, material moving, and other bargain-basement jobs function at the very bottom rung of our labor market—a precarious position, to say the least. Workers rightly fear that they will be retaliated against by their employer if they file a complaint, by being fired or by being punished with reduced hours or a demotion. This fear is especially intense for undocumented immigrant workers, who worry about being reported to immigration authorities and ultimately deported in retaliation for their complaint.[17]

Wage theft and health and safety violations are often fueled by the now widespread use of outsourcing, in which a company sheds production or services that aren't core to its company brand. It can take many forms: franchising, multiple layers of contracting, staffing or temp agencies, or misclassification of workers as independent contractors. No matter the form of outsourcing, the result is often downward pressure on wages and workplace safety standards the further down a worker falls in the human supply chain.

Who's the Boss?

Unlike the largely industrialized working-class jobs of a bygone era, where it was clear who workers actually worked for, many of today's working-class jobs lie at the end of a Rube Goldberg–like system of contracts, subcontracts, and sub-subcontracts, where one project, often for a major company, is staffed by several smaller companies, including temporary placement agencies. Fast-food workers' paychecks come not from the recognizable brand embroidered on their uniform but from the franchise operating the store. And then there's the new practice of classifying workers as "independent contractors" to avoid the pesky costs of having actual employees. All these practices result in a web of employment relationships in which accountability is hidden, making it easy for employers to flout regulations and cut corners, with workers paying the price. This "fissured workplace," the title of David Weil's illuminating book on the subject, puts pressure on each successive contractor in the chain to trim costs, whether by paying workers less than they're legally entitled to or by saving money on vital safety equipment and practices—including hiring temporary workers for some of the most dangerous jobs, which should require safety training.[18]

The splintering of employee-employer relationships is now a ubiquitous part of the bargain-basement economy. From hotel workers to fast-food workers to warehouse workers, it is often unclear which company is ultimately responsible for ensuring that wage and safety laws are followed, and as a result these laws are often overlooked—sometimes innocently, often flagrantly.

Subcontracting: Splintering the Links in the Chain

Subcontracting is one of the most common ways for lead companies to farm out work that isn't core to their brand, such as janitorial services, warehousing, and customer relations. Just a decade or so ago, a warehouse worker for a major national company like Hershey would have been an actual employee of Hershey, enjoying the same perks—high wages, health and retirement benefits, vacation and sick days—as the company's white-collar professionals who work in marketing and product development.[19] Today that's no longer the case. A few years ago Hershey became the center of a national firestorm when its overly layered subcontracting system resulted in a bruising and highly publicized story of labor violations and outright abuse at one of its distribution centers.

Illustrative of the winding, complex loop-de-loops of today's subcontracting practices, the story of what happened at a Hershey warehouse began with a plea for help to the U.S. State Department.[20] Yes, the State Department, the governmental agency responsible for maintaining our relationships with countries around the globe. Why did a worker at a Hershey distribution center contact the State Department for help? It turns out that the worker was actually a foreign exchange student, here on a long-standing J-1 Visa program designed to give international students a chance to experience American culture. The program is run by a nonprofit organization, the Council for Educational Travel, USA, known commonly by its acronym, CETUSA. In this case, CETUSA managed the visit of four hundred students from more than a dozen countries, finding them jobs, booking their travel, and arranging for housing.

The jobs CETUSA found for the students were the last link in a chain of subcontractor relationships, all leading back to Hershey. In the early 2000s, Hershey began the process of shedding operations that its managers felt weren't core to its brand, including, startlingly, the actual production of chocolate as well as the packaging and distribution of its products. The company did retain ownership of one distribution center, in Palmyra, Pennsylvania. But Hershey didn't want to be distracted with managing the center, so it contracted with Exel, a logistics company that operates more than three hundred sites in the United States.[21] Exel then contracted with a temporary staffing agency, SHS OnSite Solutions, to hire and manage the workers at the center. SHS OnSite Solutions, itself part of a larger company called SHS Group LP, contracted with CETUSA to provide four hundred international students to work at the center. For the students, all of whom rationally thought they were going to work for the very American chocolate company Hershey, their paychecks alerted them to the fact that they were not Hershey employees.

When the students' complaints to the State Department about their working conditions went unanswered, they protested and walked out on the job. That grabbed the State Department's attention, and that of the Labor Department's Wage and Hour Division. The students working in the Hershey facility, each of whom paid $3,500 to experience American culture, were being paid $8.35 per hour and often had rent taken directly out of their paychecks. They worked the night shift, from eleven p.m. to the morning, manually lifting and hauling around fifty-pound boxes of Hershey's Kisses for eight hours. With little money left after they were paid, experiencing any culture-enriching activities was out of the question.

After investigations conducted by OSHA, Exel was cited for health and safety violations and fined $283,000, and the State Department banned CETUSA from participating in its guest worker visa program.[22] Hershey, SHS OnSite Solutions, and CETUSA all publicly ducked responsibility, pointing the finger at one another and claiming they weren't directly responsible for, or aware of, the conditions at the facility.

These four hundred students came to our shores to experience American culture, which they certainly didn't define as back-breaking work at low wages in unsafe conditions. Ironically, what they experienced is indeed a quintessential feature of American culture: the exploitation of low-wage workers.

The Dependent "Independent Contractor"

One of the most common tactics used to distance companies' responsibility for their workforce is to misclassify many of their workers as "independent contractors," which exempts the company from having to provide benefits, pay payroll taxes, and comply with federal and state labor laws, such as the minimum wage and overtime rules. As a result of misclassifying workers in this way, states and the federal government lose billions of dollars in tax revenue each year that supports unemployment insurance, worker's compensation, and Social Security and Medicare, not to mention state and federal income taxes. Employers often underreport how much they pay independent contractors or pay them off the books to avoid paying taxes. Meanwhile, the workers also lose, because as independent contractors they don't qualify for most safety-net programs when they are out of work, and they fall through the cracks of most labor and employment laws.[23]

So who exactly should be classified as an independent contractor? The key term here is the word "independent." According to the IRS, what makes someone an independent contractor is that the firm paying for his or her work has direct control only over the result of the service or work provided, not over what work will be done and how it will be done.[24] True independent contractors, such as realtors and freelance graphic designers, are self-employed, responsible for finding clients on their own.

The misclassification of workers as independent contractors has jumped the fence from professional occupations to include some of the lowest-paid jobs in America, including home care, janitorial work, and trucking. Today, for instance, almost all heavy-truck drivers are "independent contractors."

Rhonda, a thirty-six-year-old white woman, has driven trucks for over nine years. She's currently a truck driver in the Port of Savannah, Georgia, where she's "leased to" C&K Trucking. As a port trucker, Rhonda moves (or "pulls," in trucking lingo) the giant shipping containers from the port to a nearby warehouse or distribution center. She owns her truck but not the chassis or other equipment needed to pull containers; that is leased to her by C&K Trucking, and under her contract she can only haul C&K Trucking's freight. Because she's classified as an independent contractor, she must pay for all expenses associated with keeping the truck running—fuel, insurance, tires—and the costs of repairs to parts she doesn't even own, like the chassis. There is nothing "independent" about Rhonda's relationship to C&K. In fact, like most port truckers in the United States, hers is a classic example of companies classifying their workers as independent contractors to avoid the costs and responsibilities of having employees. This misclassification is rampant in port trucking and has fueled ongoing strikes at major ports in the country as truckers fight to be considered employees and gain the right to join a union.

"They get to do us how they want, without any discipline—they don't have to worry about being regulated, there's no one out there governing them," Rhonda told me. "They basically treat us like sharecroppers on wheels, because we can't stop them and we can't fight them. We show up every day and are given assignments—I'm not sure how much more of a definition of an 'employee' they need to treat us like one. It's hard when you work all week, and after a week you can't afford to pay your bills, let alone take care of the truck. The joke of it is that they consider us small-business owners, yet we only take home about $500 week. What kind of business owner would make it if they only brought home $500 a week?" Rhonda gets paid by the container, earning $40 per container she moves for C&K. Last year her gross income pulling containers was $60,000. But after all the expenses to maintain and operate the truck, she filed just $19,000 in taxable income.

Rhonda's real independence as a contractor is largely fictitious. She must show up each morning, and if she isn't going in, she must let C&K know, as if she were an actual employee. "They discipline you if you don't call in like an employee. If you don't let them know you're not coming in, they won't work you the next day or so when you do come in," she said. Because Rhonda isn't considered an official employee, she doesn't get health insurance from her job. She applied for health insurance through the new exchanges created by the Affordable Care Act and found out she didn't earn enough money to qualify and needed to apply for Medicaid. She's still waiting on a return phone call after applying. For now, her whole family is uninsured and must rely on clinics for care, "praying to God" that nothing serious happens.

Because Rhonda and her husband can't afford after-school programs or summer camp, their twelve-year-old son stays home by himself when school is out. They both work in the trucking industry, and being close to home was the chief reason Rhonda bought a house so close to the Port of Savannah, less than a mile away. It gives her peace of mind to know that she's less than five minutes away if her son needs her. She could make more money driving the roads, but the expenses and maintenance are higher and the hours are longer. She chose port trucking so she could always be close to her son.

Port truckers are the backbone of our logistics industry: They are the first line in a complex web of moving goods that we literally depend on for the shirts on our backs. My conversation with Rhonda turned emotional when we started talking about politics. Fighting back tears, she talked about the indifference of elected officials who never had to struggle and don't know what it is to struggle. "If they walked a day in our shoes, this industry would change," she said. "And I would let each and every one of them ride in my truck, right up to the president, just so they could see it for themselves."

The Formidable Franchise

When you drive down any major thoroughfare in any town in any state, at some point the vista will be taken over by the blanketed sameness provided by our nation's most recognizable fast-food and hotel chains. Weary travelers or stressed-out parents know they can pull in for a quick bite to eat or to rest their head for the night, knowing exactly what they're getting before they even walk in the front door. The Olive Garden and Holiday Inn Express off the turnpike in Ohio will offer the same menu choices and service standards as those establishments in Chula Vista, California. That's the beauty, or banality, depending on your viewpoint, of the franchise.

Buying a franchise is less risky than conceiving and operating an independent small business. Big national chains offer a practically built-in customer base, no matter where you open up shop. But purchasing and running your own McDonald's or Holiday Inn Express is quite a different experience from owning and operating something that is truly all yours. In the case of fast food, when you purchase a franchise, you'll be agreeing to operating standards and procedures that are minute in their detail. You'll also be agreeing to pay an up-front royalty and then a percentage of all sales to the company, which are typically 6 percent, but for McDonald's, the leader of the pack, are 12 percent of all sales.[25] It all sounds innocent enough, and indeed, unlike other arrangements that siphon operations away from the lead company, it is a legitimate way to expand a brand's footprint.

But in an era when worker power is weak to nonexistent and labor regulators are woefully understaffed, the franchise model has devolved into a tale of big brands squeezing more profits from their franchisees under draconian operating procedures, with franchisees in turn squeezing out their profits by cheating workers out of pay.

Dion, a thirty-four-year-old African American father of six, is all too familiar with the tactics of fast-food companies. He works as a shift manager at Rally's, a burger chain in the Midwest and Southeast, and as a cook at Lee's Famous Recipe Chicken, a fried chicken chain concentrated in the Midwest, with a sprinkling of locations in the South. Juggling the two jobs is made slightly easier for him because the two outlets are across the street from each other. He's worked in fast food for the past ten years, and to help make ends meet and support his children, who live with their mother, Dion is currently living with his own mother. I talked with him the day he was written up at work for moving too slowly during his training to become a manager at Rally's, where he had started just three weeks before. Speed is the name of the game in fast food. From the time the customer pulls up to the drive-through menu, the timer starts going and employees have two minutes to take the order, collect the money, make the sandwiches and drinks, and get the customer on the way. Dion thinks this is unrealistic and leads to bad customer service, not to mention demoralizing the staff, who are watched like hawks as the timer begins the two-minute countdown. Part of Dion's training as a manager at Rally's involved instructing him to make sure that none of the employees met with representatives from Fight for $15, the union-backed movement of fast-food workers who are demanding higher wages and a union, even if they were off the clock.

Over at Lee's Famous Recipe, where Dion has worked for ten years, getting scheduled enough hours is a challenge. During the first year, most employees are given only fifteen hours a week, and after that most get scheduled for less than thirty hours. There's a reason for this: By keeping workers under forty hours, companies can lower their labor costs by avoiding paying for benefits such as vacation days and health insurance. Neither of Dion's jobs provides paid sick days, so coming down with the flu means losing pay. At Lee's, workers can earn a week of paid vacation after their first year if they've averaged thirty hours per week over the year—which means most workers don't qualify. Neither of Dion's jobs provides him with any kind of security for dealing with life's worst situations. And Dion has definitely been through the worst.

Dion's daughter was born with left-side heart syndrome, meaning that the left side of her heart was underdeveloped. When she was an infant, she had surgery to repair her heart, and as a result of complications from the surgery, she had damage to her kidney and lungs. Just before her third birthday, she passed away because of kidney failure. Because his daughter's illness was so grave, Dion stopped working for two years, racking up medical bills and debt. When he returned to Lee's after his leave of absence, he wasn't given his managerial position back, so he is now working as a cook. He took the job at Rally's to help him climb out of debt. At Lee's he makes $9 an hour, even though he has worked there for ten years. When he started he made $5.95, so he's had a $3.05 raise over ten years. Rally's pays him $10 an hour, a $1-an-hour boost for being a manager. He works at Lee's for thirty hours a week and at Rally's for twenty hours a week. "I work seven days," he explained. "I don't get any off days. I work days, nights, overnights. I work whenever they may need me or whatever I see on the schedule." The schedules are posted a week in advance.

Dion's days start early. Rising at five a.m. to catch the bus to either job, he typically works until about six or seven p.m. Because he doesn't own a car, he drives to work only when his mom is off and he can use her car. When he gets home, he washes his uniform for the next day, gets some sleep, and starts the process all over again the next morning. Juggling two jobs has come with a price that Dion wishes he didn't have to pay: a lack of time spent with his kids. He just had a new baby girl, and he regrets not getting to spend time with her. But he needs the two paychecks to get out of debt and support his family. It's a trade-off many parents in the bargain-basement economy find themselves forced to make because they work in jobs with low pay and unpredictable schedules.

Compared to the big fast-food companies, like McDonald's and Taco Bell, Rally's and Lee's Famous Recipe seem like mom-and-pop outlets. But they share the same basic franchisor-franchisee structure. It's possible to measure the effect of franchising on fast-food working conditions because many of the major companies still own and operate some of their own outlets instead of franchising them. A study comparing the likelihood of violations of wage and hour laws between company-owned outlets and franchise-owned outlets for the top twenty fast-food companies found that franchised outlets were 25 percent more likely to be in violation, and the back wages owed to workers were 60 percent higher per investigation.[26] As the researchers explain, franchise owners are less concerned with maintaining the image of the corporate brand than they are with making a profit for their individual store. Why might this be the case? The researchers suggest that franchisors are much less disposed to do anything that might damage the brand, because they profit from all sales, so they are more likely to play by the rules and avoid any negative attention that comes with a federal investigation. In contrast, franchisees profit only from the sales at their specific outlets, making their core concern protecting their profit, which leads to squeezing labor costs, often in ways that violate the law.

For too long the major fast-food companies could shield themselves from any liability over the labor practices of their franchise operators by claiming they were not the actual employer, since the franchisee controlled the hiring, firing, and wage-setting. Basically, corporate McDonald's takes the stance that workers at franchised McDonald's aren't actually employed by McDonald's. For decades the conservative-controlled National Labor Relations Board (NLRB), which is the first stop to settle these kinds of disputes, agreed with this spurious logic. That is, until July 2014.

As fast-food workers began to organize in 2012, they held a series of one-day strikes, and many were illegally fired, threatened, or otherwise penalized for their pro-labor activities. These workers filed official complaints with the NLRB, and out of the 181 complaints filed, the General Counsel of the NLRB found merit in 43 cases and said that he would include McDonald's as a joint employer in those cases.[27] The cases will now go to administrative judges; if McDonald's loses and is found liable, the company will probably appeal to the NLRB. And depending on how that goes, this seemingly commonsense ruling could wind up before the Supreme Court. Upon the initial ruling, a spokesperson for McDonald's issued the following statement: "McDonald's serves its 3,000 independent franchisees' interests by protecting and promoting the McDonald's brand and by providing access to resources related to food quality, customer service, and restaurant management, among other things, that help them run successful businesses. This relationship does not establish a joint employer relationship under the law . . . This decision to allow unfair labor practice complaints to allege that McDonald's is a joint employer with its franchisees is wrong. McDonald's will contest this allegation in the appropriate forum."[28] The stakes are high for McDonald's, so it's certain that a white-shoe law firm is on retainer and the best public relations firm is too. The company will spare no expense to shield itself from accountability for the working conditions of its (non-) employees.

On Call—Not Just for Doctors Anymore

Nancy, a fifty-four-year-old white woman, has worked for Walmart for over nine years. She's currently a customer-service manager in Baker, Louisiana. Despite the "manager" title, her position is not a salaried management position; it's hourly, and those hours are subject to change on a weekly basis. Nancy took a circuitous employment route to Walmart. She and her then husband (they are now divorced) owned a video store in the early to mid-1990s. They did well until Blockbuster came along and could afford multiple copies of hot titles, making it easier to rack up rentals. But the final death knell came when Walmart entered the VHS business. Once Walmart got into the business, studios invented the idea of "sale-thrus"—selling videos at retail stores. Within two years sale-thrus took off and the wholesale prices charged to video rental stores increased significantly. In order to break even on a title, they had to rent a video at least twenty-five times, a hurdle Nancy's mom-and-pop store couldn't clear. "I'm different from most associates at Walmart," she told me, "because I've been on both sides of the coin. I've been a small-business owner who was put out of business by Walmart, and now I work there."

When Nancy started working at Walmart in 2005, she was "shocked by how it was the best job I'd ever had. These people respect you—my gosh, it was amazing. I told everybody to go to work at Walmart." But that all changed in late 2006. The managers called the associates in to talk to them about a series of changes they were rolling out in their stores. Over a period of six to eight weeks, associates were gathered in the break room to learn of a new change, such as shifting to optimized scheduling (aka "just-in-time" scheduling) or cuts to benefits. As Nancy said, "Ever since that first day, Walmart has been horrendous to work for. If I had not had the time that it was wonderful, I just could not believe the change. It was just amazing."

Nancy started talking to her coworkers about the need to stand together. The cutting of hours and optimized scheduling (optimized for Walmart, that is) resulted in workers being scheduled all around the clock. At first Nancy's coworkers thought it was just something their particular store was implementing, but Nancy suspected it was a change being directed by the home office and put in place in all the stores. Her hunch was confirmed when she learned about OUR Walmart on Facebook. OUR Walmart, which stands for Organization United for Respect, is a group of Walmart associates supported by the United Food and Commercial Workers (UFCW) who are working to improve the working conditions at Walmart. Nancy's father and older brother were in a union, and she had learned that solidarity among workers can produce real change. In 2010 she got the chance to stand up and speak up on behalf of herself and her coworkers at Walmart's annual shareholders meeting. Walmart sends one associate from each store to the meeting, and Nancy was selected. Associates are given a tour of the home office, vendors set up booths to offer free products, and two concerts are held before the actual meeting. The big meeting always features major stars as emcees; Céline Dion, Tom Cruise, and Hugh Jackman are just some of the celebrities who've lent their name to the company. The year Nancy attended, Jamie Foxx, the actor, was the emcee.

As part of the show, Bill Simon, then CEO of Walmart, opened the floor up to associates to ask questions. When one associate received a condescending response to his complaint about how hot the stores were in the summer, it was the last straw for Nancy. She felt she had to get in the line to speak, but she was overcome by anxiety. She prayed for the Lord to give her a sign that she should speak up, which she got when Bill Simon pointed to her and said she'd get the last question. So she began talking about the changes in working conditions, focusing particularly on the new scheduling practices. As she spoke, the three thousand-plus associates began clapping in support, and when she finished, they gave her a standing ovation. Bill Simon was not too happy, quipping, "I guess we're having fun now" when Nancy finished speaking.

Four years after fighting for change, Nancy admits she was naive. When she first got involved, she truly believed that if the CEO and Rob Walton (chairman of the Walmart board from 1992 to 2015 and son of Walmart founder Sam Walton) were aware of how the new policies were negatively affecting workers' lives, not to mention the quality of the shopping experience for customers, they would make changes. She reached out to OUR Walmart looking for a bridge to the home office in the hope of improving Walmart, not in order to destroy it. She examined the company's financial statements and was just left wondering, "Why are they cutting everything when they're making such a high profit?"

Nancy and the rest of the OUR Walmart members have made a difference. In April 2015 the company raised its minimum wage to $9 an hour, and it is scheduled to raise to $10 an hour by February 2016. In July 2015 the company announced additional raises for managers in service-oriented departments, such as electronics and auto care.[29]

Nonetheless, the havoc wreaked by "just in time" (JIT) scheduling remains a major problem at Walmart and across the retail and food-service industries. Basically, JIT is typically done using advanced software that allows managers to calibrate workers' hours with consumer demand. So when the mall is empty and store traffic is lighter than anticipated, managers send workers home before their scheduled shift is over, essentially cutting their pay. Managers are often under pressure to meet targets for payroll as a percentage of sales, and since they can't easily drum up more customer traffic, their only real tool is to cut workers during slow times. But the scheduling issues, a major source of frustration and insecurity for the new working class, aren't just about being sent home early without pay. Just-in-time scheduling also means that workers' schedules are rarely shared more than a week in advance, and their hours may vary from week to week. Workers may be scheduled fifteen hours one week, thirty hours the next week, twenty-two hours the next week—and those schedules may be posted just days before each workweek. According to the Economic Policy Institute, 17 percent of the workforce has an unstable work schedule, which wreaks havoc not only on their budgets but on their lives more broadly. For parents, unpredictable scheduling makes child-care arrangements nearly impossible to nail down, leaving them few options for good and stable care. The pervasiveness of on-call scheduling in retail and fast food illustrates the kind of stance toward employees that makes them feel disrespected by their employers, as if they were little more than machines to be turned off and on to meet demand.

The issue of just-in-time scheduling got a major profile boost thanks to an in-depth article in the *New York Times*.[30] The article chronicled the troubles these scheduling practices visit on families, upending child-care arrangements and making budgeting nearly impossible. One of the workers in the story was a barista at Starbucks, where she often wouldn't get her weekly schedule until three days before. She also endured what workers call "clopening"—closing down the store and returning only hours later for the opening shift. Just a few days after the article ran in the paper, Starbucks announced that it was committed to providing stable schedules for its workers, which the company defined as posting schedules at least one week in advance.[31]

Whether it's wage theft, skimping on safety equipment, or misclassifying workers as independent contractors, the thread connecting all of these practices is unbridled corporate power and a punitive workplace culture that places the blame for bad working conditions squarely on the worker. After all, these workers should be able to "just get another job" or "go back to school." And the new working class is all too aware that their labor is deemed disposable and rather unremarkable in its skill. It's manifest in every nook and cranny of the bargain-basement economy. To a person, workers experience a painful desire for respect and dignity on the job that remains unfulfilled. The Fight for $15, which now includes retail, fast-food, and airport workers, adjunct faculty members, and home care workers, isn't just about a pay raise. It's about bringing basic decency and humanity back to the workplace.

As the Sleeping Giant stretches its arms to the sky, waving placards demanding a better wage, workers appear to be winning this burgeoning battle in the court of public opinion. Whether the fight will change our politics and shift the ground on which national and state candidates run for office will be proved in the long months of the hotly contested 2016 presidential race. Can the needs of the working class punch through our money-drenched, elite-driven political campaigns? And what would a politically potent working class demand? The answer is different than you might assume. It turns out that much of the conventional wisdom about working-class politics is just plain wrong.

CHAPTER THREE

Meet the New Populists

Every four years we Americans become spectators in a circus known as the presidential election. For most of us, participating in the process of electing the next president involves watching televised debates, discarding flyers from local and state candidates, and muting the slugfest known as campaign advertising. We're spectators in the sense that we are watching, listening, and processing the event, but most of us remain far from the table of influence, which is increasingly reserved for a very small, very white, very male, and very rich group of individuals. These individuals—titans of industry, captains of retail, lords of finance—are the pipers calling the tune.

That's not to say that politics hasn't always been a game dominated by elites. But generations ago the power elite included the labor movement and the millions of working-class people organized through that now threadbare remnant of economic democracy. Over the past fifty years, as labor's political influence has waned, the power of the wealthy has mushroomed, aided in great part by several Supreme Court rulings that opened campaign spending floodgates. But perhaps one of the most effective, and cynical, strategies to trample the interests of the working class has been a very strategic and deliberate use of race to undermine class-based solidarity. Finally, there's the stubborn and historical gap in voting, in which college-educated and more affluent voters almost always show up at the polls while the working class watches from the sidelines.

But speculation about how the working class will vote—especially white working-class men—is a favorite topic of the political pundits. The conventional wisdom is that this group is solidly and impenetrably conservative and a predictable base for Republican candidates. But on some key issues about the role of government and the power of big money in our political system, the white working class is actually much more liberal than its college-educated counterparts, revealing key opportunities for progressive candidates to earn their votes.

Let's be clear. The Sleeping Giant, with its larger share of women and people of color, is shifting the center of gravity in politics. Thanks to largely working-class movements such as the Fight for $15 and Black Lives Matter, candidates of both political parties have been compelled to address economic and racial inequality in the months leading up to the 2016 presidential election. There is more working-class solidarity right now in the United States than at any time since the 1970s, and on almost every measure this new working class is much more progressive than its college-educated counterparts. But it would be a mistake to consider the working class a monolith when positions on some key issues still diverge by race and gender.

Who Are the New Populists?

One of the most stubborn pieces of conventional wisdom about the white working class is that they are red-meat conservatives, with a strong knee-jerk reaction against anything that smacks of a government program. But an extensive survey conducted by the Public Religion Research Institute (PRRI) uncovered a populist streak among the white working class that is way more Elizabeth Warren than Jeb Bush or Rush Limbaugh. Take, for example, the fact that white working-class Americans are more likely than white college-educated Americans to report that a lack of good jobs (67 percent vs. 52 percent) and a lack of opportunities for young people (56 percent vs. 46 percent) are major problems facing their communities.[1] Moreover, 70 percent of working-class whites believe that the economic system in this country unfairly favors the wealthy, 53 percent say one of the biggest problems in this country is that we don't give everyone an equal chance in life, and 62 percent favor raising the tax rate on Americans with household incomes of over $1 million per year. And finally, nearly eight in ten white working-class Americans say that corporations moving American jobs overseas are somewhat (25 percent) or very (53 percent) responsible for Americans' current economic distress.

But this populism fractures when it comes to issues of race. Six in ten white working-class Americans (60 percent) believe that discrimination against whites has become as big a problem as discrimination against blacks and other minorities, compared to only 39 percent of white college-educated Americans. And nearly half (49 percent) of white working-class Americans believe that over the past few decades the government has paid too much attention to the problems of blacks and other minorities, compared to 32 percent of white college-educated Americans. It's important to note that the belief that too much attention has been paid to blacks and other minorities garners majority agreement only among southern white working-class voters, reflecting a racial anxiety steeped in the region's brutal history of racial antagonism and terror. Today the racial anxiety expressed by working-class whites also extends to other people of color, namely immigrants. White working-class voters, unlike college-educated whites, blame immigrants for taking jobs that would otherwise have gone to them. Again, the PRRI survey shows a gulf between southern white working-class voters and their counterparts in the rest of the country. In fact, the South has retained its racial animosity to an incredible degree, and there is no dearth of politicians who still tap those reserves to win elections and stoke antigovernment sentiment. As I discuss later in this chapter, the use of race to appeal to white working-class voters has a long and ignoble history.

The Big Class Divide

When we look at how Americans view the role of government in addressing poverty and providing opportunity, it becomes very clear that there are two Americas, one in which the people who live in comfort exhibit little empathy for those in the other America, who struggle. In one of the more illuminating yet depressing examinations of the difference between the fortunate and unfortunate, the Pew Research Center for People and the Press compared the responses of financially secure and financially insecure individuals to one of their major surveys conducted in 2014.[2] The groups were created using an index of ten measures of financial security and financial distress, with individuals categorized into five groups, each representing roughly 20 percent of the population. At the ends are the most well-off and the least well-off. A glimpse at the demographics of the two most financially insecure groups reveals a near perfect overlay with the new working class—women, people of color, and people without four-year degrees. In fact, only 7 percent in the least secure group had a college degree.

The findings reveal, unsurprisingly, that when it comes to support for the safety net, views about poverty, and perceptions of business, financially insecure Americans hold much more consistently liberal views than their better-off counterparts. When given a choice between two statements about government's role in helping the needy, over 60 percent of the most financially secure Americans chose "The government can't afford to do more to help the needy," while 60 percent of the least financially secure Americans chose "The government should do more for the needy, even if it means more debt." One of the likely reasons the well-off don't support providing more help for the needy is that they think the poor have it easy in this country. Just over half of the most secure Americans agree with the statement "Poor people today have it easy because they can get government benefits without doing anything in return," while two-thirds of the least secure Americans agree instead that "poor people have hard lives because government benefits don't go far enough to help them live decently." Keep in mind that in 2013 just twenty-six out of every one hundred poor families received Temporary Assistance for Needy Families, down from sixty-eight families for every one hundred in poverty in 1996, the year that President Bill Clinton "ended welfare as we know it."[3]

This polarization by class extends to views about business, with two-thirds of the least secure Americans believing that corporations make too much profit, while less than half of the well-off believe that to be the case.

What the Pew analysis shows is that on pocketbook issues, the new working class desires more action from government to improve their lives while the affluent exhibit very little support for such action. The implications are profound, given what we know about who participates in our political system, who contributes financially to our elections, and whose opinions get preferential treatment once candidates are in office. But the views of the least secure aren't consistently liberal. In fact, of all the questions Pew asked, there was one economic item on which the least secure held more conservative opinions than the financially secure, and that was on the economic impact of immigrants. Forty-four percent of the least secure, compared to just over a quarter of the most financially secure, say that immigrants are a burden on the United States because "they take our jobs, housing, and health care."

On other social issues, America's class divide disappears. The well-off and the working class have similar views on regulation, government's effectiveness, and national security. And on the question of black progress, the working class and the well-off are nearly identical in their opinions, with close to two-thirds agreeing that "blacks who can't get ahead in this country are mostly responsible for their own condition."

Working-Class Moderates, Privileged Conservatives

The conventional wisdom that white working-class voters are monolithically conservative Republican voters doesn't conform to the way these voters actually identify themselves. Data from American National Election Studies (ANES), the premier source for public opinion on issues, elections, and political participation, show very little difference between college-educated and working-class individuals in whether they think of themselves as a Democrat, Republican, or independent. In fact, if anything, white working-class voters are slightly less likely than their white college-

Table 3. Political Party Identification of the Working Class: "Generally speaking, do you think of yourself as a Republican, a Democrat, an independent, or what?"

POLITICAL PARTY	ALL		WHITE		BLACK	
	COLLEGE DEGREE	WORKING CLASS	COLLEGE DEGREE	WORKING CLASS	COLLEGE DEGREE	WORKING CLASS
Democrat	32%	37%	25%	26%	71%	74%
Independent	36%	39%	38%	42%	24%	24%
Republican	31%	24%	36%	31%	6%	2%

POLITICAL PARTY	HISPANIC		MALE		FEMALE	
	COLLEGE DEGREE	WORKING CLASS	COLLEGE DEGREE	WORKING CLASS	COLLEGE DEGREE	WORKING CLASS
Democrat	45%	50%	28%	32%	36%	42%
Independent	32%	36%	39%	43%	34%	35%
Republican	23%	14%	33%	26%	30%	22%

Source: Author's analysis of American National Election Studies, 2012.

educated counterparts to identify themselves as Republican and slightly more likely to identify as independent (see Table 3). Both working-class men and women are more likely to be Democrats than their college-educated counterparts. Where conventional wisdom does carry the day is that both blacks and Latinos consider themselves Democrats over Republicans by a very large degree. College-educated and working-class blacks are three times as likely as whites to be Democrats, and Latinos are twice as likely to be Democrats as whites.

In addition to asking about party identification, the ANES survey asked people to place themselves on an ideological scale. Again the stereotype of a white working-class die-hard conservative isn't quite justified. While whites self-identified as more conservative than blacks or Latinos (see Table 4), it's actually college-educated whites who are most likely to identify as conservative, while working-class whites are more likely to identify as moderate. In fact, working-class whites are equally likely to identify as moderate or conservative, belying a well-worn stereotype about their politics.

Table 4. Self-Identified Description of Political Views

IDEOLOGY	ALL		WHITE		BLACK	
	COLLEGE DEGREE	WORKING CLASS	COLLEGE DEGREE	WORKING CLASS	COLLEGE DEGREE	WORKING CLASS
Liberal	29%	20%	27%	18%	36%	30%
Moderate	25%	37%	23%	36%	36%	34%
Conservative	42%	32%	47%	35%	19%	22%

IDEOLOGY	HISPANIC		MALE		FEMALE	
	COLLEGE DEGREE	WORKING CLASS	COLLEGE DEGREE	WORKING CLASS	COLLEGE DEGREE	WORKING CLASS
Liberal	39%	22%	29%	20%	29%	21%
Moderate	27%	34%	22%	34%	28%	39%
Conservative	28%	26%	47%	35%	37%	29%

Source: Author's analysis of American National Election Studies, 2012.

What about on more cultural issues? Again, the white working class is less conservative than one might expect, though modestly more conservative than college-educated whites (see Table 5). Overall, the majority of Americans no longer support the man-as-breadwinner/woman-as-homemaker situation as some kind of nostalgic ideal. This idea remains popular among only 21 percent of college-educated individuals and 38 percent of the working class. But working-class people of all races are more likely to agree with the statement that "it is much better for everyone involved if the man is the achiever outside the home and the woman takes care of the home and family." Working-class Latinos were the most likely to agree with the statement, with 44 percent in agreement, compared to 33 percent of working-class blacks and 37 percent of working-class whites. Most Americans have removed their rose-colored glasses about America's idealized *Leave It to Beaver* era.

Table 5. "It is much better for everyone involved if the man is the achiever outside the home and the woman takes care of the home and family."

% WHO AGREE OR DISAGREE	ALL		WHITE		BLACK	
	COLLEGE DEGREE	WORKING CLASS	COLLEGE DEGREE	WORKING CLASS	COLLEGE DEGREE	WORKING CLASS
Agree	21 (3)%	38 (7)%	22 (2)%	37 (7)%	21 (3)%	33 (6)%
Disagree	79 (33)%	62 (17)%	78 (34)%	62 (18)%	79 (32)%	66 (20)%

% WHO AGREE OR DISAGREE	HISPANIC		MALE		FEMALE	
	COLLEGE DEGREE	WORKING CLASS	COLLEGE DEGREE	WORKING CLASS	COLLEGE DEGREE	WORKING CLASS
Agree	9 (6)%	44 (7)%	26 (1)%	40 (7)%	16 (4)%	37 (7)%
Disagree	91 (35)%	56 (11)%	74 (25)%	60 (13)%	83 (39)%	64 (20)%

Source: Author's analysis of General Social Survey, 2010. Figures in parentheses represent the percentage who strongly agreed or strongly disagreed.

Missing at the Ballot Box

There is no doubt that the United States has a serious voter turnout problem. Over the past four decades, turnout in presidential elections has hovered around 60 percent. In 2012, 62 percent of eligible voters cast a ballot. And among that meager percentage, wealthier and white voters show up in greater numbers than others. In 2012, 26 million eligible voters of color did not vote, and among eligible voters earning less than $50,000, 47 million did not vote.[4] The big questions are why this is the case and whether it matters. For decades political scientists concluded that voters and nonvoters essentially held the same views, in essence meaning that low turnout among working-class voters or voters of color was insignificant in terms of representation. But this research examined only candidate choice—whether nonvoters would have voted for the Republican or the Democrat. There are lots of practical reasons that working-class and poor voters may not vote, such as time constraints and registration obstacles. But what if they don't vote because they sense there isn't much difference between the two candidates' positions? It turns out that compared to higher-income voters, low-income voters have a much harder time discerning meaningful differences between the two political parties.

In their book *Who Votes Now?*, Jan Leighley and Jonathan Nagler examine differences among lower-income and higher-income voters in rating each of the presidential candidates' ideology on a liberal-conservative spectrum and on the question of government's role in guaranteeing a job for everyone who needs one. What they found is that in both the 2004 and 2008 elections, high-income voters perceived a much greater difference in the ideology of the two candidates, while low-income voters saw each candidate as less ideological and had a harder time perceiving his stance on the issue of government guarantee of jobs.[5] This matters because the perception of a real difference in the positions of the candidates affects whether someone thinks it matters to vote. The finding that lower-income voters don't perceive candidates to be either strongly liberal or strongly conservative is telling, and reflects how neither party is directly speaking to the economic concerns of the working class while being quite effective at communicating the party's positions to people with higher incomes. Without a meaningful perception of a difference between the presidential candidates, many working-class voters make the rational decision not to cast a ballot—and our nation's policy priorities are skewed as a result.

Since 1972 the difference in the policy preferences of voters and nonvoters about government's role in our society has widened, with voters much more aligned with conservative preferences and nonvoters more aligned with progressive policy preferences. Missing voters, who are more likely to be low-income, are more liberal on questions of redistribution in particular, specifically on the need for government to provide jobs, services, and health care.[6]

Politicians focus their campaigns, and all of their polling, on motivating "likely voters" to cast their vote for them. But structural barriers, including burdensome registration procedures, combined with an enthusiasm gap means that the working class is more likely to be missing from the pool of "likely voters." And so the agenda is set by an electorate that is more white and more affluent than the nation as a whole. This has profound consequences on the types of issues candidates campaign on and what they prioritize once in office. And those decisions have deep implications about the kind of social contract our elected leaders deem appropriate for our country, generation after generation.

Research on turnout and policy outcomes in other countries

corroborate the idea that countries with less class bias in voting and higher turnout have more generous social welfare policies. Researchers examining our nation's depressed levels of voting came to the conclusion that "low turnout offers a potentially compelling explanation why the American welfare state has been so much less responsive to rising market inequality than other welfare states."[7] A study of eighty-five democracies found that higher voter turnout leads to higher total revenues, higher government spending, and more generous welfare state spending.[8]

One could conclude from this research that the recent conservative attacks on voting rights—from requiring photo identification to shortening early voting opportunities, both of which dampen turnout among younger, lower-income voters, as well as voters of color—are clearly designed to preserve an ideological hegemony that doesn't reflect the needs of all the people in our democracy. Most recently, in 2013 conservative legislators were given even more leeway to curtail voting rights by the Supreme Court. In *Shelby County v. Holder*, the justices struck down a provision in the Voting Rights Act that required states with a history of voting discrimination (mostly southern states) to get pre-clearance from the Justice Department before making any changes to their voting laws or practices. In the year immediately following the decision, Texas, Alabama, North Carolina, and Mississippi all enacted strict new voter identification laws, which either had been blocked under "pre-clearance" or would likely have been blocked. North Carolina went a step further and repealed a series of laws that increased turnout, including early voting.[9]

Our democracy is far from inclusive of all the people it purports to represent. And that status quo is highly desirable to, and vigorously defended by, elites of all stripes, using a combination of suppressive voting laws and big-money donations that undermine the Sleeping Giant's political power.

The Big Influence of Big Money

There's an old adage that if you ask a simple question, you'll get a simple answer. So here's the question I posed to the individuals I interviewed: "Who has power in this country?"

"People with money." "Rich people." "The politicians and all big companies." "Anybody who has money." "Once upon a time, I would have said the people. Now I say it's the ruling class." "Rich people do." "The companies have the power." "Whoever has the money has the power." "The rich." "Big business."

Simple, yes. But pithiness often comes from great clarity. And today it is abundantly clear that instead of our democracy writing the rules for capitalism, capitalism is writing the rules for our democracy. The decline in working-class economic and political power mirrors the rise of power among corporate and wealthy elites. And this shift was anything but accidental—a political thriller of a story that we'll visit in the next chapter. For now, let's stick to how the views of the rich and the working class diverge significantly on fundamental economic issues, and how the affluent almost always win in this tug-of-war.

There's a saying in Washington, D.C., that if you're not at the table, you're on the menu. And America's big business lobbies and high-powered donors have gotten fat off a menu of free trade, financial deregulation, weak labor protections, and tax cuts. The power to set the agenda in Washington and in state capitals across the nation—the menu, if you will—rests almost entirely on having the money of a big corporation or trade association behind you, or a very fat bank account that can easily support checks containing six or seven zeros in the amount box. This cozy connection between big money and government has prompted many respected journalists and academics to declare that the United States is no longer a democracy but a plutocracy or oligarchy.[10]

Money has always played a role in our nation's elections, but there used to be commonsense rules about where that money could come from, how it could be spent, and how much any individual or corporation could contribute. The principle of political equality—that the size of a person's wallet shouldn't determine the strength of his or her voice in our democracy—was at the heart of these rules. In addition, laws protected our democracy from corruption—the kind of pay-to-play, "I rub your back, you rub mine" relationships that the Watergate scandal exposed. But in 1978, in *Buckley v. Valeo*, the Supreme Court struck down many features of our campaign finance laws and dealt a fatal blow to the ability to promote political equality by limiting the amount of money that can be spent to win elections, either directly by a candidate or by outside groups.

Since that watershed decision, the Supreme Court has ruled on several additional campaign financing cases, all of which resulted in the loosening of restrictions and the weakening of the average citizen's voice. The fatal blow to our democracy's bedrock principle of all citizens having an equal say in the decisions that shape their lives came in 2010 with the Supreme Court's ruling in the *Citizens United* case. In *Citizens United v. Federal Election Commission*, the Court struck down previous restrictions prohibiting corporations from spending money to influence elections through what are known as "independent political expenditures," which essentially means any spending that is not directly coordinated with a political party or candidate. Corporations are still prohibited from giving money directly to candidates. Unfortunately, there are countless indirect and influential ways for corporations and wealthy individuals to stack the political deck in their favor. While some donations to certain kinds of groups must be disclosed (such as those to PACs and Super PACs), money given to tax-exempt "social welfare organizations" or trade associations does not have to be disclosed. In the 2012 presidential election, the first after the *Citizens United* ruling, this secretive spending or so-called dark money accounted for 31 percent of all outside spending.[11] Whether the money does or doesn't have to be disclosed, the amount these organizations can spend to influence federal elections is completely unlimited.

Demos, the organization where I oversee research and policy, analyzed the amount of money spent in the 2012 elections and detailed the findings in a report called "Billion-Dollar Democracy: The Unprecedented Role of Money in the 2012 Elections." In the 2012 presidential election, just over $1 billion was spent during the national elections to influence House and Senate races and the big kahuna, the race for president of the United States.[12] That amount was more than was spent by the Republican and Democratic parties combined—a first in American elections (see Chart 1).[13]

American elections have become dominated by slush funds in which major individual donors can place their bets, doubling down to advance their interests and protect their privilege in a game we used to call democracy. In the 2012 presidential race, Mitt Romney and Barack Obama raised a combined $313 million from over 3 million individuals giving less than $200. But that's nothing compared to the largesse of America's superdonors, who with an average contribution of $9.9 million to Super PACs were able to match the combined giving of over 3 million citizens with

Chart 1. Total Federal Spending by Type, 2012 Election Cycle

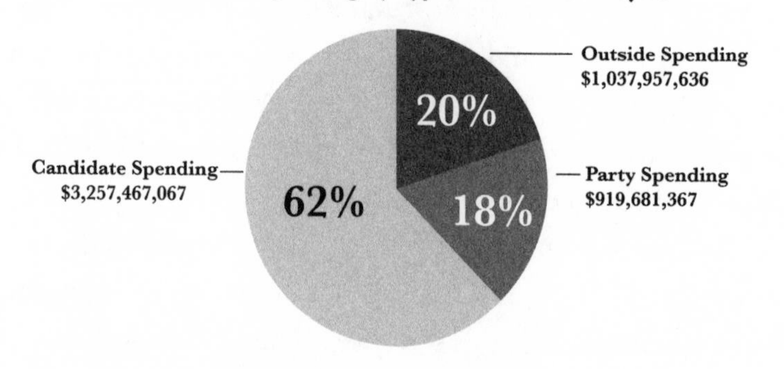

Source: Demos and U.S. FIRG Education Fund analysis of FEC and Sunlight Foundation data.

just thirty-two people.[14] These über-donors reflect a small sliver of an already nefariously narrow group of big political donors. Consider that nearly 60 percent of Super PAC funding came from just 159 donors who contributed at least $1 million. And nearly all the money (93 percent) raised by Super PACs came in the form of $10,000 contributions, from just 3,318 donors.[15] Think about that. Through the ability to write very large checks to political organizations whose sole purpose is to sway the outcome of an election, just 0.0011 percent of the U.S. population is controlling the messages and the agenda of our federal elections through television spots, radio commercials, and public events that now form the backbone of election season. The 2016 election cycle is already breaking records for outside money from a small cadre of donors. As of August 2015, more than $303 million had been raised by Super PACs, a much higher amount than was raised at the same point in the 2012 presidential election.[16]

Now, it's important to say explicitly that the amount of money spent in our elections isn't inherently bad. What makes it so toxic and dangerous to our democracy is that the money is overwhelmingly from a very small number of wealthy individuals and special interests who use their generosity to promote their messages and their agendas and to elect candidates who share their priorities and positions on issues. Today in America, economic clout is easily translated into political clout, ultimately driving the very governance of our country.

Thanks to a body of new research from political scientists, we now have empirical evidence that confirms our gut instinct that the wealthiest among us dominate our democracy.[17] In his seminal book *Affluence and Influence: Economic Inequality and Political Power in America*, Martin Gilens looked at several decades of public opinion on economic, social, and foreign-policy issues. He compared the policy preferences of different income groups to the actual policies that were passed by Congress to identify which, if any, income groups had more or less influence over policy. It turns out that the American government does respond to the public's preferences, but that responsiveness is strongly tilted toward the most affluent citizens. Indeed, under most circumstances, "the preferences of the vast majority of Americans appear to have essentially no impact on which policies the government does or doesn't adopt," Gilens writes of his findings.[18]

Of course, average Americans don't always disagree with the opinions of the affluent. In many areas there is consensus among Americans of all income levels. But, importantly, Gilens found that "the starkest difference in responsiveness to the affluent and the middle class occurs on economic policy, a consequence of high-income Americans' stronger opposition to taxes and corporate regulation."[19] In fact, if policy outcomes more generally reflected the preferences of the poor and the middle class, it's probable that we'd have a higher minimum wage, more generous unemployment benefits, stricter regulation of big business, and a more progressive tax code.[20] Given what we know about the causes of the Great Recession and its devastating and disproportional impact on the working class, the outsized role of the affluent on economic policy is particularly concerning. The deregulation of the financial industry—a long-pursued goal of Wall Street titans and the investor class—played a key role in the financial collapse and allowed millions of working-class homeowners to be preyed upon by mortgage brokers whose compensation depended on duping homeowners into refinancing their safe loans with ones with exploding interest rates. These subprime loans were aggressively marketed in working-class communities, particularly black and Latino neighborhoods. When the dust settled and the investigations ended, it was clear that the big banks had exploited America's strapped working class for their own profit, and in the process vacuumed up what little wealth so many homeowners had scraped and sacrificed to accumulate. All told, this unregulated morass of mortgage brokers and lending companies (often financed by America's top banks) created widespread suffering, causing over 4 million foreclosures[21] and 8 million lost jobs.[22] While America's economic elite eventually recovered from the financial collapse, the working class is still reeling even several years after the official end of the Great Recession. And while President Obama and the then Democratic-controlled Congress were able to pass some economic regulations and stimulus spending during the darkest days of the collapse, they were considered by most economists to be far too weak to offer broad relief to people battered by the crisis.[23]

America's economic elites, including big business, had a different agenda. While the overwhelming majority of Americans agreed that the government should be doing more to create jobs, the top 1 percent were more concerned about deficit reduction and reducing the nation's long-term debt.[24] This finding was part of a larger, groundbreaking survey conducted by Benjamin Page, Larry Bartels, and Jason Seawright examining the policy preferences of the affluent, defined as individuals with annual incomes greater than $1 million, compared to those of the general public. The survey found that 87 percent of affluent households believed that budget deficits were a "very important" problem—the highest percentage of all listed perceived problems.

But it's not just in choosing fiscal austerity over job creation that there are distinct differences in policy preferences between the general public (which includes the sizable working class) and the richest among us. As you can see in Table 6, the donor class isn't very supportive of a robust minimum wage, affordable college tuition, public schools, or ensuring that people can meet the most basic of needs. Differences of opinion about public policy are part of democracy; the problem isn't disagreement. The problem is that the donor class wins almost every time. In fact, America's elites are

Table 6. Policy Preferences of the Affluent Versus Those of the General Public

	WEALTHY IN FAVOR	GENERAL PUBLIC IN FAVOR
Government must see that no one is without food, clothing, or shelter.	43%	68%
The minimum wage is high enough that no family with a full-time worker falls below the official poverty line.	40%	78%
The government in Washington ought to see to it that everyone who wants to work can find a job.	19%	68%
The federal government should provide jobs for everyone able and willing to work who cannot find a job in private employment.	8%	53%
The federal government should spend whatever is necessary to ensure that all children have really good public schools they can go to.	35%	87%
The federal government should make sure that everyone who wants to go to college can do so.	28%	78%
The government has an essential role to play in regulating the market.	55%	71%
Spending on domestic programs like Medicare, education, and highways should be cut in order to cut federal budget deficits.	58%	27%

Source: Benjamin I. Page, Larry M. Bartels, and Jason Seawright, "Democracy and the Policy Preferences of Wealthy Americans," Perspectives on Politics *11, no. 1 (March 2013): 51–73.*

very effective at translating their wishes into legislation while the preferences of the working class are by and large ignored.

Research by the political scientist Larry Bartels finds that in contrast to the affluent, working-class Americans have little or no influence over policy outcomes. As he writes in his 2008 book *Unequal Democracy: The Political Economy of the New Gilded Age*, "The preferences of people in the bottom third of the income distribution have no apparent impact on the behavior of their elected officials."[25]

Although the working class is more liberal than the affluent or the middle class on questions of economic policy, that doesn't necessarily translate into the political will for change. What opinion surveys measure is the starting point for any kind of policy preference or ideological belief. But once active debate happens, underlying support can easily be made to erode. And politicians of both parties have found a very effective way to turn support for activist government into downright vehement opposition by using a weapon as old as our nation's history: race.

The Dog Whistle Still Blows

In this chapter we've shown that the majority of working-class voters believe the government does too little to help the needy, and are sympathetic toward those who are in need. Yet an examination of how these issues were portrayed during the elections following the Great Recession, when a great many Americans were reeling from the financial collapse, reveals the toxicity of using racial anxiety to diminish support (and sympathy) for struggling Americans.

In his illuminating book *Dog Whistle Politics: How Coded Racial Appeals Have Reinvented Racism and Wrecked the Middle Class,* Ian Haney López details the long history of politicians triggering racial anxiety to stymie the expansion of government. It's a strategy with roots in the 1968 presidential campaign of Richard Nixon, now widely known as the "southern strategy"—the Republican Party's infamous and calculated winning of votes in the South by appealing to racism against black Americans. When President Johnson signed the Civil Rights Act of 1964, he fretted that he had just signed away the South for the Democrats for a generation. The Republicans largely made that fear a reality.

In the decades that followed, starting with President Nixon and his championing of "states' rights" and moving on to President Reagan's "welfare queens," the first President Bush's demonizing of Willie Horton, and President Clinton's calculated "Sister

Souljah moment" and pledge to "end welfare as we know it," white political candidates have effectively used coded racial language to court the white vote and provoke antigovernment sentiment.[26]

In a shockingly honest admission, Lee Atwater, a leading political strategist and adviser to the Republican party, explained the southern strategy during an anonymous interview with political scientist Alexander P. Lamis, which appeared in his book *The Two-Party South* and was subsequently reprinted in *Southern Politics* magazine in the 1990s, this time with Atwater's name revealed. He described both the strategy and President Reagan's use of it:

> You start out in 1954 by saying, "Nigger, nigger, nigger." By 1968 you can't say "nigger"—that hurts you. Backfires. So you say stuff like forced busing, states' rights and all that stuff. You're getting so abstract now [that] you're talking about cutting taxes, and all these things you're talking about are totally economic things and a byproduct of them is [that] blacks get hurt worse than whites. And subconsciously maybe that is part of it. I'm not saying that. But I'm saying that if it is getting that abstract, and that coded, that we are doing away with the racial problem one way or the other. You follow me—because obviously sitting around saying, "We want to cut this," is much more abstract than even the busing thing, and a hell of a lot more abstract than "Nigger, nigger." So any way you look at it, race is coming on the back burner.[27]

Our nation's inability to confront its history of racial oppression and the continued racial anxiety and bias that exert a powerful influence in our society are among the reasons that we can't have nice things like affordable college tuition and child care, pensions, world-class infrastructure, and the higher taxes to pay for all these things, which countries without our destructive racial history simply consider the requisites of an advanced society.

Since the passage of the Civil Rights Act, through their use of racially coded language—up to Newt Gingrich's characterization of President Obama as "the food stamp president" and our racially fraught present moment—Republicans have deliberately used race to pursue their broader objectives of shrinking government and deregulating the economy. And it has worked. As Haney López explains, in 1964 almost two out of three whites voted for Lyndon Johnson, who embodied the support of activist government, but in 2012 nearly the same proportion of whites voted for Mitt Romney, a candidate clearly hostile to activist government. Additionally, in every presidential election since 1964, a majority of whites have voted for the GOP candidate, while rarely have more than one in ten blacks done so.[28] Something is clearly up. That something is race. But not racism in the vein of vitriolic name-calling and beating with clubs; it's something much more subtle but just as powerful. And as we'll see in the next chapter, for the black and Latino working class, the experience of racial exclusion and exploitation in the labor market and its associated institutions that began centuries ago still echoes today.

CHAPTER FOUR

The Great Power Shift

Javier wanted to be an architect—a big dream for a kid in East L.A. born to Mexican immigrants and living in the projects. If he had achieved that dream, it would have been one of those great modern-day Horatio Alger stories that allow us to tell ourselves that America really is a land of upward mobility, where we all have an equal chance to meet our aspirations. But alas, that America has always been a bit more fairy tale than real life—and it is even more fictional today in the midst of historic economic and political inequality.

Javier didn't become an architect. The bridge from the projects to a college campus was far too long to cross by himself, with neither his parents nor a school counselor able to provide guidance. Today Javier finds his creative outlet in drawing, carving wood, and writing rap and hip-hop songs in his free time. Now thirty-one, he works at Walmart stocking shelves in the frozen food department. Over the past eleven years he's worked in the food business at both hotels and fast-food chains. At Walmart he earns $10.20 an hour, which includes a one-dollar-an-hour bonus for working the overnight shift. But as is the case for many workers in food and retail, Javier's hours and days off vary from week to week, and his hours are deliberately kept just under full-time so that he does not become eligible for benefits.

Despite the fact that Javier and his wife work as close to full-time as they can (she works at Big Lots), the couple has needed to rely on payday loans to pay their bills, which perversely became harder to meet after their household income rose high enough to disqualify them for food stamps. The payday loan payment comes directly out of Javier's paycheck—a $300 bite out of a $700 paycheck, accumulating interest at an annual rate of 200 percent. These are hard facts for Javier to swallow. "I really don't want to be stuck with those payday loans," he told me. "Everything else, God provides. We have clothes. We go to food banks, they provide food." But a bigger paycheck would get him free of the payday lenders and maybe even allow him and his wife to afford things like his kids' school pictures or the yearbook his daughter wants. His new dreams are for his kids' future. He wants them to live in a society where they can provide for their own families without struggling too hard, and he wants them to know the importance of hard work.

That's why Javier joined OUR Walmart, the association of Walmart workers who are trying to improve working conditions at stores across the country. Javier got involved with the organization when a friend at Walmart introduced him to a United Food and Commercial Workers organizer. The organizer taught him about labor law and his rights to organize in the store and generally gave Javier the tools he needed to study his store's policies and local laws. Javier remembers attending his first action and seeing a woman marching, holding a sign with one arm and her baby with the other. "If she can be out there with her baby for a cause that's so right, then I can do it . . . There's no excuse for anybody to not speak up," he said. Javier takes his children to the actions and meetings of the organization so he can "teach them about their inner strength and the movement."

With OUR Walmart and the Fight for $15, the major unions

have dusted off their playbook and recommitted to labor's historical mission of "organizing the unorganized."

They have a lot of work to do.

Today the percentage of private-sector workers who are unionized is lower than it was before the Great Depression—that is, before President Roosevelt signed the Wagner Act, often known as labor's Magna Carta, which established the National Labor Relations Board and created firm legal rights and concrete procedures for workers to unionize. In 2014, just under 7 percent of private-sector workers, or about 7.3 million workers, belonged to a union, whereas nearly one-third of workers belonged to a union in the mid-1950s and one out of five private-sector workers belonged to a union in 1980.[1]

When President Obama was elected, the labor movement and millions of members of the new working class rejoiced that they might finally get real labor law reform, as the former U.S. senator Obama had cosponsored legislation to that effect and pledged to get it passed under his administration. But it wasn't to be. For years the major unions had been building support for labor law reform, commonly known as "card check" or "majority sign-up," which would require employers to recognize the union once a majority of workers sign cards stating they want the union; and those cards are submitted to, and verified by, the NLRB. Currently employers have the right to demand a separate secret ballot election conducted by the NLRB, which they inevitably do to buy significant time to thwart the union drive. Labor law in the United States is heavily skewed toward employers, who have more rights than the unions do to communicate with the workers. For example, employers have exclusive rights to talk to employees on company premises. They can require workers to attend captive-audience meetings where they present anti-union arguments without any obligation to let the union representative also speak. And in most cases management conducts its anti-union drive by hiring outside "union avoidance" consultants, a trend I discuss in more detail later in this chapter. Card-check reform was the key provision in a package of labor law reforms known as the Employee Free Choice Act (EFCA), the bill President Obama cosponsored when he was a senator. Along with card check, the act would have required binding arbitration between employers and the union if a contract had not been settled within 120 days, and increased the penalties for employers who retaliate against workers involved in the union effort.

With Democratic majorities in Congress and a Democratic president, the labor movement saw this as the window of opportunity to pass EFCA. The legislation was expected to sail through the House but face some difficulty in amassing a sixty-vote majority in the Senate (to stave off a Republican filibuster), because of a handful of conservative Democrats from states with low levels of unionized workers. Sensing that the card-check provision was too controversial to win all sixty Democratic votes needed to overcome a filibuster, the sponsors drafted an alternative that jettisoned card check in favor of expedited NLRB elections and stiffer penalties for companies that break the rules during a union drive.[2] But it turned out that EFCA wasn't a major priority for the president, who used neither his bully pulpit nor his political muscle to build public support and alignment in the Senate.[3] Meanwhile, big business pulled out all the stops in a blizzard of lobbying on the Hill and major advertising buys in Democratically vulnerable states. In an investigative report on the corporate-driven campaign to kill EFCA, Ken Silverstein of *Harper's Magazine* shared a quote from Glenn Spencer of the Chamber of Commerce about Obama's position on the issue: "The administration is working on a lot of serious issues, the kind of things that make a legacy—health care, the economy, immigration reform. This is just a distraction. It will split the Senate right down the middle, and you still may not win.

[Obama's] not going to ignore the unions. But will he sink a lot of political capital into a radioactive issue like this? I don't think so. Congress has noted the lack of engagement. They know what his priorities are."[4]

The new compromise version of EFCA, without card check, had a chance of passing the Senate. It would be a fight, but it was possible. But President Obama asked the Senate leadership to hold off on a vote until after the passage of health reform, which occurred just a few months before the bruising 2010 midterm elections, in which Democrats lost their congressional majority. The window closed again.

And so, for the fourth time in a half century, Democrats (President Johnson in 1965, President Carter in 1979, and President Clinton in 1994) who held power failed to stand up for the working class and the only institution dedicated to improving their lives.[5] Not to mention the only institution that consistently delivers working-class votes—including the elusive white working class—to Democratic candidates. So why the timidity? Because at the end of the day, Democrats have failed to challenge the power shift, and too often have aided and abetted the corporate hegemony. "The Democratic Party has always been only half enthusiastic about labor," is how Robert Master, assistant to the vice president for District 1 of Communication Workers of America, explained the repeated defeat of labor law reform on the Democrats' watch.

Unlike the Great Depression, the major financial crisis of 2007 that spawned the Great Recession did not spark any progressive resurgence or a rethinking of the fundamental rules of capitalism. There was nothing remotely close to the New Deal. No updating of our grossly antiquated and inadequate unemployment insurance. No federal jobs plan to rebuild our fraying infrastructure and put people back to work. No renewed push to restore workplace democracy to check the power of CEOs. Instead there was an anemic stimulus followed by enormous cuts to federal spending.

In the wake of the financial collapse, America's working class got No Deal.

By the time of the Great Recession, questions of power—who has it in the economy and who doesn't—had long been excised from the Democratic playbook in favor of a neoliberal, market-centered orthodoxy. (They were never in the Republican playbook, as the answers for Republicans have unwaveringly been that business should have the power and neither government nor workers should constrain people's right to run their companies however they want.) So as it became increasingly clear that America's biggest banks had manipulated, gambled, and grossly mismanaged their affairs, resulting in millions of lost jobs and $16 trillion in lost wealth, $6 trillion of that in home equity alone,[6] the Democratic establishment didn't see it as a wake-up call that something was terribly wrong in American capitalism. In fact, pretty much the opposite was the case.

President Obama, who won his election in large part due to working-class voters, nevertheless recruited his closest advisers from the very heart of Wall Street. Unlike FDR, Obama didn't welcome the hatred of America's financiers. Instead he kept them on speed dial and hand-plucked economic sages from their number. And instead of maneuvering a win to help save the main institution that helped create the middle class, he dithered and went back on his promise. Making matters worse, he gave in to the corporate class's deficit hysteria and lent his support to the idea that America needed a new era of austerity. In early 2011, when the unemployment rate was still nearly 9 percent, Obama released his proposed budget with the following statement:

> I've called for a freeze on annual domestic spending over the next five years. This freeze would cut the deficit by more than $400 billion over the next decade, bringing this kind of spending—domestic discretionary spending—to its lowest

> share of our economy since Dwight Eisenhower was president. Let me repeat that. Because of our budget, this share of spending will be at its lowest level since Dwight Eisenhower was president. That level of spending is lower than it was under the last three administrations, and it will be lower than it was under Ronald Reagan.

It's unfair to blame Obama alone for the failure of much-needed labor law reform for a working class on its knees, or for appeasing corporate America with a shrunken budget. The political calculus and ideology displayed by the administration reflected decades of shifting allegiances and power in the country, including the formerly proud "party of labor."

In fact, you, reader, may even be thinking to yourself that unions are some kind of industrial-age relic with no relevance in today's economy—that they're dying because they make no sense in today's tech-rich, global-scale economy. So let's take a quick look back and remind ourselves of what unions have done for American society.

The power of unions transcends the collective bargaining done on behalf of their workers. The real power is that through union dues, the labor movement can amass significant resources to engage in voter turnout, agenda setting, and issue advocacy, all on behalf of ordinary Americans. It's that amassing of political power that is so threatening to conservatives and corporate America. After all, big labor has been responsible for advances in our day-to-day lives that still make conservatives livid: Medicare, Medicaid, and, yes, Obamacare too; unemployment insurance; Social Security; the forty-hour workweek; pensions (what's left of them, anyway), and the minimum wage. These are just the greatest hits; many other humane advances in our lives owe their existence to labor unions. Power in America might be thought of as being historically represented by two scales. On the left is labor and on the right is capital. When one side loses political clout, the other side gains it. Today the right side of the scale overpowers the left. And that was no accident. So, with that brief reminder about the historic and continued need for a labor movement, let's get back to the story of just how those scales got so out of balance.

Labor's long decline to near extinction, and the growing invisibility of America's working-class majority, is a story of success, neglect, corruption, apathy, betrayal, and avarice, with powerful actors from politics, business, and labor contributing each of these elements at some point in the past six decades. The story begins shortly before the 1950s, when the first backlash against worker power was initiated by big business and conservatives in Congress. We have to go that far back because what Congress did in that year, as long ago as it seems, greatly constrains working-class power today.

Of Birth and Backlash

As part of his package of New Deal reforms, President Roosevelt signed into law the National Labor Relations Act, commonly referred to as the Wagner Act. The act gave workers the explicit right to select their own union by majority vote, and it guaranteed their right to strike, boycott, and picket.[7] The act also prohibited a set of contrary practices by employers, including company-sponsored unions, the intimidation or firing of workers who are attempting to unionize, and the blacklisting of union activists. The government would play an active role in mediating conflicts and union certification through a new agency created under the law, the National Labor Relations Board. It's hard to overstate the radical nature of this law at the time it was enacted. In fact, given the Supreme Court's long-standing animus to government involvement in the economy, the law seemed destined to be overturned by the Court and left in the dustbin of history. Indeed, most of the big corporations at the time—DuPont, General Motors, and Republic Steel—ignored the law under this assumption, carrying on their normal business of fighting union attempts by firing activists, hiring spies, and stocking up on guns and tear gas.[8] They funded the legal challenge to the National Labor Relations Act and a major public relations effort to smear the law in the court of public opinion. But in a 1937 decision in *National Labor Relations Board v. Jones & Laughlin Steel Corporation*, the Supreme Court declared the Wagner Act constitutional by sustaining Congress's power to regulate employers under the commerce clause.

To seize the opportunity to organize a greatly expanded swath of the industrial working class created by the Wagner Act, John L. Lewis of the United Mine Workers and Sidney Hillman of the Amalgamated Clothing Workers created a new labor federation, the Congress of Industrial Organizations (CIO), after leaving the American Federation of Labor (AFL). At the time, the leaders of the AFL, which comprised the various crafts unions representing cigar-makers, tailors, and the like, held great disdain for black and immigrant workers, particularly the "unskilled" laborers in America's growing mass-production factories. The CIO grew quickly, successfully launching historic strikes against industrial behemoths like GM. Within a year and a half, 3 million new workers voted to be represented by a union in the CIO.[9] As America entered World War II and demand for machinery, ammunitions, and aircraft soared, another 5 million workers voted for a union in just three years, including many women and black workers, who had gained new protections under federal contracts related to the war effort.[10]

During the war years, almost all the major unions abided by labor peace agreements and promised not to strike, which would impede the war effort. That meant that by the time the war was over, millions of workers had a host of grievances: long hours, speed-ups, lower wages. Like a powder keg, the end of the war brought widespread strikes to the homeland. In 1945, 3.4 million workers went on strike, followed by 4.6 million in 1946. No industrial sector was spared. And the workers won. By the end of the 1940s, nearly one-third of American workers were unionized, winning contracts for better wages, job security, and benefits.[11] Big labor was triumphant, and America's industrialists and conservatives were bitter, not just about the growing ranks of union members but about the whole shebang—the shifted balance of power and government protections for the working class ushered in by the New Deal.

It was time to strike back and put big labor in its place. So the Republicans in Congress drafted a bill that would amend the Wagner Act by gutting many of the hard-fought labor rights it guaranteed. The bill, known as Taft-Hartley for its cosponsors, Senator Robert Taft and Representative Fred Hartley, made it much tougher for labor to organize the workforce. Most important, it allowed states to pass so-called right-to-work laws, which gave workers, even in a unionized workplace, the right to refuse to join the union and to refuse to pay what are known as fair-share fees. Under these laws, workers can free-ride—enjoy the benefits of representation without having to pay for it—which makes the establishment and sustenance of a new union a much riskier proposition. The law also provided so-called free-speech rights to employers during an NLRB election, providing companies ample time and leeway to spread false and anti-union information to their workers. Employers could now hold mandatory meetings with workers to detail the perils of welcoming a union into the workplace, intimating that their jobs or indeed the entire factory might up and disappear. The Taft-Hartley amendments also outlawed industry-wide strikes, secondary boycotts, and sympathy strikes and gave the president more expansive authority to obtain injunctions against strikes if they jeopardized national interests. And its most ideological mandate was to require all union officers to sign an affidavit saying that they were not members of the Communist Party. At the time, some of the most effective organizers in the labor movement were Communists. After Taft-Hartley was passed, some unions collapsed and others were purged from the CIO or left rather than signing the pledge. As the Republicans intended, this provision of the law neutered the most radical and effective elements in the labor movement and washed the labor movement free of its most ardent supporters of women's and civil rights.[12]

The bill, passed in 1947 with enough votes to override the veto of President Truman, marked a significant triumph for big business. The bill was written by the National Association of Manufacturers and the Chamber of Commerce, which put significant resources into a public relations campaign to support it.[13] Big business saw the weakening of union rights as the first step in a campaign to bring down the entire New Deal order, and weren't shy about saying so. At the end of the war, Alfred Sloan, CEO of General Motors, spoke honestly about his disdain for the New Deal, saying, "It took fourteen years to rid this country of Prohibition. It is going to take a good while to rid the country of the New Deal, but sooner or later the ax falls and we get a change."[14]

In the aftermath of Taft-Hartley, a number of states passed "right to work" laws. Ten states, mostly in the South, passed them immediately in 1947, followed by another half dozen or so in the early 1950s.[15] Still, despite the restrictive new parameters of labor organizing, unions continued to build power and sign on millions of new members in every industrial sector, providing a working-class politics and social unity that brought security, respect, and dignity to America's wage laborers. But as big labor would soon learn, the constraints imposed by Taft-Hartley wouldn't always be so easy to overcome. And they wouldn't be the only impediment to maintaining working-class solidarity. Alfred Sloan's words would prove remarkably prescient.

Boom Times and Populist Power

America was booming: the smokestacks were billowing, the cars were rolling off the assembly lines, and the homes of the new suburbanites were sprouting. Much of this was fueled by postwar investments in the national highway system, federally backed mortgages, and the G.I. Bill. Of course, it's important to remember that all these investments were racially exclusive. The highways cleaved black neighborhoods from white neighborhoods; black people were disqualified from receiving mortgage loans through covenants in home contracts barring sale to them and by discrimination in federal mortgage insurance; and the G.I. Bill overwhelmingly benefited white veterans, since university administrators barred many black veterans from their universities. The civil rights movement was just getting started, and it would be two decades before our nation's laws mandated equal treatment of black Americans under the law. America's great economic expansion was overwhelmingly a white affair, with implications that I discuss more deeply in the next chapter.

But it was a historic expansion. Backed by the force of law, workers who were paid wages and built this industrial, consumption-soaked era had the nation's politics and spirit on their side. American workers experienced rising living standards that would have been unthinkable at the turn of the century. Quite extraordinarily, incomes grew fastest among workers at the bottom of the wage scale between 1947 and 1979.[16] Workers in the bottom fifth experienced income gains of 116 percent, compared to 86 percent among those in the top fifth of the income distribution.[17] Gross domestic product (GDP) grew a whopping 37 percent in the fifteen years after the war.[18] Productivity gains enriched both corporations and workers, and for the first time in the nation's history, large numbers of workers found themselves with enough disposable income to consume well beyond their daily needs. The working class (at least the unionized, industrial workers) became middle class through negotiated union contracts providing strong wages, vacation benefits, health care, and pensions.

America's industrial working class held center stage in American politics. In every presidential election between 1948 and 1964, the Democratic candidate launched his campaign with a Labor Day rally in Detroit's Cadillac Square.[19] In the prosperous decades of mid-twentieth-century America, organized labor was an influential power broker, and not just around the bargaining table. The AFL and the CIO merged in 1955 and combined their resources to build a formidable political operation, the Committee on Political Education (COPE), rooted in mobilizing workers around major legislation and turning out the union vote during elections. COPE focused on a nationwide voter registration drive of union members. At its inception, only about one-third of union members were registered to vote, but by 1961, COPE's effort had edged union voter registration to over 50 percent.[20] Incentivized with matching funds from the federation, union locals were encouraged to conduct member political education and voter turnout drives. The AFL-CIO also became a major player in the Beltway machine, as its in-house think-tank operation provided research, policy development, and analysis on a broad range of economic and social policy issues. Indeed, this internal brain trust developed the health-care policy that would eventually become Medicare.[21] By all accounts, the union movement's political power was central to the 1960 and 1964 presidential elections, and in some ways the federation functioned like a labor party within the larger Democratic Party. Critical to its electoral strength, labor dedicated significant resources to registering and mobilizing black voters. In 1964, 86 percent of union members supported Lyndon Johnson.[22] And owing to labor's political power, many Republican officials, particularly in heavily unionized states, supported union-backed legislation, including increases in the minimum wage and labor law reform.

The labor movement aligned early with the civil rights movement, with Walter Reuther, the president of the powerful United Automobile Workers, fighting to move the Democratic Party to a more liberal position on civil rights. Prior to the merger of the AFL and the CIO, the CIO was much more in the vanguard on civil rights. CIO activists in strong labor states pushed the Democratic Party to embrace stronger civil rights platforms, creating a groundswell that the national party couldn't ignore. In negotiations over the Democratic Party's 1952 platform, national leaders tried to moderate the party's statement on civil rights, fearing a revolt from the party's southern members. Upon learning that southern delegates might leave the convention if a strong civil rights platform was adopted, Reuther said, "If it so chooses, let this happen; let the realignment of the parties proceed."[23] (The southern Democrats stuck with the party until President Lyndon Johnson signed the 1964 Civil Rights Act, prompting him to predict, rightly, that the party would lose the South for a generation.)

By the 1960s, with a merged and powerfully dynamic AFL-CIO in the forefront, the nation's labor leaders were strongly aligned behind the push for national civil rights legislation. But there remained deep racial divisions among the rank-and-file, an issue the civil rights community argued the national federation was negligent in addressing. Racial discrimination at union locals was rampant, and not just in the South. White union members were often vehemently opposed to opening up apprenticeship programs to black workers and to integration efforts in society more broadly, particularly the use of busing to desegregate the nation's schools. By 1960 African Americans were more likely than any other racial or ethnic group to be union members (this is still true today), giving black union leaders considerable leverage within the larger federation. That leverage coalesced with the formation of the Negro American Labor Council (NALC), led by A. Philip Randolph, president of the Brotherhood of Sleeping Car Porters. NALC effectively pushed the AFL-CIO, led then by George Meany, to step up its efforts to combat racial discrimination in unions. Meany became a vociferous advocate for the inclusion of the equal employment opportunity section of the 1964 Civil Rights Act, testifying before the House in 1963 that "we need a federal law to help us do what we want to do: mop up those areas of discrimination which still persist in our own ranks."[24] But as I discuss more in the next chapter, racial tensions and discrimination remained deep problems in the labor movement, with many white union members abandoning the Democratic Party as policies around affirmative action and housing integration were implemented.

The 1960s were a high-water mark for what is referred to as social movement unionism. Labor was an advocate not just for its members but for the entirety of the working class. In 1967, 25 percent of all political activity, such as voting and contacting legislators, was performed by union members.[25] The working class was political, and its voice reverberated through state capitals across the country and through the halls of Congress. And much of what labor and its allies accomplished provoked the ire of the nation's corporate elites.

Big Business Fights Back

To big business, the 1960s and early 1970s brought nothing less than an all-out assault on corporations and free enterprise. A revolution was under way, and big government and big labor were leading the charge. The working class flexed its muscle in a wave of major strikes, shutting down production at GM, stopping the railroads, and even halting mail delivery. The strike wave from

1967 to 1976 was the biggest since the immediate postwar years. In 1970 alone there were thirty-four major work stoppages, each involving more than 10,000 workers.[26] But labor wasn't the only thorn in business's side. The consumer movement had achieved new regulations around health and safety, with Ralph Nader's Raiders focused on breaking corporations of their nasty habit of making profits at the expense of public safety and well-being. The environmental movement blamed the problems of pollution directly on negligent and careless factories, effectively advancing a major new federal law to control that pollution, the Clean Air Act of 1963, followed with expanded authority in 1970. Finally, the student antiwar movement included a broad critique of American big business, which the students saw as profiting from the war—particularly America's biggest banks and chemical and weapons manufacturers.[27] In May 1971, the *New York Times* reported that "since February 1970, branches [of Bank of America] had been attacked 39 times, 22 times with explosive devices and 17 times with fire bombs or by arsonists."[28] In that sense, the assault was direct.

The inflationary spiral only added to the growing set of problems that the American people blamed on big business. Rising food and gas prices pinched household budgets, and many concluded that business was behind the energy shortage and escalating bread prices. As David Rockefeller, then chairman of Chase Manhattan Bank, said, "Some people are blaming business and the enterprise system for all the problems of our society."[29]

Of course, business and conservative politicians viewed the situation quite differently. In their eyes, corporations weren't the problem; organized labor and an overreaching government were the culprits, dragging down the economy with high wages and onerous regulations. They were tired of being on the defensive and being pushed around by all manner of activists—labor, environmental, and antiwar. As political scientist David Vogel remarked of this time of sweeping reforms, "From 1969 to 1972, virtually the entire American business community experienced a series of political setbacks without parallel in the postwar period."[30] Business wasn't being paranoid—it *was* besieged by a great spurt of participatory democracy—and it was furious.

It was in this climate, two months before Lewis F. Powell Jr. was nominated by President Nixon to the Supreme Court, that he penned his now famous memo making the case for business to get organized, get political, and get going. At the time Powell was a successful corporate attorney in Richmond, Virginia, who sat on eleven corporate boards and was the neighbor and friend of a man named Eugene Sydnor Jr., a national director at the Chamber of Commerce and the chair of its Education Committee.[31] Sydnor asked Powell if he would write a memo to the chamber outlining the threats to free enterprise and providing a blueprint for business to fight back. On August 23, 1971, Powell delivered nothing short of a call to arms in an eight-page manifesto titled "Attack on American Free Enterprise System." The memo indicts a broad range of institutions engaged in the destruction of capitalism, including unions, the consumer movement, colleges, the media, and politicians. To Powell, the business community had not only sat on its hands, it had even facilitated the attack on free enterprise by appeasing and compromising with its critics. It was time for business to organize itself. Powell wrote that "the time has come—indeed, it is long overdue—for the wisdom, ingenuity and resources of American business to be marshaled against those who would destroy it." He provided a rather comprehensive plan for changing the hearts and minds of the American people and elites by aggressively promoting the ideology of the free enterprise system on America's campuses and in major broadcast media, with a network of scholars supported by business. The effort to remind America of the benefits of unfettered capitalism should be spearheaded by the Chamber of Commerce, which Powell saw as uniquely poised to coordinate and align the corporate community. After all, without a front group providing cover, corporate America might be reluctant "to get too far out in front and make itself too visible a target."

Powell acknowledged that changing public opinion would be a gradual and long-term process. But he said that the political fight must begin immediately, the payoff being changing the role of government and its stance toward business.

> But one should not postpone more direct political action, while awaiting the gradual change in public opinion to be effected through education and information. Business must learn the lesson, long ago learned by labor and other self-interest groups. This is the lesson that political power is necessary; that such power must be assiduously cultivated; and that when necessary, it must be used aggressively and with determination—without embarrassment and without the reluctance which has been so characteristic of American business.
>
> As unwelcome as it may be to the Chamber, it should consider assuming a broader and more vigorous role in the political arena.

He concluded the memo by articulating the narrative that must undergird all these efforts: that any attack on free enterprise is an attack on individual freedom.

Just a few short months after Powell submitted his memo to the chamber, he was nominated to the Supreme Court. Somehow the memo never surfaced during any of his confirmation hearings, and he slid into the permanent robe of justice without controversy. But a year after his ascension to the nation's highest court, a copy of the memo was leaked to the journalist Jack Anderson, who quoted it liberally in his syndicated *Washington Post* column. While Anderson's intentions were to embarrass and undermine Powell, the attention instantly made Powell's memo a sensation. The chamber publicly released the whole document, and copies were distributed throughout the nation. CEOs passed the memo along to each other, and in short order several rich capitalists stepped up to respond to the call, establishing and generously funding what are now the dominant conservative think tanks in America: the Heritage Foundation, the American Enterprise Institute, the Manhattan Institute, and the Cato Institute.[32]

It didn't take long for Powell's call to arms to be realized. Kim Phillips-Fein catalogs in *Invisible Hands* the growing army that was assembled to advance the free enterprise idea. The number of corporate PACs grew from 89 in 1974 to 821 in 1978. These PACs quickly became a giant tributary of political campaign funding, rapidly outpacing the number of union PACs, which stabilized at 250.[33] The business lobbying brigade was also formed during the 1970s, mushrooming from only 175 companies employing lobbyists in 1971 to over 2,500 by 1982.[34]

Meanwhile, the Chamber of Commerce grew exponentially, doubling in membership and tripling its budget between 1974 and 1980, while the National Federation of Independent Businesses doubled its membership over the same time.[35] The membership of these two groups covered a wide range of American small and midsized businesses. The corporate titans needed their own group. So in 1972 three organizations were merged to form the Business Roundtable, a CEO-only association. By 1977 the Roundtable counted 113 CEOs of the Fortune 200 as members—a conglomeration representing nearly one-half of U.S. economic activity.[36]

Prior to the coalescing of organized business, labor PACs greatly outnumbered and outspent corporate PACs. But by 1975 labor and business PACs were spending equally on congressional campaigns. The stalemate wouldn't hold. By 1980, just in time for the presidential campaign, union contributions represented only one-quarter of all the money spent on PACs.[37] The corporate political spigot widened thanks to a ruling by the Federal Election Commission that loosened restrictions on how corporations could fund their PACs. Before the 1975 ruling, corporations could establish PACs, but only funds from shareholders and executives could be used. With the FEC ruling, corporations could now solicit funds for their political entities from all their employees.[38]

We are now living, and have been for at least two decades, in Powell's imagined world, where big business calls the shots in democracy. The Chamber of Commerce has emerged as one of the most powerful and successful special-interest groups in the United States, leading America through a sharp right turn in economic policy. Between 1998 and 2012, the chamber spent $1 billion on lobbying.[39] In her book *The Influence Machine*, Alyssa Katz chronicles the rise of the chamber, examining its major role in some of the biggest policy debates of our time. From financial reform to tax policy to environmental regulations, the chamber has amassed an army of political operatives, litigators, lobbyists, and regulatory experts who can flood the nation's capital on a mere moment's notice. In addition to funding the chamber, nearly all American companies today engage in their own independent lobbying and political activity. In 2012, 372 companies reported spending at least $1 million on lobbying. All told, individual corporations spent $1.84 billion in lobbying in 2012. But that's still just the tip of the iceberg. Trade associations spent $553 million and businesswide associations $175 million, bringing business lobbying to a grand total of $2.57 billion—78 percent of all the money spent on lobbying in 2012.[40] By comparison, unions spent $45 million that same year. It is alarmingly clear that capitalism writes the rules in our democracy, and the needs of the working class are nowhere on the agenda.

Union-Busting Goes Mainstream

There's a very sanitized name for the thriving industry whose mission is to help corporations defeat a union drive: "union avoidance." But make no mistake, this is a profession based on intimidation and veiled threats. These well-paid professionals know exactly how far to push or even break the rules to snuff out working-class solidarity. Larger companies often contract with union-busting firms to do their dirty work, but smaller ones may rely on the head of labor relations or human resources to fight the bad fight.

It's no coincidence that the union-busting industry grew rapidly in the 1970s; after all, this was the decade in which business decided it was time to put up a fight, and quashing union attempts was ideologically and practically aligned with its goal of rescuing the free enterprise system. And the union-avoidance industry proliferated. There were only one hundred union-avoidance firms in the 1960s. By the mid-1980s, there were one thousand.[41] Whatever truce had been established between labor and management in the postwar decades was decidedly over. These union-busting firms created what are still tried-and-true forms of halting a union drive: employee "vote no" committees, anti-union videos (and now websites)[42] for use in captive-audience meetings, and literature articulating the potential dire consequences of voting in a union. Three-quarters of employers hire union-busting consultants when confronted with a union campaign.[43]

The Burke Group is the largest firm in the industry, with over 1,300 clients and over 800 counter-organizing campaigns under its belt since it opened its doors in 1981. Burke claims to have a 96 percent success rate and is especially good at turning back the union tide when the majority of workers have signed union authorization cards. A glance at Burke's roster of clients exposes a wide and diverse group of blue-chip companies—Heinz, NBC, Coca-Cola, Blue Shield, Lockheed Martin, Honeywell, and General Electric among them.[44] With consultants being paid between $180 and $250 per hour, anti-union campaigns can cost a company millions of dollars, especially if campaigns continue for multiple years. For example, Baltimore Gas & Electric (BGE) paid over $50 million to the Burke Group to successfully fight off three NLRB elections in 1996, 1998, and 2000 with the International Brotherhood of Electrical Workers (IBEW).

Labor law gives employers pretty wide latitude in campaigning against a union because of the free-speech provision in Taft-Hartley. Management can hold captive-audience meetings, basically mandating that workers attend and listen to predictions about how voting in a union would jeopardize the well-being of workers.

Joe, a thirty-three-year-old white man, has experienced the stridency of an anti-union campaign firsthand. He works at McKesson Pharmaceutical, just outside of Atlanta. McKesson, ranked eleventh in the Fortune 500 in 2015, is the largest U.S. pharmaceutical distributor, shipping pallets of drugs to major drugstore chains, hospitals, and pharmacies. Joe is a materials handler, a sanitized title for a job that basically means he hoists large totes (plastic bins) onto pallets until they're eight feet tall. In one night he lifts about 3,500 totes, which can range from less than a pound to twenty-five pounds. He works the night shift, when he and about ten other workers process $25 to $30 million worth of inventory per night. He admits that the job isn't rocket science, but the stakes are high: one mistake could amount to a $3,000 error. Joe is paid $16.83 an hour, earning an extra dollar per hour for the night shift.

Joe is leading an effort to unionize the McKesson facility in Atlanta because of the way management treats the workers. "I've never been treated as terribly as I've been in Atlanta. I've never seen a management team use so many threats. I couldn't believe it," he told me. He went on to describe a system of supervision based on favoritism, in which a small handful of workers are granted privileges and a lot of leeway to antagonize other workers. The issue of favoritism, which really translates into some workers getting easier assignments on their shifts, being cherry-picked for raises, and, in Joe's case, given leeway to verbally abuse and threaten other workers, is particularly nettlesome. So Joe is trying to unionize the distribution center. McKesson has other facilities that are unionized, most of them up north and already unionized when McKesson acquired them from another company. According to Joe, McKesson used to tout that the company had never had one of its facilities vote in a union that started out as McKesson, but that changed in October 2011, when local Teamsters 78 unionized the distribution center in Tampa, Florida.

But McKesson isn't rolling over easily on this one. A tape-recorded session of one of the captive-audience meetings is available online.[45] In one of the forty-five-minute sessions, the director of labor relations for McKesson gives a presentation on "how collective bargaining works." He tells the employees that "if the union gets voted in, everything that you have goes on the table and we negotiate it. So the current wages you have goes on the table, your benefits, your UPTOs [universal paid time off], and all your working conditions go on the table. And through the process of give-and-take, we bargain a contract. Now we give and take. So if I give something, I take something. That's my job. McKesson pays me to negotiate contracts. To get the best deal for McKesson. Nothing is guaranteed—both sides can make proposals, and the company can simply say no because we don't like what they're asking for."

If you depend on your paycheck to make ends meet, the brutal implication is, are you going to take the risk of losing it all by voting in a union? Where once the union calling card was that it offered workers job security and stability, employers have effectively turned the argument upside-down to make it seem like voting in a union entails risking everything you have.

The no-holds-barred attack by business, from the political arena to the workplace, left labor in the rearview mirror. Business opposition to everything from government spending to unionizing attempts has grown more brazen since the Powell memo delivered what turned out to be a plug-and-play strategy that would catapult the interests of the free market and its titans to the center of the economic and political world. Big business was the person everyone wanted to dance with at the party, even if it was someone else (like workers) who got you in the door.

Hard Hats Are Out, Briefcases Are In

During the 1960s and 1970s, through the civil rights movement and then the antiwar movement, a growing rift was occurring within the union movement and within the Democratic Party. On one side were the so-called hard hats—auto, steel, and construction workers—and on the other were America's growing legions of college students who heeded the moral call of the civil rights movement and spearheaded the protest movement against the Vietnam War. To put it mildly, these two groups did not see eye to eye. Rank-and-file union members—mostly white men—bristled at integration efforts both in the workplace and in their children's schools, viewing the progress of equality for black Americans as a direct threat to their own modest comfort and hard-won security. Republicans and southern Democrats exploited this new vulnerability among the white working class by appealing to their racial anxiety, epitomized by Nixon's "silent majority" strategy and Reagan's very deliberate and often not-so-silent dog-whistle appeals to white working-class voters. As the cultural distance between the hard hats and the activists widened, economic populism became decidedly passé, and cultural and consumer issues rather than labor captivated a burgeoning population of newly credentialed, upwardly mobile professionals. Major new membership groups such as Common Cause and Public Citizen captured the attention of these newly affluent white professionals, who were increasingly alienated from the white working class ideologically and culturally. More and more public activism was aimed at environmental protection, governance reform, and consumer protection. It's not that these interests were antithetical to the working class. It's just that they were decidedly not about living standards or working conditions, at a time when the very livelihoods of the working class were being ripped out from under them. As the working class faced dwindling jobs and shrinking pay, these "new class" Democrats were energized more by car safety and air pollution than by the falling minimum wage and inadequate labor laws. Violent attacks on antiwar activists by union-card-carrying hard hats—white men all—further eviscerated the prospects of solidarity within these diverging groups of Democratic voters. Adding to the out-of-touch positions of labor, the AFL-CIO maintained an intractable opposition to immigrants and immigration reform until 2000.

This battle for the heart and soul of the Democratic Party occurred at precisely the same time that organized business was ascending in power, and unions were inexorably caught in a downward spiral. As America entered the 1980s, this was the context for the shifting allegiances of the working class and the political direction of the Democratic Party. We know how this battle turned out. The Democratic Party, led by its more moderate southern flank, orchestrated a major shift in the party's identity, away from a pro-worker, pro-union stance toward a business-friendly, neoliberal panoply of platforms such as deficit reduction, welfare reform, and trade expansion. This was Republican Party Light, and it would shift the center of gravity of the Democratic Party away from working-class interests for twenty-eight years, until the election of

Barack Obama and a financial collapse that reignited progressive populism and severely wounded the reputation of big business and finance.

The Next Battle

Today the battle within the Democratic Party is a fun-house mirror image of the one fought during the civic upheaval of the late 1960s and early '70s. This time it's bold economic populism, fueled by a multiracial and broad class solidarity, that is catching fire. It's the business-friendly, free-trade and wishy-washy-on-government Democrats who are fighting to remain relevant. Meanwhile, the Republican Party seems to do nothing but double-down on the platform spawned nearly two generations ago—the anti-everything platform, call it. Anti-union, antiregulation, antigovernment, anti-inclusion, anti-immigrant, antiblack, anti-women, antitaxes. The new working class, beaten down by corporate elites and job-killing trade deals and largely abandoned by both Democrats and Republicans, is rebuilding the progressive voice in America largely outside the two-party system. The Sleeping Giant is stirring. Whether a full-scale awakening happens during the 2016 election largely depends on whether the Democratic candidate offers the new working class an authentic and robust platform for which to cast their vote.

CHAPTER FIVE

The Legacy of Exclusion

From the abolitionists, to the suffragists, to the unionists, to the civil rights and feminist activists, the bravery of a few to challenge the power of the many is part of our national heritage. But power, even when successfully challenged by underdogs, does not go gentle into that good night. So while the civil rights movement in many ways has beaten the racists and the feminists have beaten the sexists, many of the institutions and structures created by once legally sanctioned hierarchies continue to marginalize black people, women, and immigrants.

These racial, gender, and ethnic hierarchies still reach deeply into nearly every aspect of our society, including our labor markets. Although Title VII of the Civil Rights Act of 1964 outlawed racial and gender discrimination in the workplace, most of our workplaces remain deeply segregated. And people of color and women still disproportionately work in the lowest-paid jobs. These are the occupations that shape the new working class, a proliferation of underpaid, undervalued jobs in all sorts of service industries, from health care to restaurants. History shows up in the wallets of the new working class.

As the manufacturing footprint in the working class has shrunk, so has the white male archetype that has historically defined the working class. And as the share of private-sector workers in unions shrank along with those jobs, and working-class jobs became more diffuse and spread across numerous sectors, the idea of a coherent working class has lost its force. The racial and gender diversity of today's working class facilitates its invisibility in two important ways. First, a unifying, single archetype of the new working class remains elusive. Would it be a Latina hotel housekeeper? A black home care worker? A white warehouse worker? An Asian cashier? Definitions want to be neat and tidy, but this working class lacks the defining center of gravity that manufacturing provided the old working class. The second way in which the racial and gender diversity of the new working class undercuts its power is by the very fact that it is so disproportionately black, brown, and female, carrying the lingering residue of second-class citizenship status.

As discussed in Chapter 3, our political system, especially our politicians and the people who fund their campaigns, remains very much a white male establishment. The old working class had political and economic power on its side, aided and abetted by unassailable white male privilege. White men in manufacturing had all the best jobs, despite legal progress that was supposed to make it otherwise. And while white women and people of color, especially black women, have made significant progress into managerial and supervisory positions, these positions remain dominated by white men.

The decades-long destruction of American manufacturing profoundly changed the working class—the neighborhoods, the jobs, the families. What had once been nearly universal guaranteed well-paying jobs for young men fresh from high school graduation were yanked overseas with little regard for the devastation left behind. To add insult to injury, the loss of manufacturing jobs was often heralded as a sign of progress. Black men, who had fought for decades for their right to these well-paying jobs, watched them evaporate just as they were finally admitted to competitive apprenticeships and added to seniority lists. When capital fled for Mexico or China, the shuttered factories in America's biggest cities left a giant vacuum in their wake, decimating a primary source of jobs for black men that would never be replaced.

The invisibility of today's working class reflects deeply rooted, often unconscious biases about the worth and value of work done by women and people of color. And for the once privileged white working-class man, the dignity and sense of self-worth that came with a union contract and the trappings of middle-class life are sorely missed and their absence bitterly resented. These are the contours shaping, and sometimes constraining, the economic and political power of the new working class.

The Fight of Our Lives

Until the 1964 Civil Rights Act, neither women nor people of color had a right to equal employment. It was totally legal, as well as common practice, for employers to be explicit about who they wanted to hire—a man or woman, a white person, a black person, or a Latino. If you were a black woman looking for work, your options were clearly spelled out for you in the newspaper classifieds. Anything that didn't align with your race or gender was out of the question. This legal segregation translated into an earnings hierarchy that mirrored the racial and gender hierarchy in the country. The best jobs were for white men. All managers, supervisors, and professionals were white men and had been since the days of the American Revolution. Black men came next in the earnings hierarchy, but it was a steep drop from the flagship positions reserved for white men, as blacks worked the dirtiest and most dangerous factory jobs or in the fields. White women came next in the pecking order, consigned to low-paid clerical work and a smattering of entry-level factory jobs. Black women were mostly restricted to serving as domestics, cleaning the homes and caring for the children of middle-class and more affluent white families, or working in sweatshops in America's textile mills or garment factories. In 1960 the vast majority of Latinos lived in the Southwest, where legally they were designated as white but were never truly seen as citizens.[1] Most Latino men at the time worked in manual labor, filling jobs that employed few white men. Unlike black men and women, some Latino men were able to break into higher-skilled factory jobs and some Latinas were able to secure clerical jobs.[2]

As a result, in 1964 men and women didn't work the same jobs. Blacks, Latinos, and whites didn't work the same jobs. And even if the hiring preference wasn't explicit, pervasive cultural norms made it clear which positions were for whom. In factories, seniority lists and apprenticeship programs were structured in ways to ensure that only white men could advance into higher-paying positions and that a woman would never get a job previously held by a man. In the building and crafts trades, apprenticeships and jobs were controlled through tight kinship or ethnic networks, passed down from fathers to sons and among cousins for generations.[3] White women were expected to quit their jobs upon marriage, and were commonly fired upon becoming pregnant. When white women held jobs, they were largely in clerical positions—typing, filing, and answering phones. The same was not true for black women. One hundred years after slavery ended, black women were doing the same work their female ancestors did under bondage: cleaning, cooking, and caring for white people's homes and children, or working in the fields tending to white people's crops. In 1960 nearly two-thirds of black women worked in private homes, with earnings only half those of white working women.[4]

The Civil Rights Act of 1964, with its inclusion of both race and sex as categories protected from discrimination in employment, represented a landmark expansion of freedom and opportunity for the majority of American citizens. The muscle behind the bill was a cross-race movement made up of America's industrial unions and civil rights organizations, along with millions of working-class black people who marched, protested, picketed, and stood up against a brutal racial hierarchy. At the time a *Business Week* editorial noted, "The summer of 1963 may well go down as a landmark in the history of American industry. With a forcefulness few businessmen ever expected, Negroes nationwide are pressing, individually and in well-organized groups, for more jobs and better jobs. In its drama and impact, the campaign is comparable to the American workers' drive to unionize at the turn of the century."[5] The entrenched racism and bias of whites at the time of the civil rights movement, particularly in regards to hiring, is hard to overstate. One study found that fewer than one in four whites believed that companies should follow the same rules in hiring blacks and whites.[6] At the same time, with profound illogic, nearly half of both southern and northern whites believed that blacks "had as good of a chance" as whites "to get any kind of job for which they are qualified."[7] These two survey responses illuminate two deeply entrenched beliefs: that black people are inferior to white people, and therefore not deserving of equal treatment, and that the playing field is level (even in 1963), belying the structural disadvantage operating in our society.

The reason for inclusion of the category "sex" in the final bill is a source of debate among historians. There is some evidence that it was added by segregationists in an attempt to derail the bill. There's also evidence that the amendment was prompted by racial anxiety from white women, who worried that black women would be given preferential treatment if gender was not included. There's also some evidence that black women in the civil rights movement argued for its adoption to ensure that racially focused efforts didn't leave them behind.[8] Whatever the motivation, the amendment remained in the final bill, much to the dismay of most men, white, black, or Latino. The very idea that women should be able to have the same jobs as men was seen as both ridiculous and contrary to human nature. Executives at the time deemed women fundamentally, biologically, and emotionally so different from men that it was incomprehensible that the sexes could work side by side, let alone do the same job. The head of the Equal Employment Opportunity Commission (EEOC), charged with enforcing the law, said at a press conference that "the whole issue of sex discrimination is terribly complicated," which was not exactly reassuring. After the White House held a conference on equal employment, a *New York Times* editorial ridiculed the idea by saying that "it would have been better if Congress had just abolished sex itself," while the paper's news coverage focused on the hypothetical problem posed by a man applying to be a Playboy bunny. Meanwhile, over at the *New Republic*, the editors railed against the White House for taking the sex provision seriously, asking, "Why should a mischievous joke perpetrated on the floor of the House of Representatives be treated by a responsible administrative body with this kind of seriousness?"[9]

Dealing with married women's employment really confounded the EEOC. Cultural norms at the time assumed that married women were dependent on their husbands, leading employers to pay women less in both wages and benefits. Working-class women were much more likely to work outside the home than their middle-class counterparts, and black working-class women even more so. These middle-class and white-centric norms ignored the needs of working-class women of color, who were more likely to be co-breadwinners or the sole breadwinner in the family. While the EEOC immediately banned race-explicit categories in help-wanted ads, it dragged its feet for four years before banning ads designating specific jobs for men or women. In fact, upon passage of the Civil Rights Act, the EEOC made it clear to employers that the agency was solely focused on the advancement of black men.[10] It wasn't until the women's movement achieved political clout in the 1970s that enforcement of the gender-discrimination provisions were taken seriously by the EEOC, and thus also by employers.

In the decades since the act was passed, black men and working-class women of all races have fought hard to open the doors to better jobs and benefits. They joined forces through the trade union movement, launching the Coalition of Black Trade Unionists and the Coalition of Labor Union Women. Working-class union women, particularly in the Amalgamated Clothing Workers of America, led their unions and the AFL-CIO to take up the cause of child care and put it at the top of the agenda.[11] Black unionists led by A. Philip Randolph campaigned for a so-called Freedom Budget for All Americans that would provide a government guarantee of full employment, a higher minimum wage, and a basic income for those who couldn't work, along with major new investments in education and health care. Randolph unveiled the plan at a White House conference in 1966, just three years after the March on Washington for Jobs and Freedom. At the time, arguing for full employment was a strategic way to end the often zero-sum politics between whites and blacks, where a gain for one race was often seen as a loss for the other. As Randolph wrote with great prescience, "The tragedy is that the workings of our economy so often pit the white poor and the black poor against each other at the bottom of society. We shall solve our problems together or together we shall enter a new era of social disorder and disintegration."[12] Though the Freedom Budget gained champions in the labor movement, the faith community, and even among some business leaders, its aims were never fully embraced by the political establishment. Toward the end of his life, Randolph explained his thinking: "My philosophy was the result of our concept of effective liberation of the Negro through the liberation of the working people. We never separated the liberation of the white working man from the liberation of the black working man."[13]

Fifty years have passed since labor and civil rights groups joined forces to promote economic freedom and good jobs as critical to the advancement of civil rights for all people. It was the fight of our lives. And it still is.

Work: Still Separate and Unequal

The largest number of jobs that will be added to our economy in the future are going to be working-class jobs, requiring little education, if any, beyond a high school diploma. These jobs are heavily segregated by race and gender, paying wages that still reflect the long-standing hierarchies that the civil and women's rights movements fought tenaciously to overcome.

The two charts on page 127 examine the stubborn racial and gender segregation within the ten occupations that will continue to comprise the largest source of new jobs for the foreseeable future, with nine out of ten of these occupations squarely located in the bargain-basement economy. All but one require little to no education beyond a high school diploma. Nine of the ten jobs are rigidly segregated by gender, with women making up overwhelming majorities in all but three occupations. And seven of the ten largest-growing jobs are disproportionately filled by people of color.

In some of America's biggest cities, undocumented immigrants toil in pockets of the economy where wage theft is rampant, pay below the minimum wage is common, and abusive and degrading work environments are pervasive. In cities like Los Angeles, New York, and San Francisco, immigrant labor makes possible the many conveniences desired by the affluent, professional elite: cheap manicures and pedicures, drivers for hire, food and grocery delivery, and care of infants and young children. And for Americans across the country of every socioeconomic background, our nation's crops are still primarily picked and harvested by immigrants.

Chart 2. Top Ten Largest-Growing Jobs by Gender

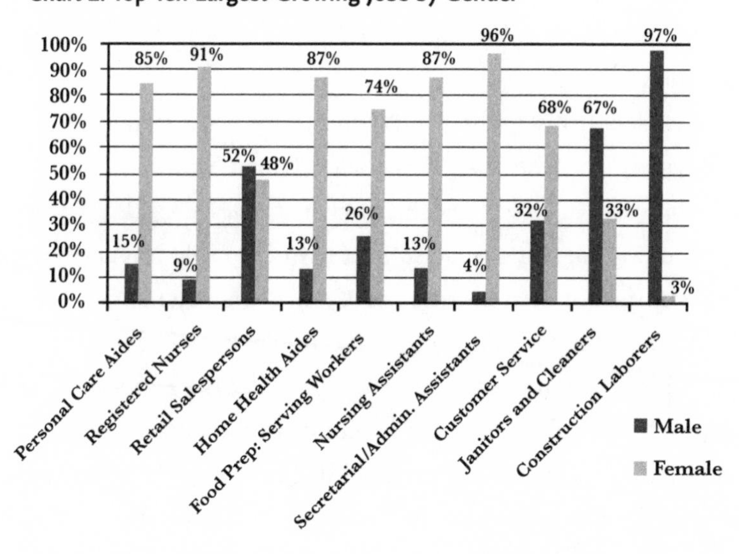

Source: Author's analysis of the 2012 U.S. Census and the 2011 American Community Survey of the ten largest-growing occupations as identified by Department of Labor's U.S. Bureau of Labor Statistics at http://www.bls.gov/emp/ep_table_104.htm.

Chart 3. Top Ten Largest-Growing Jobs by Race

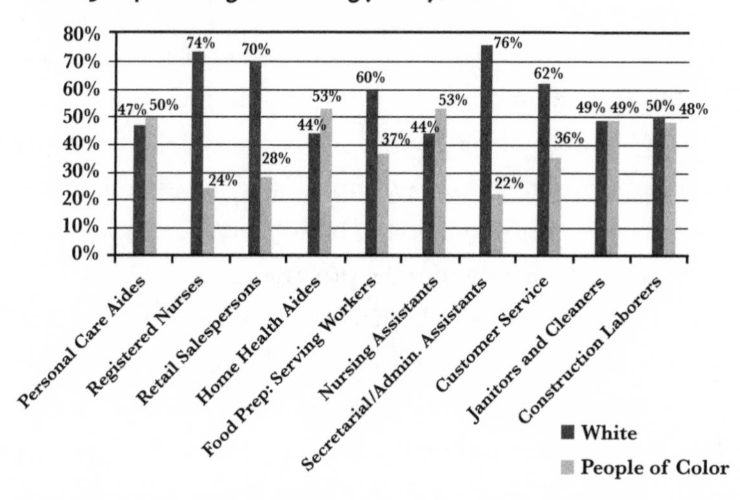

Source: Author's analysis of the 2012 U.S. Census and the 2011 American Community Survey of the ten largest-growing occupations as identified by U.S. Department of Labor, U.S. Bureau of Labor Statistics at http://www.bls.gov/emp/ep_table_104.htm.

What happened to the promise of Section VII, the provision of the Civil Rights Act that would provide equal opportunity in the workplace?

In a deeply researched and quantitative assessment of the drive to desegregate America's workplaces, Kevin Stainback and Donald Tomaskovic-Devey tell the story in *Documenting Desegregation* of substantial progress despite stubborn and durable privilege. In the years immediately following the Civil Rights Act, from 1966 to 1972, major gains were made among black men, black women, and white women—but, importantly, not at the expense of white men, who actually got a major bump up the advantage ladder.[14] As black men and black women made big gains into working-class jobs, white men got propelled upward into even more managerial positions.[15] Working-class jobs became more integrated, with more black women and white women working together than before, and more black men and white men working together on an equal-status basis. But at the top, white men still had the perch all to themselves, rarely interacting as equals with anyone besides other white men.

The hardened gender segregation began to unravel in the 1970s, as pressure from newly formed feminist groups such as the National Organization for Women (NOW) forced the EEOC and thus employers to enforce the sex provision of the Civil Rights Act of 1964. Between 1972 and 1980, both black women and white women earned their way into the professions, with black women actually outnumbering black men in professional occupations.[16] White women were the biggest winners during this era, gaining access to both managerial and professional occupations at much higher rates than either black women or black men. Black men made substantial inroads into higher-paying working-class jobs, while women remained largely locked out of those jobs. Overall, white women benefited more from Title VII, securing jobs that once were held by mostly white men in the professions.

By 1980, sixteen years of organized activism and formal federal oversight had resulted in remarkable gains for black women, black men, and white women. But progress ground to a halt in the 1980s, with only white women advancing over the next three decades. At the national level, our political debate became increasingly racialized, particularly around the issue of affirmative action. Conservatives successfully recast affirmative action as "reverse discrimination," and when they secured electoral advantage, they were able to transform this rhetoric into action. Upon winning the presidency, Ronald Reagan quickly knocked the teeth out of federal enforcement, slashing the budget of the EEOC and the office responsible for federal contracting.[17] He appointed Clarence Thomas (now a Supreme Court justice) to head the EEOC and ordered a near stoppage to enforcement of the law. Class-action lawsuits by the EEOC, the easiest way to secure remedies for discrimination, dropped from 1,106 in 1975 to just 51 in 1989.[18]

Today progress has stalled on all fronts. The integration of black men into jobs formerly held only by white men advanced rapidly in the 1970s, but this halted in 1980 as factories were being shuttered in favor of cheaper labor overseas. White women made significant gains in the 1980s but stalled out in 2000 as well. Black women made the least progress of the three groups after the Civil Rights Act. In her book *Opportunity Denied*, Enobong Hannah Branch describes black women as being "between a rock and a hard place," explaining that "the occupational advancement of black men occurred because of male privilege, and the occupational advancement of white women occurred because of white privilege. However, black women had no point of privilege by which they could advance."[19] By 2005 it was still the case that black men and women, especially black women, rarely worked in the same job in the same workplace as white men. As a result, in order to achieve completely integrated workplaces in the private sector, more than half of all workers would have to switch jobs.[20]

According to research by the Institute for Women's Policy Research, only four of the twenty most common occupations for men and the twenty most common occupations for women overlap.[21] Why does gender segregation in the labor market matter, especially for working-class women? Because any job that is performed primarily by women pays less than a similar job performed primarily by men. Home health aides earn less than janitors. Secretaries earn less than construction workers. Elementary-school teachers earn less than computer software engineers.[22] What's more, even women working in the same jobs as men get paid less than the men do. Women's work is still undervalued, and women of color suffer a disproportionate share of that legacy. The paychecks of women of color are undercut by both the gender and the racial wage gap, resulting in many of the lowest-paid jobs being disproportionately performed by women of color: home health aide, child-care worker, and nursing assistant. Women of color, both native-born and immigrant, are bound together at the bottom of America's wage hierarchy, despite the fact that many of these jobs carry an enormous responsibility—the development of and caring for people.

Of course, all men are not equal in our labor market either. Research by the Economic Policy Institute finds that black men are represented proportionately in only 13 percent of all occupations.[23] This occupational sorting has significant implications. The average annual wages in occupations in which black men are underrepresented is $50,533; that's a nice middle-class wage. However, the average in occupations in which black men are overrepresented is $37,005; that's a working-class wage. This research controls for any differences in education or skill level, leaving one remaining explanation for the lower earnings of black men: discrimination. This discrimination works similarly for black men as it does for women. Essentially, employers steer black men into lower-paying jobs, and the more an occupation becomes associated with black men, the less the boss is willing to pay for the work.

The composition of today's working class is a direct reflection of decades of gender and racial discrimination, with a pecking order constructed in the past. As immigration from Latin America increased in the past two decades, Latinas found their lot cast with that of black women—they were relegated to our nation's poorest-paid jobs, disproportionately likely to be engaged in the work of cleaning or caring. Today 88 percent of maids or housekeepers are women, 43 percent of whom are Latina. Among janitors, more than two-thirds are men, 30 percent of whom are Latino.[24] Forty-three percent of groundskeepers are Latinos, and in many of the lower-paid construction jobs, Latinos make up the overwhelming majority of workers, many of them day laborers who do the hardest, most backbreaking work at the end of a long subcontracting chain where cost containment can operate in the form of subminimum wages and unsafe working conditions.[25] Latinos now occupy the lowest rung in the American economic hierarchy, with wages below those of their white or black counterparts. While the white-black and white-Latino wage gaps have narrowed slightly since 1970, there is still clearly a white wage premium and a male wage premium (see Chart 4). In 2012 white working-class men earned $4.27 more per hour than black working-class men and $5.32 more than Latino working-class men. White working-class women earned $1.79 more than black working-class women and $3.18 more than working-class Latinas.[26]

While race- and gender-specific help-wanted ads are no longer legal, numerous studies conclude that employers exercise implicit bias that reveals strong preferences for white people, particularly men. One study found that white men with a criminal record were more likely to be called in for an interview than black men without a criminal record.[27] Another study found that résumés with white-

Chart 4. Working-Class Median Wages, by Race and Gender, 2012

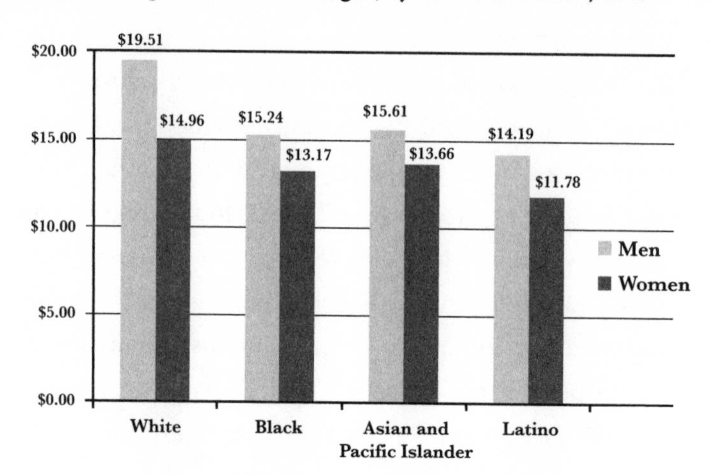

Source: Author's analysis, U.S. Department of Labor, Bureau of Labor Statistics, Current Population Survey Annual Social and Economic Supplement.

sounding names, such as Emily and Brendan, were 50 percent more likely to receive a call than were résumés with black-sounding names like Lakisha and Jamal.[28] A study examined bias against mothers and sent résumés that were otherwise identical for both men and women, with one difference: the "test" résumés included information indicating the man or woman was a member of the parent-teacher association. Women whose résumés indicated they were mothers were half as likely to be called as women whose résumés did not indicate they were mothers, while men whose résumés indicated they were fathers were more likely to receive calls than men who weren't parents.[29] Discrimination unquestionably exists; it has just learned to camouflage itself bureaucratically.

Women and people of color have made great strides in the past fifty years, but there's no turning away from the reality that our society is still organized along relatively rigid gender and racial hierarchies. As the quality of the new jobs being created in America continues to deteriorate, the inequities by race and gender are further exacerbated.

Who Cares?

Nearly twice as many women as men work in jobs paying wages below the poverty line. In fact, five of the most common occupations for women—home health aides, cashiers, maids and household cleaners, waitresses, and personal-care aides—fall into that category, compared to just two of the most common jobs for men.[30] With the exception of waitresses, these jobs are either primarily or disproportionately done by women of color. Two are caring jobs and two are serving jobs, which means that they involve high levels of interaction with human beings from a subordinate position.

Jennifer, a forty-three-year-old white woman, describes her job as a preschool teacher as a huge responsibility and one that she loves because she knows how important emotional, social, and cognitive development is at an early age. She told me, "Now is when you can make a big impression on their lives. I'm with them more than their parents are. I'm with them eight hours a day. Their parents are with them for a couple hours and then they go to bed. I feel like I can make a difference in their lives." And she's right. The care and learning environments experienced by young children will have ripple effects throughout their lives, as well as throughout society. Getting it right or wrong during this age can have huge benefits or huge costs. Research shows that it's an investment worth making, returning between $7 and $11 for every $1 invested.[31]

For filling such an important job, Jennifer earns $9 an hour, up from the $7.50 she earned for two years before getting a raise. To become a preschool teacher, she had to earn a CDA (Child Development Associate) credential by taking a thirteen-month course that includes 480 hours of experience working with young children combined with 180 hours of formal training.

Like most women who work in the so-called caring professions, Jennifer derives deep satisfaction from seeing the impact she is making on people's lives. Her biggest complaint, shared by most women in the caring professions, is that the value she creates is diametrically opposed to how much she earns. "I wish we got more credit for what we do," she said. "I have a big responsibility. I take care of anywhere from ten to fourteen kids a day. And I get paid nine dollars an hour for it. Their lives are in my hands every day. And I don't think we get enough credit for what we do. It's not a small job. It's a big responsibility, what we have to do. People are trusting me with their kids." It turns out that choosing a profession focused on developing and maintaining the well-being of people—whether old, young, disabled, or sick—means sentencing oneself to a life of penury.

America's demand for these kinds of caring jobs will only increase over the next several decades. The aging of the baby boomers means that the population of the very elderly—those over age eighty-five—will more than double by 2035, to 11.5 million.[32] Millions of new jobs will be created to help these boomers age with dignity, in their homes, as their bodies begin betraying them, making it difficult for them to feed, bathe, and dress themselves. As a result, home health aides will be the largest and fastest-growing occupation in the country, more than doubling in number over the next decade.

To understand how historical racial and gender hierarchies still echo through our society, one should look no further than the caring professions. Paid care work, whether for the elderly, the disabled, or the young, has always been the job of women, and traditionally of black women.

Home health workers are disproportionately women of color, often immigrants from around the globe. In New York City, home health workers hail from the Caribbean, Africa, and Latin America, leading one *New York Times* reporter to observe that "home care aides are the garment workers of the modern New York economy."[33] In their book *Caring for America*, Eileen Boris and Jennifer Klein track the historic devaluation of care work. They tell the story of Evelyn Coke, a seventy-three-year-old Jamaican immigrant who worked as a home health aide for twenty years, often pulling twenty-four-hour shifts without overtime pay. When her own health was failing, Evelyn became the plaintiff in a lawsuit seeking compensation for all those extra hours of unpaid work, challenging the Labor Department regulations which stated that home care attendants were not covered by federal minimum wage or overtime laws, even when, like Evelyn, they were employed by a for-profit agency. The case made its way to the Supreme Court, where, in June 2007, Evelyn lost her case and millions of home health workers lost their right to finally be treated as real laborers. During oral arguments, Justice Breyer expressed concern that if home health workers were paid overtime and minimum wage, millions of families would not be able to afford the care.[34] The Bloomberg administration and federal government allied against Evelyn, citing the concern that higher wages would greatly increase Medicaid and Medicare costs (which pay for the lion's share of home care services), squeezing state and federal budgets.[35] While the Court's unanimous opinion focused on procedural and interpretative analyses of congressional intent and regulatory authority, the reality remains that it is entirely acceptable, culturally and morally, to argue that home health workers shouldn't be paid minimum wage or overtime because it would be too costly for Medicare and Medicaid. Can you imagine the same argument being made about doctors? Can you imagine the same argument being made if the work was done overwhelmingly by white men?

In Evelyn Coke's case, the justices and her opponents basically removed the workers' lives from the equation. The costs to the state and to the patients were paramount; the livelihood of the workers was rendered completely invisible and inconsequential. But like their union ancestors in the garment industry and textile mills, these women are standing up for themselves and getting organized. After a decade-long campaign in California involving dozens of protests, some policy jujitsu, and creative organizing, 74,000 home health-care workers voted by a ten-to-one margin to join the Service Employees International Union (SEIU).[36] The organizing win was made possible by legislation that allowed counties to establish public authorities defining themselves as joint employers of the workers and thereby able to negotiate with the union, and created a registry so families could find home care workers.

The SEIU has since taken this strategy to other states, resulting in 27,000 home care workers in Minnesota voting to join the union in 2014—the largest union election in the state's history.[37] The contract negotiations with the state delivered a raise from $9 to $11 by 2016, the first-ever paid sick days, investments in training, and protection from wage theft. At the federal level, President Obama's proposal to change the rule that exempted elder-care workers from minimum wage and overtime pay made its way through the courts and was ultimately upheld by the U.S. Court of Appeals for the D.C. Circuit in August 2015.[38] The proposed changes were favored by some states (Connecticut, Illinois, Iowa, Maryland, Massachusetts, Minnesota, New Mexico, and New York), all of which submitted briefs in support of the new rule, while other states (Arizona, Georgia, Kansas, Michigan, Nevada, North Dakota, Tennessee, Texas, and Wisconsin) submitted briefs opposing the new rule.[39] The win both delivers material gains for the workers and, as important, finally recognizes their occupations as "real work"—a major victory for a workforce that is expected to grow from 2 million workers to over 3 million by 2022.[40]

SEIU represents about 600,000 home care workers, a scale that lends itself to comparisons with the great industrial union organizing of the last century.[41] This is substantial progress, but unlike the contracts negotiated for the mostly white and mostly male blue-collar manufacturing workers, these jobs don't remotely provide the wages and benefits that allowed the previous working class to live a middle-class lifestyle. And thanks to another Supreme Court ruling, the ability of unions to organize home care workers took a big hit. In states without right-to-work laws, all workers who benefit from a union contract must pay an agency fee, even if they decline union membership. The agency fee basically represents the worker's fair share of the costs of the union's providing collective bargaining and other benefits. This is a smaller fee than the overall union dues, which cover broader costs, such as political funding and lobbying. Without an agency fee, workers in companies that have voted in a union can essentially take a free ride, enjoying the benefits of an enhanced contract without supporting the union's costs of making the contract happen. That loss of revenue makes organizing in right-to-work states much more financially risky and is a major reason that union density in those states is so much lower.

Now enters the landmark case that dealt a major blow to organizing home health workers, *Harris v. Quinn*. The SEIU has been successful at organizing home care workers by getting states to adopt joint employer status, making the state as well as the individual client receiving care the official employers of the workers. This makes sense, since a majority of the workers' pay comes from public funds. But the Court ruled that the home care workers, who were still hired by and could be fired by individual clients, were not wholly public employees. They were "partial public employees" and therefore exempt from being required to pay agency fees like public employees represented by a union.

Now, to be sure, this was a major blow to organized labor. But it was not the fatal setback many thought was coming. This case hinged on an earlier Supreme Court ruling (*Abood v. Detroit Board of Education*) that found it constitutional to require public employees who choose not to join a union to pay an agency fee to cover the costs of representing them. In writing the majority opinion, Justice

Alito created a wholly new category of worker—this "partial public employee"—as a way to undercut the unionization of a workforce that is overwhelmingly composed of women of color. The fatal blow would have been if the Court had overruled its *Abood* decision and declared that requiring non-union workers to pay agency fees was unconstitutional for all public employees. However, legal experts agree that in the majority decision, the justices all but invited new cases that would directly challenge the *Abood* precedent, implying that the agency fee requirement of public-sector employees was on very shaky constitutional ground. And indeed, the Court quickly accepted a new case directly challenging the constitutionality of mandated agency fees. Arguments in the case, *Friedrichs v. California Teachers Association,* will be heard in early 2016.[42] If *Abood* is overturned, it will eviscerate public-sector unionism by making all union dues voluntary, essentially allowing far too many workers to free-ride on union benefits without paying dues, or covering their fair share of the costs of collective bargaining. In the private sector, this kind of exclusion is known as right-to-work, and it has essentially made unionization in right-to-work states exceedingly rare.

From Smokestacks to Barbed Wire

When America's great industrial factories were locked up and denuded of equipment, some of our nation's biggest cities were left with barren stretches of wasteland. What once symbolized productivity and ingenuity would become an anachronistic remnant of blue-collar America, either destined for decay or converted into expensive lofts for a new, upwardly mobile professional class. The pace of job losses was swift, a hard jerking away of people's livelihoods and dignity, leaving a reverberating pain that would last for decades. The Civil Rights Act of 1964 opened up opportunities for black men to work in the reigning industrial sector of the time, but predominantly in the hardest, lowest-paid jobs—the very jobs that were most susceptible to being replaced by machines.[43]

As a result, black men experienced more than their fair share of dislocation as a result of deindustrialization. Thanks to a generation of discriminatory housing policies, black Americans were also more likely to be living in the central core of urban America. So when major steel factories on the outskirts of major cities—Los Angeles, New York, Detroit, Cleveland—shut down, the communities closest to these economic hubs faced severe economic isolation and collapse. The depth of the loss was substantial. Between 1972 and 1982, New York City lost 30 percent of its manufacturing jobs, Detroit 41 percent, and Chicago 57 percent.[44] White residents in those cities were better positioned to move to the suburbs in search of employment, while black Americans were left behind because of active redlining, designed to keep black people out of the suburbs. In 1970 more than 70 percent of black workers held blue-collar jobs; by 1987 only 27 percent were employed in industrial jobs.[45] Unemployment among black men soared, while black women did somewhat better in securing jobs in the exploding new service sector. As companies shipped entire industries overseas and the central cities lost white middle-class residents to the job-exploding suburbs, urban black people found little support or sympathy from our political elites. Laissez-faire, trickle-down economics was gaining prominence and power just as globalization tore through American manufacturing. After the widespread shedding of factories in the urban core, Ronald Reagan made it to the White House, in no small part thanks to his astute use of racial anxiety to win over white working-class voters. Help most assuredly would not be on the way.

Patrisse Cullors, one of the three founders of Black Lives Matter, directly experienced the simultaneous havoc created by closing factories and the "war on drugs." Her father worked for General Motors in Van Nuys, California, a job that made her dad exclaim with pride, "I could build a car from scratch." Open since 1947 and employing 2,600 workers at its peak, the plant closed in 1992, when Patrisse was about eight years old. Growing up, Patrisse and her brothers were supported by her mom, who "worked three part-time jobs to keep a roof over our head." Her dad's job had provided the family with excellent health insurance and additional resources to supplement her mom's earnings. Patrisse recalls exactly how the factory closing affected her life, explaining that it "was such a major blow to him, and to our family. And really, to the community at large. My grandfather worked at General Motors, then my dad worked at General Motors. So many children, parents, and families literally inherited the job in the factory." And the loss of her dad's job quickly plummeted the family from "being working class to being super-poor," Patrisse remembers. Instead of having access to private doctors and world-class care at Kaiser Permanente, she and her brothers now had to go to the public county hospital. Her dad was never able to rebound to his previous salary, instead relying on a series of low-paying jobs at auto-repair franchises like Midas.

Cullors describes the connection between deindustrialization and mass incarceration as happening "fast, fast, fast." Her neighborhood, Van Nuys, was poor in the 1990s, and right next door to the affluent community of Sherman Oaks, which made Van Nuys susceptible to gentrification and its black residents undesirable. "The neighborhood became super-surveilled and super-policed. I witnessed my brothers and their friends being harassed on a daily basis, stopped and frisked. They were eleven, twelve, and thirteen. There was no community center or community organization for the neighborhood kids to go to, leaving them with nothing to do but sit and hang out all day." In his teen years, her older brother was brutally beaten by a sheriff while in the L.A. County jail, an experience that fundamentally shaped Cullors's life. Years later, after graduating from UCLA in religion and philosophy, she made a decision to make her life's work tackling the state-sanctioned violence she witnessed in her neighborhood. So when the ACLU filed an eighty-six-page complaint in a class action suit against the Los Angeles Sheriff's Department for abuses in its jail system in 2011, Patrisse answered the call. She read the report in one evening and decided she was going to do an art piece with the complaint. She created a forty-five-minute performance piece which included recordings of the notes her mom kept while her brother was incarcerated, news clippings from the sheriff and undersheriff denying the allegations, and the eighty-six-page report, which was pasted onto giant boards sectioned off with police caution tape. "It was a beautiful and very intense piece," she recalls. She toured the piece for six months, and the repeated requests from viewers for information on how they could get involved and fight back prompted Cullors to start Dignity and Power Now. That group's major demand was permanent civilian oversight of the Sheriff's Department, which they won in September 2014; they are currently negotiating with the county supervisors about implementation. For Cullors's family and millions of others living in former industrial belts, the loss of manufacturing jobs and the rise of extensive incarceration were inextricably linked.

Let's take a short look back at Chapter 4 and recall the hyper-racialized politics of the 1970s and 1980s. By the mid-1970s the Republican Party was determined to peel away white working-class voters by playing to their increasing racial anxiety after the civil rights reforms opened up competition to jobs, mandated busing to integrate schools, and developed affirmative-action policies to redress the long-standing exclusion of African Americans from opportunity. As several scholars have observed, it was the white working class who bore the brunt of integration efforts. As Thomas and Mary Edsall explain in their book *Chain Reaction*, white working-class men felt they had worked hard to buy a home near good schools, only to find that now their kids would have to be bused way across town. It didn't sit well, and it bred resentment. On the other hand, most affluent whites lived in communities so far from either black or white working-class people that their children were rarely affected by busing orders.[46] The Republican Party used the detachment of white elites from the implementation of integration to charge the Democratic Party with liberal elitism: championing the rights of minorities from a lofty perch on which they remain unaffected. In addition, the Republican Party cleverly began describing affirmative action as "reverse discrimination," arguing that better-qualified whites were losing jobs to less-qualified minorities. It was a cynical and ugly ploy, but it worked.

And it's still working. Charges of reverse discrimination have resulted in Supreme Court rulings that have all but ended affirmative action. The Republicans pursued a narrative of "color blindness," arguing that the way to overcome past and current discrimination was to bar government from considering a person's race at all, often co-opting and distorting Martin Luther King's famous statement that "we should judge people on the content of their character, not the color of their skin." In addition, ever since Nixon's campaign focused on law and order, the Republican Party has found electoral success in framing urban problems as ones of lawlessness, disorder, and dysfunction. The problem—rising drug-related crimes—was addressed not as the symptom of economic blight and marginalization but instead as a moral and character defect of black people—one that required a war to fix. That war, which is still officially under way, was the "war on drugs." As Michelle Alexander observes in her stunning and critically acclaimed book *The New Jim Crow*, "Conservatives found they could finally justify an all-out war on an 'enemy' that had been racially defined years before."[47]

By the time Reagan took office, two things were crystal-clear about the ideology of the Republican Party: 1) it would use race to divide the working class to win elections; and 2) it would use race to fuel antigovernment sentiment to shrink the role of government. So just when urban America was reeling from the economic upheaval of deindustrialization and black working-class men and women found themselves either jobless or underemployed, the narrative about what was happening in these neighborhoods depicted black people as morally and culturally defective, mired in a web of self-destruction that included drugs, out-of-wedlock births, and crime.

Ronald Reagan masterfully spun dog-whistle narratives, turning racially coded language into electoral gold. He was an equal opportunity offender, demeaning black men and black women alike. In addition to the mythical "welfare queen" with "eighty names" and "twelve Social Security cards," whose tax-free income alone was "over $150,000," Reagan described the criminal as "a staring face—a face that belongs to a frightening reality of our time: the face of the human predator."[48] He promised to crack down on crime by bringing more federal resources to bear on the problem—law and order being the one exception to a rigid intolerance for government spending.

As neighborhoods in our greatest cities cried out for help in dealing with the spasms of joblessness and a rising drug trade, there was no New Deal. Or new War on Poverty. There was a war on drugs. And it was, and still is, being waged with near impunity in black and brown communities.[49] Today 2.2 million people are incarcerated in prisons or jails, up from just 350,000 in 1980.[50] A full 60 percent of incarcerated individuals are people of color, and two-thirds of all people in prison for drug offenses are people of color. Today one out of three black men and one out of six Latino men is likely to be imprisoned at some point in his life, compared to one out of seventeen white men. And it's working-class men of color who have been cast as the enemy in this sprawling dragnet. The new working class is missing millions of black men who instead of punching the clock are now serving time as a result of the economic wasteland wrought by deindustrialization. The United States spends $80 billion annually on incarceration, and the economic and social toll expands the amount. A criminal record casts a long shadow, with an often lifelong sentence of social and economic exclusion. Even the most entry-level of jobs require a criminal background check, and most states restrict an ex-offender's right to vote. In 2010, 5.8 million people weren't allowed to vote because of a criminal conviction, with black Americans more likely to be disenfranchised. In three states—Florida, Virginia, and Kentucky—more than 20 percent of black Americans were disenfranchised.[51] Imagine if the cumulative resources spent on the war on drugs had instead been allocated to rebuilding the communities left barren by closing factories and isolated by white flight.

Today almost one in twelve black men is behind bars, a staggering loss to families, neighborhoods, and society.[52] And for the partners and wives left behind, most of whom are working-class, the challenges of making enough money to get ahead have only intensified with the rise of the bargain-basement economy. Nearly half of all child-care and home care workers have to supplement the incomes they earn from their jobs with public assistance.[53] These are the "welfare queens" that Reagan was so fond of demonizing and that President Bill Clinton called to mind in his successful effort to "end welfare as we know it."

Today young activists like Patrisse Cullors and thousands of others are fueling a new civil rights movement that brings together economic, social, and racial justice, which I cover in more detail in Chapter 7. In working-class black neighborhoods, as in Ferguson, Baltimore, Staten Island, the Bronx, and Cleveland, this new generation is connecting the issues of joblessness, police brutality, and the prison industrial complex. It's by and large a movement of, by, and for working-class people of color, and like the earlier civil rights movement it has generated significant white allies, particularly among college-educated whites.

History Repeats Itself: The Immigrant Story

Since the beginning of wage labor at the dawn of industrialization, immigrants have been central to building working-class power (in addition to establishing and building the country). Today, with people of Latino descent making up the largest percentage of the nation's immigrant population, it's easy to forget that their white ethnic predecessors—Polish, Irish, and Italian—were once considered nonwhite and marginalized in both society at large and in the economy. These white ethnics led major strikes in the early 1900s, sometimes by joining forces with blacks, as was the case in the great shutdown of U.S. Steel in 1919.[54] At the turn of the twentieth century, these immigrants lived in tenements and ghettos and were considered to be of a lower class and status than their native-born, "genuinely" white-skinned counterparts. That changed with the "all hands on deck" ethos needed to fight World War II. With near-universal participation by American men, albeit still segregated by race, returning white ethnic veterans were granted full economic and political citizenship, their ethnic identities subordinated as the privileges of whiteness expanded through free college, federal housing loans, and better wages through the labor movement.[55] It's unimaginable that the labor movement in the postwar years would have achieved the scale and power it did without the substantial population of European ethnics becoming "white" and therefore being granted the highest legitimacy and status as workers and citizens. But their inclusion as whites further marginalized black people and Mexican Americans, who now formed a smaller group of "others" who could be consistently compared to or, more important, contrasted with the archetypal white working-class male.

Our nation has a long history, one that continues to this day, of viewing Latino immigrants as cheap and often disposable labor. We want them here when we need them but quickly turn our backs when the going gets tough. We want their labor but refuse to acknowledge the cultural contributions or full humanity of our brothers and sisters from Latin and Central America. In the early days of America's industrial expansion, many of the railroads were built and our crops harvested by Mexicans, who were recruited for these jobs. It's estimated that between 1920 and 1930 more than 1 million Mexicans crossed the border to answer the call of America's farmers and industrialists. But when the Depression hit and jobs became scarce for all Americans, the Mexican workers were swiftly and forcibly deported.[56] During World War II, when immigration from Europe and Asia was curtailed, and then after the war, when the great engine of American productivity seemed destined to deliver endless prosperity, American companies actively recruited Mexican workers to perform some of the most backbreaking, menial, and lowest-paid jobs. Migrant Mexican workers helped fill labor vacuums in the fast-growing Southwest, much of it fueled by major agribusinesses, which provided a bountiful supply of crops to be harvested. In 1950, 450,000 Mexicans were recruited to the United States as part of what was called the *bracero* program. But as before, when another recession gripped the United States in 1954, white Americans again expressed their economic anxiety by lashing out against Mexican workers. In an operation officially titled (this is no joke) Operation Wetback, the federal government rounded up something between 1 and 2 million Mexicans and quickly deported them.[57] And as always happens in the well-established boom-and-bust cycle, all was forgiven and the *bracero* program was reinstated once the economy bounced back.

The program continued until 1964, but the practice of drawing migrant Mexican workers for cheap labor in the Southwest continued unabated, just under a different name. By 1960 fully one-quarter of the southwestern workforce was made up of immigrants from Mexico. Eventually these farmworkers, along with their Filipino counterparts, would band together in one of the longest, most tumultuous, and most sophisticated labor-organizing triumphs in our nation's history under a motto that still resonates with oppressed workers and can be heard chanted in the new labor battles today: *¡Si Se Puede!*

While Mexicans make up the largest group of Latino immigrants in the United States today, about 50 percent, great waves of migration from Puerto Rico, Cuba, El Salvador, Guatemala, Bolivia, Nicaragua, Colombia, and the Dominican Republic fill out the broad Latino working class that is a huge part of our Sleeping Giant. Some people from these countries came fleeing brutal dictatorships, civil wars, and sinking economies—a good share of which were the result of U.S. foreign policy and trade policy—hoping that *el Norte* would provide a better life for themselves and their families.

The first large wave of Puerto Ricans, who, though officially citizens, are more often treated as visitors or outsiders, came to the United States in the postwar period; many clustered in barrios in New York City. But not insignificant numbers were also bound for factories in the great blue-collar cities of the Midwest. Generations of Puerto Rican families were able to move their families out of the barrios and into public housing being built for the working class, a story made more familiar to Americans by the ascension of Sonia Sotomayor to the Supreme Court. But like their black counterparts, Puerto Ricans experienced severe dislocation in America's cities when factories packed up in search of ever-cheaper labor.

During the 1980s and 1990s, as Central American countries erupted in violent civil wars, often with our country providing the weapons to one side, millions of Salvadorans, Guatemalans, and Nicaraguans sought refuge in the United States. While Nicaraguans were granted refugee status, Guatemalans and Salvadorans were not, so they became a large workforce for Americans' growing demand for largely off-the-books jobs as nannies and landscapers and in the underregulated shadows of our labor market in janitorial and housekeeping services.[58] Coming from countries marked by coups and liberation movements, Central American immigrants were far more politically sophisticated and schooled in protest movements than Americans had been for a generation. And they brought some much-needed fuel to a labor movement that had at the time been focusing on stemming losses rather than organizing new workers. Beginning in the early 1980s in Los Angeles, the largely Central American janitorial labor force began organizing for better wages. The Justice for Janitors campaign gained national attention when Los Angeles police violently attacked immigrant workers who were striking for their right to organize their workplaces in Century City, Los Angeles. The campaign, which eventually spread to over thirty cities and was led by the SEIU, won huge victories that not only improved the lives of hundreds of thousands of janitorial workers but provided the labor movement with a new vitality and courage it desperately needed. It also inspired a major Hollywood movie, *Bread and Roses*, penetrating pop culture in a way the union movement hadn't in decades. The Justice for Janitors campaign in many ways set the stage for the Fight for $15 movement, which has set its sights on disrupting the major multinational corporations that employ significant numbers of the new working class.

Between 1960 and 2008, over 40 million immigrants made the United States their home, more than half of them from countries in Latin America, with the largest group of newcomers coming from our neighbor to the south, Mexico.[59] The large influx of Latino immigrants has engendered vehement backlash and awakened racial insecurity, particularly among English-speaking whites. Today's Latino population, both documented and undocumented, is the new scapegoat used to apportion blame for all manner of social and economic problems. "They" are stealing our jobs, pushing down our wages, straining our schools, and bringing crime to our neighborhoods. In 2015, Donald Trump became the Republican front-runner during the primary season by developing an incendiary anti-immigrant platform, with widespread deportation as his central plank. Even President Obama, who has been a vocal and ardent supporter of comprehensive immigration reform, has succumbed to the political pressure to increase deportations. In fact, more immigrants have been deported under his administration than during George W. Bush's presidency.

Beginning in the mid-1990s, migration of Mexican workers to the United States picked up dramatically. Between 1990 and 2000, the population of Mexican-born people living in the United States doubled, from 4.5 million to 9 million, then grew a bit slower in the new century, to 12.7 million in 2008. About half of these immigrants are undocumented. What's unacknowledged is the profound role the North American Free Trade Agreement (NAFTA) has played in spurring this migration. If there was ever an issue that could form common cause between the white and Latino working class, it should be the destruction wrought by American trade policy. As Juan Gonzalez richly details in his book *Harvest of Empire*, NAFTA eviscerated the ability of small farmers in Mexico to make a living in the wake of U.S. agribusinesses exporting heavily subsidized and industrially raised cheap grains to the country. Of the Mexican immigrants moving to the United States in the years since NAFTA, 44 percent have been from rural areas, despite only 25 percent of Mexico's people residing in such areas.[60] The rise of American-built factories in *maquiladoras*, sprawling free-trade zones where manufacturing is centered, depressed demand for goods from Mexican-owned factories, contributing to the loss of 159,000 jobs. Today foreign-owned companies employ the same number of manufacturing workers as Mexican-owned factories. When you combine the job gains from the new factories with the losses from the old, only about 500,000 new jobs were created in Mexico during the fourteen years after NAFTA was implemented—not even close to the 1 million jobs Mexico needs to create each year to keep up with its growing workforce. Most important, the development of booming *maquiladoras* didn't produce any real improvement in the quality of life for the Mexican people. Only 10 percent of Mexican households have seen any increase in their incomes in the years since NAFTA.

American trade policy, which wrecked the livelihoods of so many working-class families in this country, is also a major driver of Mexican immigration to the United States. The United States lost over 1 million factory jobs, evenly split between Canada and Mexico in the first ten years after NAFTA was implemented.[61] Millions more would follow. South of the border, millions of Mexicans also found their livelihoods destroyed by this neoliberal economic regime and were pulled north in search of work. This enormous migration of people is the new beating heart of today's working class, and the key to its revival as a political and cultural force in America. Which is why the Republican Party has returned to its playbook of division, exploiting the economic anxiety of the white working class by making Latino immigrants the villains. The fact that Donald Trump, who profits immensely from an empire created by cheap labor and unrestricted global capital, is running for president by stirring up anti-immigrant sentiment is both a farce and a tragedy—and yet another reminder that the latent power of the new working class is threatening to America's elites and will remain politically contested. As this new working-class generation comes of age, it remains to be seen whether the racial, ethnic, and gender divides that have impeded solidarity can finally be dismantled.

This new working class faces a triple-headed challenge: overcoming entrenched corporate power, defeating the economic hegemony of neoliberalism, and tackling pervasive and stubborn racial, ethnic, and gender oppression. And as we'll see in the next chapter, rising inequality and the social distance created in its wake means that the first challenge to toppling such powerful and historical injustices is making visible the cause and the claim.

CHAPTER SIX

The Privilege of Visibility

Rick, a forty-five-year-old white computer engineer in Maineville, Ohio, realized he was really good at fixing things as a young child. But he never liked getting dirty, so his dream job was to fix things without getting dirty. Computers were just the ticket. After five years in the navy, Rick finally finished getting his two-year associate's degree, and, determined to set a good example for his children, completed his bachelor's degree right before turning forty. As a computer engineer, he has earned between $85,000 and $101,000 a year and considers himself middle-class. He's also been laid off twice, at two different companies, both times when his job was offshored to India. The last time, he actually had to train his replacement in order to receive his severance. His entire department was being transferred to India, and the company flew the new workers to the United States to be trained by the very people whose jobs they were taking.

Rick's layoff came after the company was bought out by a big, publicly traded corporation. The original company was privately held and described by Rick as a "tight-knit group, and more of a family culture." But now the culture was much more siloed and corporate. And, more important, the company was now "beholden to shareholders." In addition to Rick's department being offshored, a total of 120 staff members were laid off and their jobs outsourced.

The layoffs came after the company missed its third-quarter earnings goal and needed to initiate a "course correction." And there went the jobs.

Rick is incredulous about his situation. "This is cold-blooded at a level I've never seen before," he said. "How is this even legal? How can you fire a hundred and twenty people and then ship in folks from another country to take their jobs? Even if it is legal, it shouldn't be. It's just wrong." In Rick's mind, there's a very clear reason that this happened: "We have no union. There's nothing we can do to fight this."

Rick's story is becoming much more common now among professions once considered safe from the lure of cheaper labor. But no more. Companies are now sending many so-called skilled positions offshore, including once high-paying jobs in the financial and tech sectors. The transfer to cheaper sources of once safe occupations is just one of the ways in which work has become less secure for many people in the middle class. Recent college graduates are increasingly working in jobs that don't require a degree, at least until a career path opens up somewhere else. Journalists of all kinds are likely to be freelancers, forced to be constantly pitching new work to new outlets to earn a living. Faculty members are increasingly hired as adjuncts, paid by the course in what amounts to roughly the minimum wage. The spoils are preserved for corporate executives and managers, who now face intense pressures from the financial class to lower costs and boost profits. All of these trends lead, in some fashion or another, back to the outsized and extractive role Wall Street now plays in our economy. If you snoop around and look at corporate boards, financial statements, and shareholder proxies, chances are that the people doing the squeezing are at the very top of the food chain—private equity firms and hedge funds.

The middle class is no longer safe, as the trappings of secure life fall further out of reach: housing, child care, college, retirement, and even a decent vacation. Getting ahead is harder today. College-educated workers are feeling the pinch, and the pain, of a neoliberal economic system that is systemically rotten to the core. Much has been written about the strain facing the middle class, and I've even contributed to that growing chorus of experts, pundits, and politicians concerned about the disappearing middle class. I've tried in my writing to emphasize that it's the entry points into the middle class that have evaporated, focusing on the reality that it is harder now either to work or to educate your way into the middle class. When I wrote my first book, *Strapped*, which focused on what was happening to young people trying to get ahead in an era of inequality and finance-driven capitalism, I purposefully told the stories of young people who hadn't finished college. But the media interviews for my book almost exclusively focused on the problems confronting young professionals. There are real issues there, but when you compare those issues—doubling or tripling up in an apartment in a hip neighborhood to afford rent, say—to those of a thirty-something working as a cashier with unstable hours, struggling to find and pay for child care, it's the mom in a crumbling neighborhood who needs much more of our political attention and public concern. And it's her challenges that are faced by many more Americans than the issues confronting an upwardly mobile urban professional.

Unless we can coalesce around the need for a much higher quality of life for the new working class, then anyone who is not truly affluent and upper-class will remain living on a precipice of economic anxiety and insecurity. Why? Because the philosophy that allows employers to schedule their hourly workers week to week, with little advance notice, is the same philosophy that allows employers to expect their salaried workers to be "on" 24/7, responding to emails and taking conference calls that disrupt family and leisure time. The policies that stripped away our factories are the same policies that are now yanking professional jobs out of the country. The political hostility toward people who are down on their luck and need help buying food is delivered by the same politicians who drastically cut higher-education funding. The three biggest threats to the middle class are the same culprits behind the degradation of the working class: Wall Street, "trickle-down" economics, and antigovernment activism. These forces hit the working class first and hardest, but they inflict plenty of damage on the middle class too.

So if we want to save the middle class, we've got to start from the bottom up.

That means that the new working class, which will be primarily Latino and black in less than a generation if current trends hold, must be at the center of our public debate. And that means a major recalibration of how we view each other and whether we can finally agree that we are all in this together—native-born Americans and immigrants, blacks and whites and Latinos, poor, working-class, and middle-class. As I detailed in Chapter 5, the New Deal consensus fractured when black Americans and women finally got the legal right to the good stuff white men had hoarded for so long. So what will it take for Americans to stand shoulder to shoulder, when for so long race and class have divided us?

Three significant barriers stand in the way of this new, racially diverse working class regaining moral, economic, and political power and bringing the primarily white, college-educated middle class along with it. The first is the gaping social distance between Americans, which has certainly hardened by both race and class. Today's working class lives in a completely different orbit from the middle and upper classes, with whom they often interact only in commercial transactions. Yet our policymakers, journalists, and thought leaders are overwhelmingly culled from the more privileged parts of America, a bias that distorts the narrative about working life today in profound ways.

The second barrier is the very American tradition of pathologizing struggle and strife, which was once aimed mostly at the poor and the black underclass but has been extended to the entire working class, undercutting support for much-needed pubic policies that could help both the working class and the middle class. And finally, for the new working class, the most fundamental challenge remains the racial divisions that exist in the United States and, more important, our long aversion to either acknowledging or addressing them.

Socially Distant, Sometimes Clueless

As part of my job at Demos, I talk to journalists and producers fairly frequently. Without fail, when I talk about the fact that most Americans, even most twenty- and thirty-somethings, don't have bachelor's degrees, this "news" is greeted by surprise on the other end of the phone. Keep in mind that a full two-thirds of people in this country do not have bachelor's degrees, even among twenty-five- to thirty-four-year-olds, whereas 92 percent of journalists today—print, television, digital, and radio—have bachelor's degrees, up from 58 percent in 1971.[1] Fewer than 10 percent of journalists are people of color, an increase for sure since 1971 (5 percent), but not even close to reflecting the percentage in the population of people of color, who account for more than one-third of our country. As media outlets, particularly in digital and cable, have proliferated, journalism is no longer about "reaching the widest possible audience." Only 12 percent of journalists think this is an extremely important goal, down from 39 percent in 1971. Niche online sites tend to draw younger and better-educated readers. The Internet revolution in journalism now brings competition into the news, with each reporter or producer striving to hit the "most read" or "most clicked" on their site each day. Given who combs these news sites—think *BuzzFeed, Salon,* and *The Huffington Post*—if you were a journalist aspiring to the top ranks (or even a decent living), which story would you be more inclined to pitch, "College graduates increasingly priced out of most popular cities" or "Homelessness among the working class surges in top cities"?

In addition to speaking with journalists as part of my job, I spend a fair amount of time talking to congressional staff, whose social distance from the working class reflects an even greater gap. In 2011 the *National Journal* published the demographics of 300 top-level congressional staffers and found that 93 percent are white, 68 percent are male, and 97 percent have graduate or law degrees.[2] About half these staffers attended private colleges for their undergraduate degree, including 10 percent who went to an Ivy League school. For an institution charged with considering the interests of all people in the United States, this is pretty astounding. And it should be noted that the elitism, maleness, and whiteness of top staffers were similar for Republican and Democratic offices. Congress itself is a tad more diverse. The 114th Congress, seated in January 2015, is the most racially diverse in history, with 83 percent white members and 17 percent black, Latino, Asian/Pacific Islander, or Native American.[3] Keep in mind, however, that today 38 percent of the population is not white.

Of course, just because an individual has completed a bachelor's or an advanced degree doesn't necessarily mean he or she is not from a working-class or poor background. I'm a case in point. But I'm also a major outlier. Today, people between twenty and forty years old with bachelor's degrees are likely to have grown up in households where at least one parent also had a bachelor's degree. While more people than ever before are enrolling in college, the folks who actually manage to *complete* college are much more likely to have grown up in college-educated households than those who drop out. For example, one survey found that 55 percent of children from two-degree families reported obtaining a college or postgraduate degree, compared with just 23 percent of the children from no-degree families.[4] And those who hold advanced degrees, whether graduate or law degrees, are even more likely to come from well-educated households. What this means is that America's power brokers—our newsmakers and governing class—are unlikely to have a family background similar to that of the majority of Americans.

The social distance of America's cultural elites, its news- and policymakers, from the zeitgeist of American experience has contributed to the invisibility of the new working class. When the Great Recession hit, national news outlets focused on the falls from grace of the previously middle-class. Fairness in Accuracy and Reporting (FAIR) is a media watchdog group that extensively studied how the mainstream media covered the Great Recession. Its analysis illustrates how social distance can greatly distort the way Americans collectively view what's happening around us. Take for example, the *Washington Post.* In the first two years of the Great Recession, the *Post* did not run a single article about how the foreclosure crisis primarily hit the black and Latino working class.[5] The paper did, however, deem it newsworthy—even front-page newsworthy—to cover how foreclosures were hitting condo owners in Silver Springs, an affluent suburb of Washington, D.C., and how buyers of million-dollar homes were now facing foreclosure.[6] Stephen Pimpare, author of *A People's History of Poverty in America*, explains the class bias in our media by saying, "So much of large-audience journalism is produced by people who are not working-class and tend not to know working-class, let alone poor people. The subtext now is that this is something we need to pay attention to, because 'good, decent people' are being affected."

The *Washington Post* really takes the cake, though, for bending over backward to cover the fall-from-riches stories of the Great Recession. Keep in mind that this newspaper has a special role in agenda-setting: it is the paper of record for political elites. It is the reading du jour for anyone who works on Capitol Hill or who seeks to influence what happens in its corridors. What it reports and who it writes about matter. A lot. In August 2009, when the national unemployment rate was 9.7 percent, the *Post* ran a story with the headline "Squeaking by on $300,000."[7] A more than 3,600-word story. The main subject of the story was Laura Steins, a vice president at MasterCard who was divorced, with three children and a live-in nanny. The story chronicles the tough times to hit the leafy suburbs just outside Manhattan, where the titans of the Street were now supposedly feeling real pain. I'll admit it: I was fuming by the end of this article. At the level of humanity provided to Steins, at the expanse of words dedicated to her experience, and at the actual sympathy the reporter conveyed, writing, "Whatever fantasies the underclass may have of the good life—of small dogs in purses and Dolce and Gabbana—are not on display here. The rugs are worn. Milk is spilled. A Marmaduke of a beast named Tyson hovers at the table ready to snuffle up pork tenderloin from the plate of a distracted child." This scene unfolded in a four-thousand-square-foot home on three acres, with a swimming pool. And a nanny who does the food shopping, cooks all the meals, does the laundry, and apparently also fixes leaky pipes.

During the Great Recession, coverage by the mainstream media could give one the impression that the downturn was doing the most damage to the big banks and middle-aged professional workers. The Pew Research Center's Project for Excellence in Journalism studied the content of news stories about the economy in the early months of President Obama's first term, from February 1 to August 1, 2009. All told, the center examined 9,950 stories from television, radio, cable, newspapers, and the Internet.[8] "Citizens may have been the biggest victims of the downturn, but they have not been the primary actors in the media depictions of it," wrote the report's authors. So what did the media cover? Nearly 40 percent of the stories were about the challenge of reviving the banking industry, the battle over the stimulus package, and the struggles facing the domestic auto industry. Even though the fate of the auto industry would directly affect millions of workers, the stories concentrated on ideological questions about whether the government should bail out the industry. According to Pew, stories related to labor issues or worker layoffs registered but faintly in the coverage.

Coverage of the Great Recession was also driven almost entirely by government officials and business leaders and the press itself. The White House and federal agencies alone initiated nearly a third (32 percent) of economic stories studied, while business triggered another 21 percent. About a quarter of the stories (23 percent) were initiated by the press and did not rely on an external news trigger. Ordinary citizens and union workers combined to act as the catalyst for only 2 percent of the stories about the economy. For the average person in the United States, the two most relevant issues were the decline in housing values and rising foreclosures and the enormous increase in unemployment, but these issues each garnered just 6 percent of all the news stories generated during the deepest part of the recession.

Given that the epicenter of the financial industry is in New York and our nation's capital is in Washington, D.C., it's not surprising that so many of the stories covered would emanate from these two cities. But the proportion of all stories with datelines from either New York or D.C. even surprised the study's researchers, who refer to it as "overwhelming." Just over three-quarters of economic stories during this time were reported from these two cities alone. The struggles in the rest of the country barely seemed to exist. The one encouraging observation from the analysis was that nightly network news got it right, covering the impact on ordinary people more thoroughly and regularly than any other type of media, devoting 12 percent of economic stories to the impact on people.

In essence, not even an economic calamity—one that resulted in millions of lost jobs and foreclosed homes—could catapult the plight of the working class to headline news. Most newspapers had long ago cut their labor reporters, with only a handful left to carry the weight. Stephen Greenhouse of the *New York Times* stood out as the best in the business. But when he left the paper, the labor beat just got absorbed by other reporters. There's no dedicated reporter now at the *Times* covering issues facing run-of-the-mill workers, with the exception of Rachel Swarns's excellent weekly column, "The Working Life," in the metro section of the paper.

The new working class was able to lift the cloak of invisibility only by hitting the streets under the banner Fight for $15. As workers went on strike in hundreds of cities around the country and successfully won significant increases in the minimum wage in several major cities and states, the newsrooms finally had a story to tell and the new working class gained some visibility. Great investigative journalism by Jodi Kantor of the *Times*, for example, raised awareness about the havoc wreaked by erratic scheduling practices.[9] The morning after her piece profiling a Starbucks employee went online, Starbucks announced that it would make changes to its scheduling practices to provide more stability for its baristas.[10] The mobilization of the new working class, from retail to fast food to home care workers, has thankfully gotten the media to at least pay attention to the multiple indignities confronting the nation's lowest-paid workers: lack of paid sick days, wage theft, unstable schedules, and an incredibly low minimum wage. But it came only when a significant share of the Sleeping Giant dared to demand better treatment. The middle class and upper class bear no similar burden. Laura Steins most certainly didn't have to march to have her story of barely making it on $300,000 told.

Most college-educated workers can take a new position and pretty much not worry whether the new job includes paid sick days, offers health insurance, or provides a retirement plan. Most professionals even get paid vacation days, all without having to march in the streets and fight intractable politicians to win these benefits. Similarly, professionals don't have to wage a protest to get the media to focus on one of the biggest work-life issues confronting them, such as the 24/7 time demands facilitated by smartphones or the new expectation of working during vacation. That's the privilege of visibility. To have your life experiences acknowledged and reflected in the cultural zeitgeist is taken for granted by career professionals, providing a cocooned perception that these are the most pressing and ubiquitous problems facing workers in America.

Increasingly, Americans live in isolated similar-class, similar-race bubbles.[11] The working class and middle class aren't just separated by whether they have a degree on parchment paper declaring that they completed college. They're separated at almost every level of social and civic life. Our neighborhoods, our schools, our churches, our doctors' offices, our restaurants, our day care, and our bars are all now more likely to be filled with people just like us. And unlike in earlier generations, when class lines were more porous, today people largely marry within their own social and economic class and have children who do likewise. These class and racial cocoons are problematic, because they mean that the cultural makers, news shapers, and political agenda-setters are increasingly isolated, as well as protected, from the hardscrabble reality of the working class. Without any friends, neighbors, or relatives who punch a clock, they have fewer opportunities for authentic relationships with someone outside their social class.

Today most middle- and upper-class Americans' knowledge about working-class life comes through commercial transactions. In his widely circulated *American Scholar* article "The Disadvantages of an Elite Education," William Deresiewicz recalls the day he realized "there might be a few holes in my education." He had called a plumber to fix some leaky pipes, and when the man was standing there in his kitchen, he recalls, "I suddenly learned that I didn't have the slightest idea what to say to someone like him.

So alien was his experience to me, so unguessable his values, so mysterious his very language, that I couldn't succeed in engaging him in a few minutes of small talk before he got down to work. Fourteen years of higher education and a handful of Ivy League degrees, and there I was, stiff and stupid, struck dumb by my own dumbness."

As the more affluent among us become further cocooned in their neighborhoods, their colleges, and their workplaces, neither real life nor pop culture provides much of a window into the lives of working-class people. It's been decades since there was a hit television show about a working-class family, one that actually didn't shy away from story lines about layoffs, overdue bills, and just trying to make ends meet. *Roseanne*, which ran from 1988 to 1997, is typically held up as the last network show with working-class story lines and lead characters. In the 1970s, when the social distance between Americans was much closer, many of the hit shows revolved around working-class families, schools, and friendships: *One Day at a Time; Welcome Back, Kotter; Laverne & Shirley; Good Times; Alice; All in the Family;* and *What's Happening*, to name a few of the better-known shows. Why the vacuum today? One explanation could be that back in the 1970s, the writers and producers were probably much more likely to have families—either immediate or extended—who were working-class and could write authentic characters and story lines. Today, in contrast, a generation of screenwriters and producers bring us the very well-heeled in *Modern Family*, the bourgeoisie in *Parenthood*, and the urbane in *30 Rock*. The working class can easily get a glimpse of the affluent life by turning on the television—visibility that isn't reciprocated.

When I was growing up, I had friends whose parents were college-educated professionals and I had friends whose fathers worked at the same steel factory as mine. I lived on a block with accountants, advertising executives, teachers, factory workers, and nurses. In college, of my two closest friends, one was from a college-educated household and one wasn't. When I waited on tables during college breaks and after graduating, I was friends with single moms who were raising their children on tips like the ones I was saving up to move to New York City to start a career. Once I got into the professional career pipeline, however, my friendships and networks, once a mishmash of classes, cocooned into homogeneity. My husband's parents and his extended family are college-educated. The close friendships I've formed over the past twenty years are with people from well-educated middle- and upper-middle-class families. Most of my colleagues in the world of think tanks and progressive advocacy also hail from well-educated homes. As we raise our daughter in a mostly white and upper-middle-class enclave, her friendships mirror my cocoon. My own family keeps me grounded, and has given me a very up-close and personal look at the working class on a downward escalator over the past several decades. It's a touchstone far too few of our power brokers have today, creating a blind spot that profoundly skews our cultural and political landscape.

The cocoon bias operates by making the working class invisible, but perhaps worse than invisibility is the hostility that far too many privileged people so easily indulge toward people who are struggling. There's a noxious tradition of elites, whether public intellectuals or pundits, pathologizing people who toil for marginal wages, live in old, decaying neighborhoods, and all too frequently hit the official line designated as poverty.

Punishing and Pathologizing Struggle and Strife

Blaming people who struggle to get ahead for their predicament is something of an American tradition, one that stretches from the beginning of our nation to our current political debate. It's important to remember that of all advanced nations, the United States has the highest percentage of workers earning low pay, defined as earning less than two-thirds of the median wage. In America that describes one out of four workers.[12] As I discuss in Chapter 2, four out of ten households using food stamps have at least one adult working; the rest are children, the elderly, and disabled adults. Half of all front-line food workers and home care workers rely on food stamps to supplement their meager wages. As the Great Recession stripped millions of their livelihoods, the number of households using food stamps soared. As it should have: That's the whole point of a safety net. But according to many Republicans in Congress, the use of food stamps demonstrates some sort of moral failing.[13] The same philosophical strain also condemned unemployment benefits as a deterrent to finding a job, even when job-seekers outnumbered available jobs by a margin of four to one. Conservatives claim that people just aren't trying hard enough, and that any benefits we provide as a society to ameliorate hardship provide a disincentive for people to work or get a better job. It's fairly routine for Republicans to claim that any type of means-tested benefit is a one-way ticket to dependency and laziness. Conservative media channels like Fox News and its marquee talent, Bill O'Reilly, seem to take special pleasure in indicting the morals of people in hardship. Here's just a sample of O'Reilly's harangues against those whose struggle mightily to make it in America:

> In 2004, he ranted, "You gotta look people in the eye and tell 'em they're irresponsible and lazy. And who's gonna wanna do that? Because that's what poverty is, ladies and gentlemen. In this country, you can succeed if you get educated and work hard. Period. Period."[14]

> In 2012, O'Reilly listed what he called the "true causes of poverty" as "poor education, addiction, irresponsible behavior, and laziness."[15]

> In 2014, during the week that marked the fiftieth anniversary of LBJ's War on Poverty, O'Reilly again said that "true poverty" "is being driven by personal behavior," which included, according to him, "addictive behavior, laziness, apathy."[16]

Why does what Bill O'Reilly thinks and communicates to his audience matter? Because his is the most viewed cable news show, regularly drawing in between 2 and 3 million viewers each night. And those viewers are hit over the head with a message that people who struggle to make ends meet are bottom-feeders, "takers" in Romney lingo, who lack the work ethic and will to pull themselves up. (Just as a refresher, Mitt Romney, running as the Republican candidate for president in 2012, threw 47 percent of Americans under the bus by describing them as people "who believe that they are victims . . . who believe that they are entitled to health care, to food, to housing, to you-name-it." Well, call me crazy, but I do believe that in a country as wealthy as ours, people *are* entitled to health care, housing, and food.) And just to set the record straight, 80 percent of people who are counted as poor are children, the elderly, the disabled, students, or the involuntarily unemployed.[17]

Fox News may be the go-to channel for pathologizing individuals who work hard but can't get ahead, but the tendency to portray struggle as the result of personal failings extends far beyond the conservative media channel. Indeed, it is an analysis that enraptures many public intellectuals and academics. The inability of millions of people to get ahead—usually defined as meeting the norms and lifestyles of the white middle class—has far too often been blamed on an erosion of individual morals. This assignment of blame to the individual, as opposed to structures of exclusion created by the state, has a very long tradition in America, too long to cover here. So, with that in mind, let's start with the most famous—or infamous, depending on your viewpoint—

example of pathologizing struggle in the last half century: "The Negro Family: The Case for National Action," commonly known as the Moynihan Report.[18]

Daniel Patrick Moynihan, who went on to become a U.S. senator, was an assistant secretary at the Department of Labor in 1965, when he issued his epic analysis, which assigned the breakdown of family structure as the chief obstacle to prosperity facing Negroes (the term used in the report). Keep in mind, this report was released on the heels of both the Civil Rights Act and the Voting Rights Act, yet Moynihan focused on the breakdown of patriarchial families as the culprit holding African Americans back. In the introduction to the report, he made the case pithily and without reservation, commenting on the current economic status of African Americans: "A middle-class group has managed to save itself, but for vast numbers of the unskilled, poorly educated city working class the fabric of conventional social relationships has all but disintegrated. There are indications that the situation may have been arrested in the past few years, but the general post-war trend is unmistakable. So long as this situation persists, the cycle of poverty and disadvantage will continue to repeat itself." Moynihan did rightly attribute the root causes of the problems confronting African American families to economic and structural factors: the legacy of slavery, Jim Crow, and the racist attitudes of many white Americans. Yet the collective takeaway from the report was that the urban black working class was culturally dysfunctional because of a pattern of matriarchy and single-parent households, and because these strong black women were raising children who were less educated and more delinquent than their white counterparts. It was pseudo-social science validating the common stereotypes about black people. In fact, one chapter in the report is actually entitled "The Tangle of Pathology." Moynihan ended his report without providing solutions, other than to say that it would take a coordinated and multipronged set of strategies to address the fundamental problem facing black communities: a breakdown in family structure.

> Three centuries of injustice have brought about deep-seated structural distortions in the life of the Negro American. At this point, the present tangle of pathology is capable of perpetuating itself without assistance from the white world. The cycle can be broken only if these distortions are set right. In a word, a national effort towards the problems of Negro Americans must be directed towards the question of family structure. The object should be to strengthen the Negro family so as to enable it to raise and support its members as do other families. After that, how this group of Americans chooses to run its affairs, take advantage of its opportunities, or fail to do so, is none of the nation's business.

Fifty years after the publication of his report, Moynihan's analysis is still the subject of much controversy and public debate. To be fair, the report was written as an internal memorandum, but it swiftly got leaked to the press. Had Moynihan written the report for public consumption, it's likely he would have used less incendiary language. And apparently his motivation was a good one: He hoped to get the government to start a substantial public jobs program, using the "crisis" in black families as the rationale.[19] But for reasons we can't know, he did not explicitly call for any such plan, and in fact simply left the reader with the impression that all efforts to help achieve true equality were doomed unless black families got their act together. That meant forming two-parent families where the man was in charge. Whether fairly or not, Moynihan's report is viewed by many as blaming the victim, and it's hard not to get that impression from a straight reading. The report validated the strongly held belief of conservative readers that poverty is caused by a pathological culture, and government programs like welfare and food stamps do nothing but add another pathology to the tangle: dependency. Because Moynihan was a liberal and a Democrat, his report mainstreamed the idea that cultural breakdown causes poverty.

Our social, cultural, and economic norms have long been set by the white upper-middle class, with any failure to conform to those norms seen as deviant. In 2014, Charles Murray, well known for his infamous book *The Bell Curve*, which argued that blacks were genetically intellectually inferior to whites, broadened Moynihan's analysis to the white working class. In *Coming Apart*, Murray bemoans a white working class that has seemingly lost the hunger to work and is now engaging in all manner of activities similar to those of the "black underclass": illegitimacy, crime, and drug use. Political scientist Robert Putnam also explored the disparities in familial upbringing between college-educated and non-college-educated households in his most recent book, *Our Kids*. While Putnam's book lacks the judgmental bromides of Murray's, it nonetheless paints a picture of a working class that is mired in drug abuse, teen pregnancy, abusive marriages, and absent parents. David Brooks, the moralizing columnist at the *New York Times*, devoted one of his columns to the lessons we must take from Putnam's book. Writing in his typical condescending manner, he asserted, "It's not only money and better policy that are missing in these circles; it's norms. The health of society is primarily determined by the habits and virtues of its citizens. In many parts of America there are no minimally agreed upon standards for what it means to be a father. There are no basic codes and rules woven into daily life, which people can absorb unconsciously and follow automatically."[20]

The notion that poverty, which is a frequent way station for many in the working class, is the result of bad character traits—whether it's unwed mothers, drug addiction, or criminal behavior—is a solidly held belief in America, particularly, as we've just seen, among the elites and especially when the conversation is about people of color. We remain deeply suspicious of individuals who need any type of public assistance, harboring doubts about whether they've really done all they could do to get a better job. Maybe they just want to sit around and get high instead of going to work. And so why not force people applying for public benefits to take a drug test? Scott Walker, the Republican governor of Wisconsin and a former 2016 presidential candidate, has proposed testing people who apply for food stamps and unemployment benefits for drug use, joining twelve other states that have attached drug testing to at least some part of their public benefits programs.[21] Some people who are reading this book may agree, finding themselves nodding their heads and thinking, "Sure, I don't want my tax dollars going to drug addicts scamming the system." But here's the thing. We don't require drug testing for public benefits that accrue to more affluent people, like the mortgage interest tax deduction. We don't drug-test the real estate developers before handing over large tax abatements. We don't drug-test middle-class parents who claim the child-care tax credit. And it defies the imagination that anyone would ever propose such a policy. Why? Because there's an implicit assumption that all these individuals, by virtue of their middle-class or higher status, adhere to social norms and therefore have earned the right to such benefits. They obviously took hold of their bootstraps and climbed the ladder of opportunity and are now unassailably entitled to the good life.

The idea that anyone, no matter the circumstances in which they are born, can move up the class ladder is a bedrock principle in America. It was part of our founding ideology, conceived in direct contradiction to the rigid class hierarchy of Mother England. But there's a competing value to the individualistic ethos that if we work hard enough, the world can be our oyster. And that's egalitarianism, a very American belief in equal opportunity and the right to a level playing field. Of course there is a tension inherent in the core American values of individualism and egalitarianism. The extension of the logic that individual effort is responsible for each person's success is that the failure to get ahead is rooted in a lack of individual effort rather than in structural constraints. Hello, drug tests. However, Americans also place great importance on equal opportunity, recognizing that giving everyone an equal chance to succeed is fundamental to the American dream. An extension of this logic is that individual failures are indicative of broader inequalities and differences in opportunity. Decades of opinion research confirm that Americans change their minds about whether individuals are to blame or circumstances are, and the way these issues are covered by the media can influence how people view the failure to become middle-class.[22]

As we learned in Chapter 3, affluent Americans tend to exhibit little sympathy for the struggling masses, with two-thirds of our most financially secure citizens believing that poor people today "have it easy" because they can get benefits without having to do anything in return. They clearly missed the giant "ending welfare as we know it" reform law that was passed in 1996, which now keeps enrollment rates in public assistance very low, even during the Great Recession, when millions of working-class people lost their jobs.

So what about those drug tests for public benefits? Are they finding high rates of drug use among welfare applicants? In all but one state, the rate of drug use among applicants was found to be lower than 1 percent—much lower than the illegal-drug-use rate among all Americans, which is 9 percent.[23]

As we have seen, people of color will soon make up the majority of the new working class, a fact that creates an additional burden in reclaiming the economic and political power of the old blue-collar white working class. This working class starts from a place of larger institutional and structural disadvantage—lower pay, fewer benefits, decimated unions, and a very strong neoliberal orthodoxy that eschews government regulation and investment. But perhaps the greatest obstacle is the persistence of racial anxiety and animosity, along with a renewed xenophobia coinciding with the rise of Latino immigrants, both legal and undocumented.

The Elephant in the Room

Americans can be some of the most generous people in the world, measured by the percentage who give money, help a stranger, and volunteer in the community. When there's a natural disaster in the world, Americans in great numbers give quickly. By some measures we're the most giving country in the world.[24] I live in New York City, a place many associate with brusqueness and detachment. But that's just the reality of living in a city packed with 8 million people. When it really counts, New Yorkers can barn-raise with the best of them. Yet our nation's public spirit—the collective support we provide to everyone in the country—is decidedly miserly. If we are ever going to improve the quality of life for broad swaths of Americans by reinvesting in our common good—our state universities, child care, a humane safety net—we will need to address the legacy of our violent racial history.

If you had asked me eight years ago which identity had a more profound effect on someone's life in America, race or class, I likely would have said class. But after living through the reactionary and, yes, racial backlash to the first African American president, and after months of research for this book, I realize that the legacy of our racial hierarchy remains central to explaining the halting of American progress and the degradation of life for the working class. For readers who have been with me up until this point, I understand that this admission, and the analysis that follows, will have to cut through an instinctive and very strong shield that is erected immediately when someone mentions race. Want to clear a room at a party? Just start a conversation about race. White people tend to get defensive, offer vague regret about the state of affairs, or dismiss the claim that what is happening has anything to do with race. "I didn't have anything to do with slavery or Jim Crow." "Why can't they just let it go and move on?" "Sure, black lives matter—all lives matter."

Unlike in eras past, today's racism is covert, for the most part. Long gone are the days of "whites only" drinking fountains and casual and frequent use of derogatory language to refer to blacks and Latinos. As Eduardo Bonilla-Silva explains in his book *Racism Without Racists,* today's racism is structurally based and less about individual prejudice. But white Americans remain stuck in an outdated definition of racism. Bonilla-Silva writes, "One reason why, in general terms, whites and people of color cannot agree on racial matters is because they conceive terms such as 'racism' very differently. Whereas for most whites racism is prejudice, for most people of color, racism is systemic or institutionalized."[25]

Today's Sleeping Giant is disproportionately people of color. Many whites have escaped the working class through generations of seemingly color-blind policies and practices that provided overwhelming opportunities to white men and eventually to white women. Consider the G.I. Bill. While color-blind in its approach, it was administered locally and by states, with congressional oversight. As a result, black men were excluded from the benefits of this seemingly color-blind, universal program because of segregated colleges, redlining that disqualified them for federal mortgage benefits, and an overall racist bias against them.[26] All told, the United States spent more on higher education benefits for veterans than we did on the Marshall Plan.[27] Historian Ira Katznelson refers to the G.I. Bill as an affirmative-action program for white men. As the civil rights era produced landmark legislation outlawing discrimination, our government took similar steps to advance higher education to all Americans with the Higher Education Act of 1965, which established federal grants and loans to ensure that no one would be barred from going to college owing to cost. Almost immediately the percentage of students from low-income families going to college doubled.[28] And then, just as happened with the opening of employment and housing opportunities for people of color, states across the country began to systematically disinvest in higher education. States like California and New York, which had long made college free to in-state residents, pulled back on these programs once black students and Latinos gained access. In fact, whites in California revolted strongly against the expansion of public goods—more precisely, the racial and ethnic composition of those who had access to these public goods—in 1978, by severely curtailing revenue to pay for these goods through Proposition 13, which froze property taxes at current home values and required a two-thirds majority vote in each chamber of the legislature for any new tax increases. As the Latino population increased significantly in Colorado, its white residents fought back by passing a Taxpayer's Bill of Rights (TABOR) in 1992, which similarly constrained the legislature from raising tax revenues to meet public needs. Under TABOR, state and local governments cannot raise tax rates without voter approval, and if revenues grow faster than the rate of inflation, those revenues must be returned to the taxpayers.

These tax revolts were highly racialized: prompted by a perception among white residents that "others" were getting all the benefits and bankrupting the state in the process. Let's remember, as discussed in Chapter 3, that part of the southern strategy all along included eventually curtailing tax revenue as a way to "starve the beast" of government, by painting a vivid picture of people of color drinking from the public trough. But these revolts didn't just harm people of color, they harmed the middle class and the working class of all races and ethnic backgrounds.

The politics of austerity is also fundamentally motivated, even subconsciously, by the desire to end access to important benefits like college grants, food stamps, and child-care subsidies, all programs disproportionately needed by working-class Americans of all races and ethnicities. Congressman Paul Ryan's conception of the safety net as a hammock that lulls people into complacency is dog-whistle racism in its highest form. Without mentioning race, Ryan cleverly racializes the need to cut government spending by drawing attention to the abuse of means-tested programs, which most white Americans immediately understand (wrongly) to be used primarily by people of color.

In addition to cutting off access to vitally needed safety-net programs, austerity results in major losses of public-sector jobs. Historically the public sector has had more stringent equal opportunity and civil rights protections than the private sector, providing a haven of employment for people of color in an otherwise segregated private marketplace. As a result, black Americans and women are overrepresented in public-sector jobs, which also provide closer pay parity with white men than private-sector jobs.[29] The Great Recession prompted major cuts to both state and federal spending, resulting in half a million fewer public-sector jobs than before the recession.[30] The racial undercurrent is also present in the attacks on the collective bargaining rights of public-sector unions. In Wisconsin and Michigan, Republican governors exempted the police and firefighter unions from these attacks and restrictions—and their members are overwhelmingly white and male.[31]

As detailed in the last chapter, the reach of America's racial history is long. Indeed, it is very much still our present reality. In comparing the generous social spending of Western European countries to the miserly spending in the United States, two economists found that the racially diverse composition in the United States explains half of the gap in social spending.[32] The other half was due in large part to the presence of more left-wing political parties in Europe. At the state level, in states where the population of blacks is higher, welfare payments are less generous. Similarly, whites are more supportive of redistribution if they live close to poor whites but less supportive if they live close to poor blacks.[33]

Outright and blatant prejudice is no longer the operating principle of white supremacy in America. Today racism often seems to exist without the smoking gun of someone spewing racial epithets. But racist thinking and racist institutions and structures abound. While officially color-blind, our institutions and structures continue to deliver racially biased results. Consider that even though blacks, whites, and Latinos use drugs at similar rates, black Americans, and to a lesser extent Latinos, are much more likely to be arrested and sent to jail for drug violations. Consider that Latino and black homeowners were much more likely to be sold subprime mortgages during the housing bubble, even if they qualified for prime mortgages, than were white homeowners. Consider that today blacks and Latinos experience discrimination in approximately half their efforts to rent or buy housing. Consider that white women leaving welfare were more likely to be hired than black women, and were paid more to boot.[34]

As long as white Americans continue to insist that we are living in a postracial society, we will never truly overcome our racial past. As long as access to public goods is viewed as taking from whites to give to all the "others" in our society, we will fail to achieve greatness and continue the long slide of lower educational attainment, dilapidated infrastructure, and bargain-basement jobs that increasingly make the United States a laggard rather than a leader among advanced nations. Our present and future will continue to be constrained by insufficient public goods, a threadbare safety net, a complete lack of family-friendly policies like child care and paid family leave—all of which have shattered working-class and middle-class security and increased the population of struggling Americans.

There is hope. Working-class Americans are beginning to fight back. The Sleeping Giant is stirring. Whether we listen or act remains to be seen.

CHAPTER SEVEN

The Sleeping Giant Stirs

On May 1, 2006, millions of immigrants all across the country went on strike in what was called "A Day Without an Immigrant." On December 13, 2014, over 100,000 people demonstrated to demand an end to police brutality and violence in Washington, D.C., and New York City, united under the banner *Black Lives Matter.* On April 15, 2015, more than 60,000 workers in over 200 cities took to the streets to demand better pay and the right to unionize as part of the Fight for $15 campaign. These were the big marches and protests, the culmination of dozens, if not hundreds, of more localized protests across the country. Taken together, these three movements represent a major surge in organizing of, by, and for the new working class.

And while mass mobilizations gain strength and prominence, many progressive leaders and the organizations they lead are turning attention to building political power by creating new membership-based organizations and new strategies for community and voter engagement. Together these mass mobilizations of the public, new forms of organizations and membership structures, and new strategies and infrastructure for political engagement are starting to reshape politics in places like California, New York, Texas, Minnesota, North Carolina, and Georgia. Meanwhile, unions and new working-class groups are renewing their efforts to organize in the South, a region once deemed hopeless for progressive power-building.

The Fight for $15, the Movement for Black Lives, and immigrants' rights movements have galvanized significant portions of the new working class and achieved visibility in mainstream media. But make no mistake, a proliferation of new activists and new campaigns in major cities, in red states and in blue states, is disrupting the status quo and challenging the historic inequality strangling our nation. There is more great work happening than can be covered in just one chapter, and my apologies to the many excellent leaders and their organizations who are left out of this chapter. So, reader, please keep in mind that for every example of new working-class organizing chronicled in this chapter, there are dozens more that could have been included.

Out of the Shadows

Construction is big business in Texas. And like everything in Texas, it's bigger there than in most states. Employing close to 1 million workers, the construction industry generates one dollar of every twenty dollars in the Texas economy.[1] With a rapidly growing population, the demand for housing, new roads, schools, and other infrastructure has sustained the industry even during the economic downturn. The workers are mostly Latino, about half of whom are undocumented, working long hours for low pay and often under dangerous conditions. More construction workers die in Texas each year than in any other state. Texas's fatalities in the construction industry are almost double those of California, even though California's construction workforce is bigger.[2] Injuries are commonplace, affecting one out of five construction workers. For all the risk, construction workers in Texas earn low wages, with half of them earning income at poverty level. What's more, they often don't get paid overtime or fully paid at all; one out of five workers reports wage theft and no overtime pay.

The construction industry in Texas is a model of the fissured workplaces discussed in Chapter 2. Workers are hired by a long line of subcontractors, all of whom face immense cost pressures with increasing intensity at each link in the contracting chain. These cost pressures result in many employers misclassifying the workers as independent contractors, allowing the employer to avoid paying unemployment insurance and federal payroll taxes. And it leads to skimping on safety protections and adequate training.

Enter the Workers Defense Project (WDP). Cofounded and led by Cristina Tzintzún until the end of 2015, WDP is a statewide membership workers' rights organization composed largely of immigrants and concentrating on construction workers. With 3,500 members, WDP uses a range of tactics both to help workers directly and to pass reforms to improve working standards in the construction industry. From original survey research highlighting the deplorable conditions facing construction workers to legal support for workers seeking to retrieve back wages, WDP has managed to win major reforms in a state known to be notoriously hostile to worker organizing. In 2013 the Austin City Council passed landmark legislation that requires companies that want to build in Austin and receive tax incentives to pay a minimum wage of $11 an hour and offer the prevailing wage, worker's compensation, and basic safety training.

Tzintzún explained that the WDP's target wasn't the employers of the workers but rather the developers, who hold all the power. "In many other parts of the country, construction jobs are good blue-collar jobs. They are not in Texas," she told me. WDP estimates that about 50 percent of construction workers in Texas are undocumented, a shift that has led to increasingly abysmal working conditions. "The human cost of the Texas economic miracle that doesn't really get talked about frequently is that it's being built on the back of low-wage workers and immigrant workers. We have not just growth but massive growth in minimum-wage jobs, the majority of the workforce lives below the poverty line even though they work full-time, and it's the most deadly and dangerous place to work in the state."

The construction industry in Texas employs primarily white U.S.-born workers and Latino workers. When WDP started ten years ago, there was a lot of animosity to overcome on the part of white construction workers, who felt that immigrant workers were stealing their jobs. Tzintzún said, "One of the things I'm most proud of is that we have burly white construction workers, who are thought of as the most Texan guys you could be, standing up and fighting with us for immigration reform, and standing with a bunch of undocumented immigrant workers and seeing their struggle as one. That's one of the things I'm the most of proud of that we've done." That solidarity was built over time, with intentional efforts by WDP to work with the building trade unions. When WDP decided to focus its energies on construction workers in 2007, Cristina and her staff met with all the building trade unions to let them know that they'd be researching the industry and that they would like to work together. Only one of the unions agreed to work with them. Despite being given the brush-off, WDP let the unions know that it would leave the door open and would work with them at any time. WDP also dedicated itself to getting to know union culture and understanding their issues. As the death toll among construction workers, especially foreign-born workers, continued to rise, WDP was getting ready to release its major survey of construction workers, which found widespread abuse of both wage and safety laws. That was in 2009, and it prompted the building trade unions to come out en masse to support the workers and to apologize to the WDP for previously ignoring what was happening to foreign-born workers. Since that day the WDP and the unions, along with other civic organizations, have linked arms in the fight to improve the construction industry.

Thousands of miles north of Texas, in a completely different political environment, Casa Latina in Seattle, Washington, is organizing day laborers for better working conditions and fighting for better wages and benefits for the entire new working class. Similar to WDP, Casa Latina started out as a legal services organization to help foreign-born, low-paid workers who were fighting to get paid for work they'd already done. At first most of the workers who came to the organization were day laborers, often hired directly from the street. But as more immigrants came to Seattle, Casa Latina received complaints from foreign-born workers working in restaurants, janitorial services, and construction, often about violations from the same employers time and again. That's when Casa Latina changed its strategy from legal services to an organizing model, one in which the workers themselves decide how to price their labor. When it first became a workers' center, dispatching day laborers in 1998, its staff worked from a humble trailer on an empty parking lot. Today the organization has three buildings, which are used for leadership training, English-language classes, and workshops on job skills. In 2014 Casa Latina dispatched close to nine thousand jobs, with an average hourly wage of $16.46.[3]

As the executive director, Hilary Stern, told me, when Casa Latina first decided to become a workers' center, the staff really had no idea how to structure their organization. To develop their model, they joined and worked closely with national networks of workers' centers, including the National Day Laborer Organizing Network and the National Domestic Workers Alliance. These and other national networks like them have sprung up in the past decade to support local organizations. As an exchange within these networks, Casa Latina spent time with long-established workers' centers in Los Angeles, adopting their model of participatory democracy, which lets the workers collectively decide on their working conditions, including their wages and how the jobs are dispatched. The workers decide their minimum wage and when they can raise it based on market conditions. When Casa Latina started, the workers set their minimum wage at $9 an hour. During the tech boom, they raised it to $10. A few years later they raised it to $12 an hour, then $15 an hour. When Seattle raised its city minimum wage to $15, the workers raised their minimum wage to $16. But that's just the floor wage. For jobs that require more training and skill, such as carpentry, the wage is $20 an hour.

But Casa Latina isn't just a dispatcher for day laborers; it's also an advocacy organization that mobilizes the public and runs campaigns to improve working conditions for all of Seattle's new working class. Its first campaign, and legislative win, was a wage-theft ordinance that it introduced and helped to pass in the Seattle City Council. Stern shared an anecdote with me about how Casa Latina came to focus on wage theft. The project started over ten years ago, when workers who weren't day laborers began coming to Casa Latina. The staff would spend time trying to obtain money for their workers, but often they weren't successful in getting all or even some of their money back. So they decided it was time to organize a citywide crackdown on wage theft. Stern told me that one of the workers asked her, "Why is it that if I steal a candy bar I could be thrown into jail but someone can steal thousands of dollars from me and nothing happens to them?" Stern reached out to a council member who agreed to introduce the ordinance, which the workers and the council member worked on jointly to get the language right. She and the workers spent time educating council members through brown-bag lunches and hearings. And four years ago Seattle passed an ordinance making it a criminal offense to withhold pay from workers. Unfortunately, the council didn't dedicate funding to provide enforcement, and as a result no employer has been prosecuted. The only place to go for a wage-theft complaint is to call 911, and the police have no idea how to handle these cases. In addition, for a criminal offense you have to prove intention, and it's been fairly easy for employers to make excuses for not paying their workers. So Casa Latina and other organizations pushed for an Office of Labor Standards, which the city council approved and funded in 2015.

There are literally hundreds of workers' centers like Casa Latina and the Workers Defense Project in the United States, primarily made up of black and immigrant workers in some of the lowest-paid, most marginalized jobs in our society. Estimates suggest that there are more than two hundred workers' centers, many of them local organizations now federated into national alliances that bring together workers by sector, including the National Day Laborer Organizing Network, the National Domestic Workers Alliance, the National Guestworker Alliance, the National Taxi Workers Alliance, and Restaurant Opportunities Centers United.[4] Workers' centers are aligning around updating federal and state labor laws, which still exclude millions of working-class jobs from oversight; raising minimum wage laws; and fighting wage theft. These organizations work with local unions, faith groups, and other advocacy organizations engaging in lobbying, direct action, and education to pass reforms. And they are winning, bringing visibility to workers who have long been kept in the shadows of America's labor markets.

The success of domestic workers in winning new recognition in American labor laws, after being long excluded as a legacy of our racist history, is one of the most inspiring examples of what can happen when the new working class comes together in pursuit of justice. While today the National Domestic Workers Alliance boasts a presence in twenty-six cities and eighteen states of over ten thousand nannies, housekeepers, and care workers, it began in 2000, when Ai-jen Poo cofounded Domestic Workers United (DWU), a multiracial organization in New York City. Seven years later, in response to a growing cadre of domestic worker organizing, she helped found the National Domestic Workers Alliance, where she is currently director. But the fight began in New York City, where, after seven years of campaigning, domestic workers won their first bill of rights. The final legislation covered 200,000 domestic workers, providing an eight-hour workday, overtime pay, a minimum of twenty-four consecutive hours of rest per week, three paid days off per year, protection against discrimination and harassment, and worker's compensation insurance protection. As Poo writes in her book, *The Age of Dignity*, "The New York Domestic Workers' Bill of Rights became a flagship campaign, a symbol of the beginning of the end of invisibility for domestic workers around the country. The work in New York inspired women around the country who were part of the newly formed National Domestic Workers Alliance."[5] The fight for the New York law and the campaigns that have resulted in similar laws in Connecticut, Hawaii, Massachusetts, California, and Oregon are the result of strong multiracial alliances, including between the largely white employers and the predominantly immigrant and black workforce. The struggle for basic worker protections has brought a range of advocates together to fight side by side, including immigrants' rights groups, women's groups, faith groups, unions, and a smattering of celebrities.

From domestic workers to day laborers to taxi workers, the struggle is for dignity and visibility—the most basic components of life in a civilized society. Yet for millions of these workers, it has taken persistent demonstrations, countless acts of courage, and some kind of enduring optimism to win the right to be paid for their labor (all of their labor), time off to rest, and protection from harassment. Daniela, who worked seventeen-hour days for $3 an hour as a live-in nanny and maid in San Francisco when she immigrated from Mexico to the United States, joined the campaign for a bill of rights in California, saying, "Hopefully the bill of rights will pass so that all of this ends, so that the abuses end, and one knows her rights. And so that the worker has some time for herself. Because there are many women who live where they work and really they are like slaves—you feel like a slave. You can't say anything, move, or do anything because of your fear. The fear should end. One should be able to say things without having to be afraid."[6]

From Laughable to Doable: The Fight for $15

Back in November 2012 in New York City, a brave band of two hundred fast-food workers walked out of their jobs and into the streets to demand a better wage and the right to form a union. Just six months later, fast-food workers went on strike in six major cities across the country. As workers were joining the movement in greater numbers, the organizers added another tactic to their campaign: corporate shaming. Tipped off by a McDonald's worker, the campaign made public a website that McDonald's had created for its employees called, naturally, McResource. Part of the website was geared toward helping employees make a simple budget. Unfortunately, the sample budget revealed the behemoth to be just a tad out of touch with reality: It provided just twenty dollars per month for health-care expenses and nothing at all for gas expenses. Other parts of the site urged employees to adopt a healthy lifestyle by eschewing—wait for it—fast food. Further gaffes were exposed when a McDonald's employee called the McResource helpline and was told she would qualify for food stamps, and the website added new advice for its workers like cutting food into smaller pieces to stave off hunger. The exposure generated lots of bad publicity, even from business-friendly outlets like *Forbes* and CNBC, prompting the company to pull the website. With the press increasingly on its side, the Fight for $15 staged its first national strike in August 2013, with workers in over sixty cities participating. Two months later strikes occurred in more than one hundred cities. Then just six months later, on May 15, 2014, fast-food workers in *230 cities*, on six continents, joined the campaign, staging strikes, rallies, and protests, and bringing many supporters along with them.

But all of these actions paled in comparison to what happened on April 15, 2015, when the campaign officially expanded from fast-food workers to include retail and home care workers and even adjunct professors. It was the largest protest of low-wage workers in United States history, with at least sixty thousand people joining protests and rallies in cities across the country.[7] Mary Kay Henry, president of the Service Employees International Union, who has put the full resources of the SEIU behind this fight, said this about the movement: "There is not a price tag you can put on how this movement has changed the conversation in this country. It is raising wages at the bargaining table. It's raised wages for eight million workers. I believe we are forcing a real conversation about how to solve the grossest inequality in our generation. People are sick of wealth at the top and no accountability for corporations."[8]

I spoke with Scott Courtney, assistant to the president for organizing, about why the SEIU decided to support the campaign. He told me that when Mary Kay Henry became president of the SEIU in 2010, she asked the question "not how do we just rebuild unions and have a bigger union, but how do we make income inequality the issue that politicians in our country have to deal with?" The answer to that question over time became the Fight for $15.

The ability of the leader of the nation's fastest-growing union to ask that kind of question, one that reaches beyond the parochial goal of fighting only for its members, is the result of over a decade of work by leaders organizing people who had been excluded from traditional union membership (sometimes by laws and sometimes by the practice of labor unions). Jodeen Olguín-Tayler was active in the effort to engage union leaders to fight for the broader social struggle of the working class. Olguín-Tayler has spent fifteen years organizing the working class, first as a labor organizer at a local union and then running a national campaign to address the needs of elder-care workers and clients. She's now my partner in crime at Demos, as our vice president of campaigns and strategic partnerships, and she explained the long trajectory that made the Fight for $15 possible. "We knew that social agitation and public campaigns that reframe and transform 'worker issues' into community and social issues—that is, into *class* issues—was key to our ability to build a movement that could put economic, racial, and gender inequality back into the spotlight of public debate. This was a proactive, offensive strategy to move from protesting bad conditions to winning dignity and power for a broad, multiracial working class—a class where we, people of color, women, and immigrants, would finally be recognized as equals and deserving of our dignity," she explained. There were many successful predecessors to the Fight for $15, such as the living wage campaign of taxi drivers in San Francisco. All these wins demonstrated to the union movement that victory was possible by engaging a larger set of workers in the fight and building pressure for them to heed the call bubbling up across the country.

With the immense courage of the workers matched with the considerable financial resources of the SEIU, the Fight for $15 has taken those proven strategies and racked up major wins. In less than three years, Seattle, San Francisco, and Los Angeles have raised their minimum wage to $15. In the summer of 2015, New York State's Wage Board approved a $15 minimum wage for fast-food workers at major chains. What's remarkable is how the demand for $15 has quickly become mainstream. "We don't get laughed at anymore when we walk in the room," Courtney observed, remembering the rough times when the movement started. Back in 2012 the demand for $15 was greeted with incredulity. Fast-food workers, long seen as the bottom of the economic food chain, earning $15 an hour? It's a testament to the workers, who across race, gender, and age have shown a level of class solidarity America hasn't witnessed in at least a generation. And perhaps most important, it's brought hope to the new working class.

I asked Courtney how the movement has been able to build and maintain solidarity across such a wide range of experiences, and he talked about how the SEIU has given people the space to talk. And through that talking, they've come to realize that only by standing together will they be able to make their lives better. "People are smart. They get it. They get that they've been getting a raw deal, they've been getting a raw deal for a long time. And they haven't had hope. They have hope now. They do believe they're going to win. And when people come together and start thinking they can win, it's pretty spectacular to be a part of," he told me. This is a movement primarily, but not entirely, of people of color and immigrants, the very backbone of the new working class. And their success is made all the more sweeter by the reality that most people were skeptical at best when the first calls for $15 and a union were made. As we head into the 2016 elections, the Democratic candidates for president have already publicly supported the fight for $15, meaning that one way or another, this issue will continue to take its rightful place on the national stage.

The Fight for $15 uses a strategy well honed by conservatives: Establish a strong left flank in order to make any negotiation away from the big demand, in this case $15 an hour, seem moderate and commonsense by comparison. When the Fight for $15 started, even dyed-in-the-wool progressives thought a $15 minimum wage was ridiculous. But for cities with high costs of living, like Seattle, New York, and San Francisco, a $15 minimum is actually reasonable. So now for other cities, like Kansas City and Cincinnati, $10.10 feels not only reasonable but maybe a bit low. The Fight for $15 has fundamentally changed what's considered mainstream in our political debate about wages.

The New Freedom Fighters

In the wake of the acquittal of George Zimmerman for the fatal shooting of Trayvon Martin, three women channeled their outrage into what would eventually become the centerpiece of a new civil rights movement. Patrisse Cullors, Alicia Garza, and Opal Tometi came up with a profound yet simple rallying cry for dignity: Black Lives Matter. By the end of the night, the three women made the decision to start a movement, one that would seamlessly blend online and on-the-ground strategies. I met Cullors (whose story is featured in Chapter 5) and Garza at Demos's gala in 2015, where we honored all three women with a Transforming America Award (Tometi was not able to attend). By one estimate, there were more than one thousand Black Lives Matter protests and demonstrations around the globe between June 2014 and October 2015.[9] The demonstrations erupted after the murders of unarmed black men, teenagers, and children by police officers, from Michael Brown in Ferguson to Eric Garner in Staten Island to Tamir Rice in Cleveland, and sadly, many more black men and black women are killed with each passing month. Over time these protests grew into a broader campaign for racial justice. Like the civil rights movement a half century ago, Black Lives Matter is a broad demand for freedom from political and economic oppression. But unlike the earlier movement, Cullors, Garza, and Tometi have purposefully put black women in the forefront of the movement and emphasized the voices of queer, transgendered, and disabled black people.

Alicia Garza explained to me why it's so important that this movement not simply replicate the leadership and strategies of its predecessors. Her analysis about why there is a need to proclaim that "black lives matter" today, a half century after the civil rights act was passed, lies in part in what can now be seen as the flawed strategies pursued back then. "The time when a black man in a suit, who is typically a preacher, speaks for all of us has ended. We are coming to recognize as a society that the nuclear family only exists for some people, and that's not actually the standard that folks should be held to. Because of our social and economic conditions, we've been forced to create family where we can find it, as opposed to these really narrow definitions of what that looks like. When I hear elders talking about the civil rights movement of their time, and some of the reasons why the external optics were so much different than the reality of how things played out, it had a lot to do with appealing to white mainstream society about what we deserved as people. And so if we could mirror and mimic what white families looked like and what white social structures looked like, and show that we could do it just as well, then we would also supposedly demonstrate that we were worthy of our humanity. And that didn't work. That didn't work. For us, we're saying that this isn't about appealing to white mainstream society. This is about saying that black folks come in all different sizes, all different shapes. We're very different and complex as a people, and that deserves to be celebrated. And the humanity of all of us deserves to be affirmed, and that we all have value."

She and the codirectors of Black Lives Matter are determined to make sure that every single presidential candidate formulates a concrete position on what he or she will do to make black lives matter in this country. And they expect that answer to go far beyond criminal justice reform. "For us, it's less about endorsing candidates than it is to build the kind of coalition that can hold whoever is elected accountable to meeting the needs and dreams of our communities."

Across the country, a new generation of activists, rooted in the struggles of the poor and working class, is engaging in a new kind of solidarity, across race and gender but also across the broad issues of immigrants' rights, labor rights, and civil rights. These organizations are often led by young people of color, and they are forging deep alliances with one another, learning together how to reignite the call for racial justice in the twenty-first century. Most of the new activism began when George Zimmerman was acquitted. Because race has always been classed and class has always been raced, most of these city- or state-based organizations understand the connections between corporate power, police brutality, underfunded public schools, and low-paying jobs. There's a new beltway of activism flowing through the South, from Atlanta, Georgia, all the way down to Miami, Florida, and on over to Jackson, Mississippi.

Phillip Agnew is the director of Dream Defenders, based in Florida, and was one of the handful of young activists invited to the White House to meet with President Obama about the protests in Ferguson, Missouri. Agnew, whom I met at a Demos gala when we honored Dream Defenders with a Transforming America Award, brought the house down in his acceptance speech. Like so many other leaders, he and his group are joining the chorus of activists supporting Black Lives Matter while continuing to do local organizing and work to change policies and laws. In an interview, he seamlessly laid out the breadth of the challenge and what animates working-class people whose struggles form the backbone of the second wave of civil rights activism: "The values that our country is supposed to be built on—equal opportunity for all, the ability of all to represent our values at the ballot box—this country has never done that. What it has done, very successfully, is taken certain people—based on their color, based on their ethnicity, based on their immigration status, based on their education level, based on their economic status—and said that those people are not worthy of the values put on paper. The role of people in Black Lives Matter—the role of people who are angry about police, about the environment, about the economy—is to remind people that America has some values that it's never lived up to and that have never applied to certain people. We want to change that."[10]

In the past decade, more than a hundred thousand young immigrants, most undocumented, have built a considerable network of activism that is winning policy reforms at the state and federal level. Known as DREAMers, for their first campaign to allow undocumented immigrants in-state tuition and eligibility for federal student aid (legislation known as the Dream Act), United We Dream is the largest youth immigrant justice network, with fifty-five affiliate organizations in twenty-six states. The DREAMers are young people like Giancarlo Tello, who is currently a student at Rutgers University in New Jersey. Tello told me that he learned he was undocumented in his sophomore year of high school. He had passed his written driver's license test and was ready to go to the DMV to get his learner's permit so he could start practicing actual driving. That's when his mom told him he couldn't get a license because of his immigration status. He didn't quite understand the full implications of this until his junior year, when it came time to apply for colleges, which required a Social Security number, which he did not have. He couldn't apply for aid or scholarships, which required residency or citizenship. And he couldn't get a job, because he didn't have legal authorization. He learned he could go to Bergen Community College, thanks to his older cousin, who is also undocumented and was attending. It was there that he met another undocumented student, who invited him to a training session that was being held by the New Jersey Dream Act Coalition, one of the United We Dream affiliates. "Against my parents' advice, I decided to go, and it was definitely worth it," Tello told me. "It was the first time I'm meeting other undocumented students and seeing people who are actually affected by the issue and advocating on behalf of themselves. Not being afraid of deportation or the stigma that comes with being undocumented. That's what initially inspired me. That's where I met a lot of my mentors and other undocumented youth who had been fighting the struggle for a long time. They showed me there's a different way to go about our lives and challenge the status quo."

Tello graduated from Bergen Community College in three years, taking an extra year because he had to work and pay his way through college. He had to pay the international tuition rate because he was undocumented. He applied to Rutgers and got accepted, but again had to pay the higher out-of-state tuition rate. Each course was about $2,700, so for the first year he took only one class for two or three semesters, and then he decided to take one semester off to work and advocate for the New Jersey Dream Act. That one semester turned into a year, but it was worth it. In December 2013, Governor Chris Christie signed into law the New Jersey Tuition Equality Act, which provides in-state tuition for undocumented immigrants. (Yes, you read that correctly.) Tello took advantage of the Deferred Action for Childhood Arrivals (DACA) policy during his year off from school, which enabled him to get a Social Security number, work legally, and get a driver's license. He worked full-time during the campaign, at a law firm doing office work and for the Communications Workers of America (CWA). CWA was one of the biggest allies in the fight for the New Jersey Dream Act. Today Tello receives a full scholarship from Rutgers University, which offered him the scholarship based on his social justice activism. He continues to be actively involved in immigration justice, speaking at colleges across the state, testifying at hearings, and generally engaging and encouraging his peers to join the movement.

Tello and the hundred thousand other young, mostly undocumented immigrants are fueling a new generation of activists who are working together to challenge systems and the status quo. "There's a lot of movements on a lot of fronts, and a lot of solidarity," he explained. "We have a lot of great solidarity struggles between people of color, immigration, and LGBTQ movements."

While the children of immigrant parents have found the courage to speak out, so too have many of their parents. On May 1, 2006, millions of the new working class walked off their jobs and took to the streets in cities and towns across the country. The immigrant activism was met with solidarity from the AFL-CIO, a major shift from its historic anti-immigrant posture. By walking out of their jobs, millions of immigrants effectively shut down entire industries that day. In Los Angeles, the mostly Mexican and Central American port truckers shut down 90 percent of the port's activity, and 50 percent of the meat and poultry processing ground to a halt. The Day Without an Immigrant mobilization underscored the latent power of the new working class to disrupt business as usual.

Unions in the Most Unexpected Places

Ben Speight is exceedingly good at a difficult job. He's an organizer for the statewide Teamsters Local 728 based in Atlanta, Georgia. A thirty-three-year-old white man, he's been organizing since he was eighteen, spending eleven of the past fifteen years as a union organizer with the Teamsters. He doesn't see his work as being in the service of others but as organizing with others. As he explained, "In my fifteen years of organizing, I have never been a part of a campaign where the core of our support and the majority of our support did not come from black workers. Every campaign that I've been a part of, dozens of campaigns in the South, have all got the initial interest and the majority of their support from black workers. Black workers seek out union representation in the South more than we have the capacity to assist." Speight attributes this trend to the strong culture of resistance in the black community and the belief that collective action produces results.

And he's right. Compared to whites, African Americans are much more collectively oriented and community-centered, a worldview born of the reality that survival meant banding together. As John Powell recounts in his book *Racing to Justice*, individualism, a key value of the American ideology, is in fact a very racialized concept, and one that conflicts with the orientation toward communitarian values that are held deeply by African Americans. The tension between these two values ricochets through all our major policy debates, and generally, though not exclusively, breaks down along partisan lines, with the Democratic Party leaning more toward communitarianism and the Republican Party leaning toward individualism. The same split exists along racial lines, and it is an important contributor to the reality that today people of color are more likely to be union members than whites are.

Speight told me, "The dynamic of racism is alive in every campaign we have." In order to win, the union has to have a supermajority, and that means that the folks inside the company fighting for the union have to reflect all the workers that are employed. So when they set up the worker committee, they've got to bring together white, black, and Latino workers. And he doesn't try to evade the issue of race. He addresses it directly and openly. The Georgia local has 8,200 members, and he told me that there are some workers who come in with "Hands Up, Don't Shoot" T-shirts and members who come in wearing Confederate flag belt buckles. But when they realize that they have a common demand and a common adversary—their employer—they work through their prejudices and join together to win.

In his most recent campaign, at United Natural Food, which supplies organic food to stores such as Whole Foods, it was two white workers who sought out the union. But they realized they weren't going to win with just their own social networks in the workplace, so they actively had to build relationships with the black workers and overcome a lot of distrust about their motives.

On the other hand, at his last campaign, at Coca-Cola, the anti-union committee was all white workers, and according to Speight, Coca-Cola flouted numerous labor laws, including firing three African American workers who were at the center of the campaign.

There's a myth that you can't unionize in the South. But as Speight makes the case, industry is flocking to the South to take advantage of the legacy of hostility toward unions. It's helpful to remember here that most of the right-to-work laws were originally in the South, with the intention of maintaining a highly racialized low-wage structure. Today those laws remain, and as a result both foreign and domestic companies are moving their operations to the South, including Hyundai, BMW, Mercedes, Volkswagen, Nissan, and Boeing. Speight wants the labor movement to recommit to organizing in the South, with a new Operation Dixie. The first Operation Dixie was a failed campaign by the Congress of Industrial Unions to organize workers in the South in the postwar years. It failed largely because of the hardened racial lines of Jim Crow and the prohibitions on strikes set in place under Taft-Hartley. The defeat of Operation Dixie resounds powerfully today, both in terms of the emaciation of the unionized workforce and the race to the bottom engendered by the South's long-standing animus to anything that smacks of cross-race solidarity.

In February 2014, after months of intense organizing and even active support from the company, the United Auto Workers lost the election to unionize Volkswagen's plant in Chattanooga, Tennessee. It was a bruising defeat, made even more so by the fact that the election was exceedingly close—712 to 626, just 86 votes shy of what would have been a game-changing victory for the southern working class. The stakes were rightly seen as huge, both for labor and for corporations in the South, both of which understood that a win for the UAW would ripple across the South, opening the door to unionization at auto plants across the region. And so

Republican leaders launched an all-out assault on the campaign, despite Volkswagen officials urging third-party actors to remain neutral and stay out of the battle.[11] The antitax zealot and conservative Svengali Grover Norquist, as well as major conservative political donors David and Charles Koch, supported a well-funded campaign against the union.[12] Billboards warned residents that a union vote would turn Chattanooga into the next Detroit. The governor of the state, Bill Haslan, argued that the state would lose jobs because employers would not come to Tennessee if the UAW won. United States senator Bob Corker made similar threats, saying "they" would not expand their plants if the UAW was victorious. Meanwhile, the state proposed a $300 million incentive package for VW to expand its production by adding an SUV production to the plant, but attempted to tie the money to a no vote on the union.[13] And in the strangest through-the-looking-glass analysis of American values, state senator Bo Watson reproached Volkswagen for not vehemently opposing the union effort, saying that its approach was "unfair, unbalanced, and, quite frankly, un-American in the traditions of American labor campaigns."[14] Keep in mind that in the fall of 2013, the UAW reached the critical threshold of a majority of workers signing cards in support of the union. But with several months in between the call for an election and the actual voting, there was plenty of time for opponents to play hardball. And that they did. Eighty-six workers. Just eighty-six workers who stymied solidarity in the South once again.

When labor loses, it's not just better wages and working conditions that are left on the table. What's also lost is the civic participation and political education that unions provide. And other than churches, unions are really the only game left in town for fostering deep social and political connections. Unlike most congregations, today's unions are racially diverse, forging a deep understanding among members that blacks, Latinos, and whites share a common cause. The civic muscle-building of workers by labor unions is often overlooked but is essential to rebuilding the power of the new working class. And I'd argue that it's this political education and solidarity-building that is really behind the vehement opposition to unions within the Republican Party and conservative operatives.

Cultivating solidarity among racially diverse union members is the job Rafael Návar, political director for the Communications Workers of America, wakes up every morning to pursue. About half of CWA's 700,000 members are white, so bridging differences across race and ethnicity is his bread-and-butter. As Návar sees it, one of the chief obstacles to building that kind of solidarity is a deep class analysis about why workers, including the white working class, have lost so much ground. Without a shared understanding of how capitalism has been reengineered by elites in the past three decades to encourage financial and capital rent-seeking behavior, the working class (and the middle class as well) can be easily steered toward scapegoating a group of people as the source of their problems. Without an understanding of how the rules have been rewritten, the lack of good jobs gets blamed on undocumented immigrants by both the white and the black working class. Meanwhile, the white working class can view its inability to move up the income ladder as the fault of affirmative action, with blacks supposedly taking the best jobs that would have otherwise gone to white people.

Under Návar's leadership, CWA created a comprehensive curriculum to educate its members, which includes education about current political fights, such as the Trans-Pacific Partnership debate. But the real meat of the curriculum is the political economy, which is currently part of a presentation called "The 40-Year Class War," which tackles the biggest problem Návar sees among the working class: a lack of strong class analysis. "We have to start off from a commonality and a perspective that critiques the economic system," he said, "that is really at fault for why the white working class has been losing earnings and wages and then tie that common problem to how it is impacting people of color." "The 40-Year Class War" tells the story of the rise of organized business, which I detailed in Chapter 4, and the corporate assault on workers' rights. The curriculum also incorporates what Návar calls "other struggles," connecting the dots of other movements to the labor movement. There are three "other struggles" segments, which will be rolled out in phases: immigration, Black Lives Matter, and the environment. The union is currently engaging its members around immigration, holding a series of two-day "boot camps." Návar shows the film *Harvest of Empire*, which examines how policies in Latin America driven both by our trade policy and by major corporations fueled immigration to the United States. When Návar ran this boot camp in southern Virginia for a group of white members and one black member, it was transformative. The members were angry upon learning the story, and understood that their struggle was intertwined with that of Latino workers. CWA has run these boot camps all across the country, to audiences that are overwhelmingly black or white, and the response has been the same. One of the trainers in Georgia who ran a boot camp was very anxious about the reaction and worried that there would be backlash among both white and black members. But the day after the training, he called Návar to let him know that the members loved it, and were "pissed" at what they had learned.

Návar is doing good old-fashioned consciousness-raising, and for the progressive movement, the loss of unions playing this role is a severe blow to building the kind of shared worldview among the working class critical for rebuilding political power. And that kind of work is gaining more traction across the labor movement. In February 2015, the AFL-CIO launched a Labor Commission on Racial and Economic Justice. Carmen Berkley, director of Civil, Human and Women's Rights at the AFL-CIO, is leading the initiative, which has the full participation of the AFL-CIO's Executive Council. The initiative is an embodiment of the ideals of

AFL-CIO's president, Richard Trumka, who has not shied away from issues of race. In the wake of the killing of Michael Brown by a police officer, Trumka described the tragedy in a high-profile speech in St. Louis by saying, "Our brother killed our sister's son," referring to Darren Wilson, the police officer, and Mike Brown's mother, who is a member of the UFCW. Over the course of the year, the commission will hold discussions with local labor leaders in eight cities across the country, to directly address issues related to race and the labor movement. "Honestly, ten years ago, I don't know if we would have been able to pull off a race commission," Berkley told me. "People are not avoiding race anymore. At the AFL, we believe now is the time to talk about things we should have talked about a long time ago. And it has to be about solutions and not just lip service."

Of course, labor unions can't be the only institution providing a framework for solidarity; the major political parties have a role here too. While the Republican Party has built solidarity among the white working class through the strategic use of racially coded appeals, the Democratic Party until very recently abandoned progressivism for a more business-friendly platform. The centrist takeover of the Democratic Party was the animating value behind the formation of the Working Families Party (WFP) and a spate of newly focused state organizations working to build independent political power.

Rebooting Progressive Politics

Back in 1998, at the beginning of the Clinton administration, Dan Cantor and a handful of other individuals established the Working Families Party. Cantor, who serves as WFP's national director, remembers the founding principles behind its formation: "The Democratic Party had drifted far to the right, had abandoned its working-class roots, whose allegiance was always contested." The major planks of the Working Families Party are investments in public goods such as debt-free college tuition and child care, racial equity, and climate change with the understanding that providing a decent standard of living for working people must go beyond wages.

At this point it will be helpful to outline how the WFP functions as a third party that doesn't siphon votes away from the Democrats, like Ralph Nader did in the 2000 election. The WFP strategy concentrates on Democratic primaries at both the state and city level. Federal races remain prohibitively expensive for the WFP to engage in, though its leaders are trying to figure out how to break through the money barriers. Their candidates run as Democrats with endorsements from the WFP. When it comes to the general election, the WFP exists in states that allow fusion voting, which enables candidates who are endorsed by the WFP to run on both the Democratic Party line and the WFP line. Voters then cast their vote for the candidate on either the Democratic Party line or the WFP line. When Democratic candidates win with a significant number of votes coming from the WFP line, it helps create pressure for progressive action from the candidate, who will be held accountable by WFP members.

But the WFP isn't just about electing more progressive candidates. Its strategy is to be the left flank of the Democratic Party and eventually move the center of the party back to being the champions of the working class and of public investment in general. As Cantor told me, "The idea in forming the WFP was to be both independent and relevant. It's easy to be independent and not relevant, but that's not really helpful. And it's kind of worked better than we ever thought it would." The WFP is now active in ten states and can count some significant victories directly attributable to its work. In New York State, where the party is particularly relevant and powerful, Dan told me that fully two-thirds of voters are aware of the WFP. While most of the attention is given to the WFP's electoral work, its members actually spend 90 percent of their time working on issues, coordinating closely with various coalitions and state legislators to move progressive policy forward and "give the vote meaning." Electing good candidates isn't enough by itself, because, as Cantor told me, "We'll elect people and the next day the Chamber of Commerce has got their arm around them. 'Glad you're here—let's talk.' "

As the WFP has gained power, particularly in New York State, it has faced the problems that can come with legitimacy: whether to play ball with power or lose access as an outside actor. That's exactly the dilemma the WFP faced during Governor Andrew Cuomo's campaign for reelection in 2014. After four years as governor in New York State, Cuomo had alienated and frustrated nearly every progressive activist in the state. He made promises to enact public financing to address the deeply corrupt politics in Albany but failed to put any muscle behind the effort. Then he shut down his own creation, the Moreland Commission, established to investigate the money-drenched system and backroom deals that define Albany policymaking. He proposed tax cuts for the affluent at a time when New Yorkers desperately needed public investment in jobs, schools, and child care. So when he ran for reelection, he faced a progressive challenger in the primary, Zephyr Teachout. Teachout is one of the country's foremost experts on campaign finance and money in politics, and she made that issue a center of her platform. Her campaign generated serious attention and grassroots support, so when it came time for the WFP to vote on whether to endorse Teachout or Cuomo, the decision was about access to power. Even though Teachout was gaining ground, she faced a candidate with a considerable war chest, and her chances of winning the primary were slim. And if the WFP withheld its endorsement from Cuomo and he won, the party and its platform would face a vengeful king, losing any kind of leverage or power needed to push through policies like paid sick days and minimum-wage increases that its members and most New Yorkers supported. The vote for endorsing took place at the WFP convention, and to say this was a contentious debate would be an understatement. Governor Cuomo saw the writing on the wall and made a promise to campaign hard for Democratic candidates in the state senate, who finally had a chance to gain the majority, and he promised to deliver public financing. Mayor Bill DeBlasio of New York City supported Cuomo, and in the end the WFP gave Cuomo and not Teachout its endorsement. "Cuomo got what he wanted, and then he didn't feel any obligation to keep his promise to us and to others," Cantor explained. "We were aware that it was a risk, but we made a bet that he would keep to his word, because in politics all you have is your word. But he chose otherwise and the Republicans remained in power."

While Cuomo reneged on his promise to fight on behalf of Democratic candidates to regain control of the state senate, he nevertheless delivered a major boost to the new working class. Under state law, Cuomo can establish a wage board for certain industries, and he created one to study the pay of fast-food workers. As we've seen, the wage board voted in July 2015 to raise the pay of fast-food workers in the state to $15 an hour. This victory can be viewed in part as payback for the WFP endorsement, because the Fight for $15 set of organizations and unions who are part of the WFP voted to back Cuomo in the primary fight.

The WFP can rightly take credit for igniting a wave of paid-sick-days legislation as well. The fact that in the United States workers have to advocate and lobby for the right to take a day off when they're sick or their child is sick without losing pay is indicative of the long slide in labor standards for the new working class and the lack of bargaining power to secure basic benefits. San Francisco was the first city to pass paid-sick-days legislation, followed by a string of major cities and Connecticut in 2011. But the fight for this basic benefit was nothing short of a political showdown in New

York City. After five years of activism and lobbying, the City Council passed a fairly weak version of paid sick days that covered about 1 million workers. Then the WFP ran a progressive slate of candidates for the City Council in 2012, and they all won their seats. As Cantor told me, with the new City Council in place, it took only about three hours to amend the law to cover another 300,000 to 500,000 workers. Three hours compared to three years—that's the difference electing progressives to office can make in the lives of the working class. The City Council had more than enough votes to pass the measure, but the speaker of the council at the time was Christine Quinn, and she refused to bring the bill to the floor for a vote. Some speculate that she was appeasing the business community in anticipation of her run for mayor in the Democratic primary. In the end, the WFP brought a formidable onslaught of pressure from activists across the city, and Quinn begrudgingly brought the bill to the floor, where it passed handsomely.

Changing the Electorate in the States

In the past decade a growing number of state-based organizations realized that in order to make real gains for their working-class members, they'd need to get serious about building political power. And that meant changing the way they did business from traditional coalition work and lobbying to a long-term commitment to political education and mobilization of the new working class.

Olguín-Tayler, whom we met earlier in the chapter, explained to me the impetus for and context behind this strategic shift among working-class organizations: "It came from a growing frustration of wanting to move away from being protest movements and instead be organizations and people who are actually shaping and winning policy, and moving from just having the power to make complaints and grievances to being able to have the power to actually govern and determine our lives and conditions."

It's a formidable challenge. Many of these organizations do regular door-knocking in working-class neighborhoods, where they try to persuade citizens to vote in upcoming elections by talking about what is at stake. It's a tough sell. A standard response to a door-knocker is "It doesn't matter whether I vote or not." But these organizers are committed, and they've made some significant gains in some incredibly politically challenging environments, such as Virginia.

Jon Liss is the executive director of New Virginia Majority (NVM), an organization whose mission is to change the electorate in the state by turning out the black, Latino, Asian, and working-class vote. Liss has been organizing the working class for decades, in what he calls "new working-class organizations" that sprouted up during the 1990s and the early years of this century to fill the vacuum left by the long decline in unions. But the mobilizing of the new working class went beyond standard workers' issues to address the big challenges in their lives: access to good public schools and affordable child care, avoidance of the school-to-prison pipeline, and the need for health insurance. In Virginia, Liss led this work through Tenants and Workers United, a precursor organization to NVM. But there were limits to this approach, as he noted: "The limits of the new working-class organizing were that we were doing work in essentially one region, or one city, a lot of work in two decades. At the same time, the demographics in Virginia were changing. So we set out to change the electorate."

Over time, Liss and others in Virginia realized that without political power, their organizing efforts far too often led to dead ends. With the formation of New Virginia Majority in 2008, the goal is to build what's known in the field as "independent political power," which involves ongoing and consistent voter education and mobilization of the new working class—individuals overlooked by the Democratic Party's voter drives. In the black belt, a region stretching from Tidewater through Richmond, black voters, especially black women, are a solid progressive voting bloc and, according to Liss, a major reason that the Democratic governor, Terry McAuliffe, won his election. But Virginia is also one of the few states that take away voting rights for ex-offenders, resulting in 350,000 missing voters, most of whom are men of color. New Virginia Majority have set some ambitious goals. In northern Virginia, they've trained and hired people from the neighborhoods to go out and organize, with the goal of talking to people six times between September and November, when it's election time. Their initial list is daunting, anywhere between 60,000 and 160,000 people, and they'll door-knock about one-third of those potential voters. From there they begin winnowing their target list based on where people stand on key issues. So in 2008 they began by asking individuals if they supported universal health care, and then if they supported extending health care to immigrants. If someone answered no to either question, he or she wasn't put on the list of people whom NMV would try to turn out. The final turnout universe might be about 25,000 to 50,000, which is enough to swing an election in Virginia.

After six years of experience and practice in building a dependable working-class voting bloc, the organization created an electoral arm so it could endorse candidates and engage in electoral politics. The organizers set their sights on a thirty-year incumbent conservative Democrat backed by the local Tea Party, U.S. representative Johnny Joanou of the 79th House District. The 79th District covers Portsmouth, a working-class community with a majority black population. New Virginia Majority organized the local unions and other activists to throw their support behind a progressive city council member who was launching a primary challenge to Joanou, a man with the symbolically challenging name of Stephen Heretick. Thanks to a coordinated voter education and get-out-the-vote effort, Heretick won the primary by a razor-thin margin of two hundred votes. The vote was won by pure field muscle. "We hope to change the nature of the party over time by changing the consciousness of its voters," Liss told me.

NVM has made some progress in changing the face of who shows up on election day. But turning ideas for policy into actual law requires a robust and consistent political participation, something that has been more challenging to accomplish. Liss's goal for NVM is to create an active membership organization whose engagement goes beyond clicking on an email voicing an opinion on legislation. With twenty thousand people signed up on the email list, the organization has gotten a bird's-eye view of the challenges it faces in bridging alliances across race. When it has sent out pro-immigration emails, it has gotten push-back from some members. When it has sent out emails about mass incarceration, it has gotten push-back from some members. But Liss won't be deterred. In September 2015, New Virginia Majority brought together two hundred activists from across the state to ratify a common state agenda, which will provide alignment and shared goals across organizations working in Virginia.

Over in Missouri, Ashli Bolden, the codirector of Missouri Jobs with Justice, is fighting to build power with the new working class. "Right now we have two political parties that are being controlled by money and by corporations basically," she said. "So what are we doing to step outside of what we thought was our safety net—the Democratic Party—to see the policies we want in our communities to make our lives better? No one is talking about raising the minimum wage until it's an election year. And then after the election year, no action is happening. Nobody is talking about collective bargaining rights, or how everything is going private because nobody wants anything to be public anymore. We have to start electing people that come from our base who want the same things we do. That's why we need independent political power."

Missouri Jobs with Justice is focusing on changing the structural barriers in our democracy by working on getting campaign finance laws passed in Missouri and tackling redistricting, which right now gives disproportionate voting power to rural areas in the state. And there's a growing level of activism building throughout the state. After the killing of Michael Brown in Ferguson, Bolden told me that "people came out of nowhere." There are more activists than the existing organizations, from small informal organizations to churches, could coordinate. Missouri Jobs with Justice is currently identifying all the groups working on social justice to invite them and the local unions to a "table"—political-speak for a place where various organizations can come together to strategize.

Missouri Jobs with Justice, along with the Fight for $15 campaign, SEIU, and others, fought hard for the $13 minimum wage that the Kansas City council passed in July 2015. The law isn't perfect, because it includes a young person's exemption, which allows employers to pay subminimum wage to younger workers. The law also doesn't have an automatic cost-of-living adjustment. But its passage was significant not only for workers in Kansas City but potentially for workers across the state. When Kansas City passed its law, it created a domino effect: Kansas City County, St. Louis, and the state legislature are all now actively considering minimum-wage increases to at least $13 an hour, despite claiming that they couldn't do it just weeks before the city council in Kansas City passed its bill.

Bolden is motivated by her own experience growing up in a union household. "I know how important it is for your parents to have good health care, good wages. I had a good childhood," she explained. "When my father was laid off from McDonnell Douglas, I saw what taking all that away looks like. That's why I fight. I remember that life. And I want other children and other people to have that beautiful life of wages and benefits."

The work that both Bolden and Liss are doing is replicated in at least a dozen states across the country, including Florida, Washington, New Mexico, Minnesota, Ohio, and New York. These organizations speak to a larger fight happening within the Democratic Party, between those who want to see the party get back to its working-class roots and those who want to continue threading the needle by being both business-friendly and moderately pro-workers' rights. At the national level, this fight is epitomized by Senator Elizabeth Warren, who has become the leader in the struggle to shift the Democratic Party back to solid progressivism. It's echoed in major cities, most illustratively by the election of Bill DeBlasio, who triumphed over more moderate Democrats in the primary, as mayor of New York City. And it's reverberating throughout towns and cities, with new leaders and new organizations doing creative and innovative work to rebuild working-class power. They're not only beating back bad laws against the odds, they're also advancing proactive reforms that can make a difference in people's lives.

I am by nature not an optimist. In fact, I tend to vacillate between cynicism, pessimism, and downright despair about the state of this country. But in the past several years I've become steadily more optimistic. Through my work at Demos, I've seen the steady emergence of a new generation of activism and leadership focused squarely on revitalizing working-class power, weaving together issues of economic, social, and racial justice. It's a long-term project, to be sure. But the examples of a newly organized working class defeating attempts to scale back workers' rights or restrictive voting laws are not only too numerous to cover in this chapter but too numerous for a cynically inclined person to ignore.

Likewise, the victories bubbling up in towns and states across the country on minimum wage and paid sick days are big enough to chip away the pessimism that has gripped many progressive activists for decades. The Sleeping Giant is awaking. And our nation will be all the better for it.

CHAPTER EIGHT

A Better Deal

I miss the America I grew up in. It was a place that embraced the hard work of my parents, who without any college education were rewarded for their labor enough to build a solid and comfortable middle-class life. Bob and Sally, my parents, struggled at times, especially with four children to raise on one salary. Until my mom went back to work when my youngest brother entered kindergarten, my clothes, if they weren't hand-me-downs, came largely from our church's rummage sales and thrift stores. With my mom's paycheck, our quality of life increased pretty significantly. We began taking vacations in Myrtle Beach, South Carolina, the six of us packed into a burgundy Caprice Classic and later a minivan. For the first time I could go to the mall to buy clothes, and the teasing from other kids about my outdated wardrobe subsided. The extra money bought soccer uniforms, piano lessons, and Schwinn bikes. I remember feeling like my family had made it. We moved to a newer house, with wall-to-wall carpeting and a finished basement. Dad put up an aboveground pool and mowed the boundary lines for the backyard badminton court. As my sixteenth birthday approached, I got a job and bought a used car, with my dad cosigning the loan from the credit union. During high school I began setting my sights on an advertising career, aspiring to be like the upwardly mobile professionals in my favorite show, *Thirty-*

something. When it was my turn to go to college, I applied to one university and, thankfully, was accepted. Four years later I left without any student loan debt and worked six months as a waitress to save up money to move to New York City. Twenty-one years later I'm a New Yorker, raising my daughter in a beautiful tree-lined neighborhood.

What a gift I was given by that America.

Sadly, for the past two decades I've also had a front-row seat to watch that America crumbling, as my once middle-class family, my siblings and my mom, were pulled down by the abandonment of our nation's values and promises that set me on my way. After divorcing my dad while I was in college, my mom was able to purchase a small but comfortable home on her salary as an office manager in an orthodontist's office. She worked there for twenty-four years before being summarily let go when the owners of the practice changed hands. She and the other highest-paid (and most tenured) employee were tossed aside, presumably because their pay was considered too high by the new owners. When she was let go, my mom was making $19 an hour plus benefits, including health insurance and a small retirement account. Unemployed at the age of sixty-one, she had a hard time finding work. For four and a half years she worked part-time, earning $12 an hour with no benefits. For the first time in her life she didn't have health insurance, which was the case until Medicare kicked in when she turned sixty-five. During those years without a full-time job, she spent all her savings and racked up credit-card debt making ends meet and helping to support my siblings, all of whom have struggled to wring out a decent living in the bargain-basement economy. All told, my mom and siblings have experienced three bankruptcies, one foreclosure, and multiple spells of unemployment. My nieces and nephews know college is their pathway out, but they fear it isn't financially feasible or practical. Their America has never provided for their family the way it did for mine. They have gotten a raw deal, and so have the millions of working-class people who wake up every day, try a little harder, and yet keep slipping behind.

My family is white, and the privilege afforded to our white skin has buoyed us in some difficult times. My dad's parents left him and his siblings wealth in the form of stocks. When my dad passed away, that stock was passed down to another generation. That stock may very well put college within reach for my nieces and nephews and will definitely cushion us all from the harsh edges of today's capitalism. This legacy of wealth, especially life-altering for working-class people, provides a generational cushion that remains overwhelmingly held by whites, due to decades of discriminatory wealth-building polices and stubbornly hardened segregation in housing and jobs.

The trajectory of downward mobility experienced by my immediate family is far from unique. Those of us who, through a combination of grit, resilience, and the once-affordable state college or university, made the great crossing from the working class to the middle class or beyond, are living reminders of what was possible when life in America was more fair.

Our nation's long slide away from fairness and opportunity was in no way an accidental quirk of nature. It was created and sustained by an economic and political ideology that blesses the markets but forsakes the people—especially the people who fail to overcome the barriers deliberately constructed to make getting ahead a luxury increasingly determined by the random luck of birth.

Because America's rising inequality was man-made (our political and economic elites are still overwhelmingly men), changing our destiny is possible. It'll take a fight, but I'm pretty sure that's an American value that hasn't been eroded. Throughout history progressive transformation has occurred when the power of people and the power of ideas align. Put another way, transformative change happens when people hit the streets and ideas catch fire, making what was once thought impossible possible. The progressive uprisings in the Gilded Age and in the wake of the Great Depression ushered in the New Deal, a set of promises as much as a set of policies about what people in this country could expect from our government and our companies. These expectations weren't delivered on a silver platter; they were fought for, often bitterly. Decades later African Americans challenged our nation to live up to its promise of equality, again with civil disobedience that cost lives and involved far too much bloodshed. And then the women's movement and the gay rights movement did the same.

We are now seeing the beginnings of a new movement for justice, rooted in the intertwined struggle of race and class. As the Sleeping Giant stirs, challenging the status quo from the Central Valley of California to the streets of East New York, the new working class is beginning the tough work of changing the parameters of what's possible, opening hearts and minds to a different vision of the future.

A future where we all get a Better Deal, in both our democracy and our economy.

It's an America that most people would like to see. Where we all have a real say in the political decisions that affect our lives. Where we all have a real chance to meet our basic needs and fulfill our aspirations. Getting there will be nearly impossible without a major revival of working-class power, because the barriers standing in the way of transformative change are so formidable. The new working class is a Sleeping Giant, its latent power formidable because of its size, diversity, and a growing understanding that solidarity is the only weapon strong enough to challenge entrenched power. I realize that that might sound radical, but in an era when one-tenth of the richest 1 percent of Americans (160,000 households) owns the same share of wealth as the entire bottom 90 percent combined,[1] we must confront the issue of who holds power and the ways in which that power now dictates the rules of both our economy and our democracy.

The calls for more investment in people—rebuilding our infrastructure, meeting the challenge of climate change, providing high-quality child care for every infant and toddler, paying workers a decent wage, and reinvesting in long-excluded and isolated communities—will be immediately dismissed by pundits and politicians as too expensive. For the past several decades we've been sold the idea that somehow our country is broke. That there is simply no way we can afford the investments that would improve the lives of millions of people, not to mention modernize our nation's decayed infrastructure. Asking "How are you going to pay for it?" is an inside-the-Beltway paradigm that has seeped into our popular discourse. It's a question lobbed by reporters and politicians, aimed at exposing the futility of dreaming of something better. And we all play along. When organizations like mine develop policy proposals, there is pressure to specify exactly where the revenue would come from to fund anything better than the status quo. This is a powerful red herring, designed to obscure the real challenge of creating something better: building the political will to make it happen.

But it's not just the austerity politics of Capitol Hill that narrow our possibilities. There's also often a knee-jerk fatalism that stifles our courage to dream big and fight hard. This fatalism is represented by four little words that have become the typical response to aspirational thinking: "That will never happen." It's a Beltway mentality shared by congressional staffers, political reporters, and far too many professional progressive advocates. Let me state the very obvious truth: Nothing will ever happen if we never try to make it happen.

Back in the early years of this century, I started producing research at Demos on the growth of credit-card debt, particularly among working-class households. Part of that research led me to investigate common practices by the credit-card companies, like jacking up interest rates for late payments. This was an industry that had the power to pretty much change the terms of its contracts at any time, for any reason. So Demos, along with organizations in the consumer movement, proposed new policies to regulate the card companies. My colleagues and I would make the rounds on Capitol Hill, and we were routinely met with laughter and a bunch of dismissals about how "that'll never happen." Well, after seven years of building the case for new credit-card regulations, the financial crash opened a political window. Suddenly lots of politicians wanted to take a vote against the big banks. And what was never supposed to happen did happen. The Credit Card Act of 2009, passed with overwhelming bipartisan support, greatly curtailed fees and prohibited rate hikes on existing balances. I gleefully sat in the front row of the White House Rose Garden to watch President Obama sign the bill into law. And in the years since its passage, it has saved people over $60 billion, and that's just in fees alone. The credit-card companies can no longer do what they want, when they want, to people in debt.

So I'm going to ignore the cynical and the elite thought leaders who try to shut down change by asking the "serious" question "How are we going to pay for it?" The stakes are simply too high to start a dialogue under this narrow definition of acceptable policy discourse.

The time has come for a Better Deal.

A Better Deal would reshape our politics by replacing a big-money-driven political system with public financing, so that candidates must reach deep into their communities to attract small donations, which would be matched by public dollars. A Better Deal would finally put an end to the attempts to stymie political participation, particularly of black and brown people, through voter suppression laws. A Better Deal would ensure that all Americans know we want them to participate in the selection of our leaders by making voter registration automatic and seamless, so even if you move or are in college, your registration will follow you.

A Better Deal would transform the bargain-basement economy into one where all jobs pay a decent minimum wage, our labor laws are actually enforced, and workers are protected on the job and paid exactly what they are owed. A Better Deal would mean that workers actually have a fair chance to unionize their workplace if that's what the majority of them decide.

For our families, a Better Deal would finally give mothers and fathers the extra support they need to raise their children, by providing paid family leave and high-quality and affordable child care. The United States would no longer be the exception among democratic countries, which have provided these social benefits for their citizens for at least a generation, and most for much longer.

A Better Deal would mean our nation would finally address and repair the racial divides that still define our society. A Better Deal would invest in communities that have been isolated and excluded from society through a toxic combination of deindustrialization, discriminatory housing policies, and extensive incarceration.

Finally, a Better Deal would recommit to making America the land of opportunity, where the rungs of mobility are created through debt-free public college and a world-class system of apprenticeships and career education. A Better Deal would mean that all children would grow up in the United States with the knowledge that we want them to fulfill their dreams and have invested in a high-quality combination of higher education and training options for them to do just that.

A Better Deal would mean that Javier, whom we met in Chapter 3, who stocks shelves in the freezer department at Walmart, wouldn't have to rely on payday loans to pay his bills, because his paycheck, and his wife's paycheck from working in retail, would be enough to pay the rent and keep the fridge stocked and the lights on. It would mean that their children, unlike Javier, who dreamed of going to college but had neither the cultural nor the financial resources to do so, would grow up knowing that this country makes it possible for anyone, regardless of their background, to get the education or training they want to be their best. A Better Deal would mean that the next generation of largely Latino and black working-class children would no longer grow up in racially segregated, crime-driven projects where "getting out" is an against-the-odds tale available only to the most resilient, exceptionally bright and determined individuals.

At the conclusion of this book, I outline the key components critical to creating a Better Deal. We need a serious debate about what is really required to dismantle the hardened lines of privilege in this country. I hope we'll have that debate, and that we can at least start with consensus that the scale of the challenge will require transformative change and not just tinkering around the edges with a new tax credit here and a tax cut there.

The new working class has lifted the curtain that for so long kept hidden the indignities, injustice, and hardscrabble reality of life in America. Their fight is our fight, calling on all of us to demand more from our country. We've stalled for too long, abandoning our nation's long history of moving toward greater justice and progress. It's time for a Better Deal.

The Blueprint for a Better Deal

A Better Deal for Workers

• Modernize our labor protections by tightening the definition of "independent contractor," creating new rules for stable scheduling practices, and ensuring that the growing "on-demand" workforce is protected by labor laws and has rights to basic worker benefits. Expand federal enforcement capacity and increase the fines and penalties for companies that break the rules.

• Guarantee paid sick days and paid parental leave as universal benefits for all workers.

• Raise the federal minimum wage to $15.00 an hour by 2021 and eliminate the sub-minimum wage for tipped workers.

• Reform labor laws to ensure the ability of workers to join a union, including prohibiting so-called right-to-work laws and establishing majority sign-up as the authorization required for establishing a union.

A Better Deal for Families

• Develop a system to guarantee access to affordable and high-quality child care for infants and toddlers for all working- and middle-class families and high-quality jobs for child-care workers.

• Extend elementary school to include two years of preschool for children between the ages of three and five.

• Reinvest in state public higher education to achieve debt-free public college for all working- and middle-class students.

A Better Deal for Society

• Revitalize our nation's infrastructure, including addressing climate change, to ensure full employment.

• Establish a National Truth and Reconciliation Commission on Racial Healing to provide full accounting of our nation's violent racial history and to address its legacy in residential segregation, occupational segregation, the racial wealth gap, and oppressive criminal justice and policing policies.

• Develop comprehensive immigration reform to provide a pathway to citizenship for undocumented immigrants.

A Better Deal for Democracy

• Reform election procedures and practices, including establishing automatic voter registration to ensure all citizens are registered, and widespread adoption of same-day registration, early voting, and restoration of voting rights to formerly incarcerated citizens; restore the Voting Rights Act to provide voter protections for African Americans.

• Establish a system of public financing at the federal, state, and local levels, to reduce the role of corporate money and private wealth in funding elections and allow more racially diverse and working-class people to run for public office.

- Amend the Constitution and transform the Supreme Court's approach to money in politics to establish that money is not free speech and that corporations are not people.

Acknowledgments

I want to thank all the people who took time out of their busy lives to share their experiences with me. These individuals have deep reserves of bravery, resilience, and compassion that inspired me as I wrote, and especially kept me going when the words struggled to make it onto the page.

This is my second book with Doubleday and with the esteemed and venerable editor Gerry Howard. I thank him for his enthusiasm, commitment, and, of course, his superb editing. I must also thank my agent, Andrew Stuart, who championed this book from the start and sharpened the project along the way.

One of the smartest moves I made was hiring freelance journalist Sarah Gonser to help recruit and interview people for this book. Sarah stuck with the project, even when it took much longer than either of us anticipated, and did so with determination and persistence. The data presented in this book represent just a tiny sliver of the data crunched by Catherine Ruetschlin, former senior policy analyst at Demos, who generated reams of data and patiently generated more each time I had a new inquiry. Robert Hiltonsmith, senior policy analyst at Demos, crunched a mountain of data on wage-and-hour and OSHA violations. Juhem Navarro-Rivera, senior policy analyst at Demos with a Ph.D. in political science, lent me his public opinion expertise by carefully reviewing the GSS and ANES data crunched for the book, and generating new ideas for exploration that ended up key to the analysis. I am grateful to Baobao Zhang for her work crunching the original set of GSS and ANES data.

I am very fortunate to work at an organization with terrific people, and I thank them all for their support. I especially want to thank my friend and leader, Heather McGhee, president of Demos, who loved the idea from the beginning and gave me the organizational support to make it happen. To my colleagues on the executive team (Lucy Mayo, Brenda Wright, Lenore Palladino, Jodeen Olguín-Tayler, and Joe DiNorcia), who picked up the slack while I was busy writing and buoyed me throughout the journey, I cannot thank you all enough for your support and patience. My dear late colleague, Donna Parson, pushed me in all the right ways not just to talk about writing this book but to actually do it. I am grateful for her friendship and miss the smarts and dedication she brought to everything she touched. Lew Daly, who helps lead the research team at Demos, bore the brunt of my absence. Thank you for all you did to keep the team on track, for doing it without complaint, and, most important, cheering me on as the months wore on. To Miles Rapoport, former president of Demos and current president of Common Cause, thank you for your endless support and wisdom. Thank you to my enduring mentor, David Callahan, who reviewed many false starts and helped point me in the right direction. And finally, thank you to everyone at Demos. You've had my back since the beginning, and you constantly inspire and motivate me to do the best work I can.

To my rock-solid group of friends Zoe Diamant, Toby Williams, and Kristin Mitchell (and your partners), who are the "village" that helped keep my daughter entertained and joined my husband on many adventures while I was holed up writing. You saved me many times by picking up here or dropping off there, and I am so grateful for your help, your support, and your friendship. To my daughter, Harper, thank you for being you. Which means thank you for understanding the many weekends when Mommy couldn't go to the beach or the park because she had to write. Thank you for understanding and accepting how important this project was to me, and giving me your love and support along the way.

Finally, to my husband, Stuart Fink, my number one champion, careful critic, and steadfast partner. This book was a major undertaking for both of us, and your love, humor, and care kept me going when I didn't think I could write another page. Thank you for all you gave, and give, to our family each day.

Notes

Introduction

1. Angus Lotun, "Election Pay Day: Five States Vote to Raise Minimum Wage," *Wall Street Journal* blog, November 5, 2014, at http://blogs.wsj.com/corporate-intelligence/2014/11/05/election-pay-day-five-states-vote-to-raise-minimum-wage/.
2. Michael Zweig, ed., *What's Class Got to Do with It? American Society in the Twenty-First Century* (New York: ILR Books, 2004), p. 4.
3. U.S. Department of Labor, Bureau of Labor Statistics, "Characteristics of Minimum Wage Workers, 2013," BLS Reports, March 2014, at http://www.bls.gov/cps/minwage2013.pdf.
4. Author's analysis of *Current Population Survey Annual Social and Economic Supplement*, U.S. Department of Labor, Bureau of Labor Statistics. Data retrieved from IPUMS-CPS: Steven Ruggles et al., *Integrated Public Use Microdata Series: Version 5.0* [machine-readable database] (Minneapolis: University of Minnesota, 2010).
5. Author's analysis of 1970–2000 Decennial Census, 2011–2012 U.S. Census American Community Survey, U.S. Census Bureau Public Use Microdata retrieved from Ruggles et al., Integrated Public Use Microdata Series: Version 5.0.
6. Author's analysis of *Current Population Survey Annual Social and Economic Supplement.*
7. Ben Henry and Allyson Fredericksen, "Equity in the Balance: How a Living Wage Could Help Women and People of Color Make Ends Meet," *The Job Gap*, November 2014, at https://jobgap2013.files.wordpress.com/2014/11/2014jobgapequity1.pdf.
8. Irene Tung, Yannet Lathrop, and Paul Sonn, "The Growing Movement for $15," National Employment Law Project, April 2015, at http://nelp.org/content/uploads/Growing-Movement-for-15-Dollars.pdf.
9. U.S. Department of Labor, Bureau of Labor Statistics, "Table 5. Occu-

pations with the Most Job Growth, 2012 and Projected 2022," December 19, 2013, at http://www.bls.gov/news.release/ecopro.t05.htm.

10. U.S. Department of Labor, Bureau of Labor Statistics, "Employment and Wages for the Largest and Smallest Occupations, May 2012," March 29, 2013, at http://www.bls.gov/oes/2012/may/largest_smallest.htm.
11. Jacob S. Hacker and Paul Pierson, *Winner-Take-All-Politics: How Washington Made the Rich Richer and Turned Its Back on the Middle Class* (New York: Simon and Schuster, 2010).
12. Lewis Powell, "Attack on American Free Enterprise System," August 23, 1971. The Washington and Lee University School of Law, which Lewis Powell attended, maintains an archive of his writing and work. The complete text of the Powell Memorandum is available on the school's website at http://law2.wlu.edu/powellarchives/page.asp?pageid=1251, and from many other sources on the Internet.
13. Hacker and Pierson, *Winner-Take-All-Politics*, p. xxx.
14. Blair Bowie and Adam Lioz, "Billion-Dollar Democracy: The Unprecedented Role of Money in the 2012 Elections," *Demos*, June 2013, at http://www.demos.org/sites/default/files/publications/billion.pdf.
15. Jack Metzger, "Politics and the American Class Vernacular," in John Russo and Sherry Lee Linkon, eds., *New Working-Class Studies* (Ithaca, NY: ILR Press, 2005), p. 198.
16. Author's analysis of *General Social Surveys, 1972–2010* [machine-readable data file] /Principal Investigator, Tom W. Smith; Co-Principal Investigator, Peter V. Marsden; Co-Principal Investigator, Michael Hout; Sponsored by National Science Foundation—NORC ed.—Chicago: NORC at the University of Chicago [producer]; Storrs, Connecticut: The Roper Center for Public Opinion Research, University of Connecticut.
17. Cole Stangler, "Walmart, TJX, Target Raise Wages: What's Behind the Pay Hikes in Retail?" *International Business Times*, March 23, 2015, at http://www.ibtimes.com/wal-mart-tjx-target-raise-wages-whats-behind-pay-hikes-retail-1856022.

Chapter One: The Bargain-Basement Economy

1. U.S. Department of Labor, Bureau of Labor Statistics, "Occupations with the Most Job Growth: Table 1.4. Occupations with the Most Job Growth in 2012 and Projected 2022," December, 19, 2013, at http://www.bls.gov/emp/ep_table_104.htm.
2. Ibid.
3. Ibid.
4. Nick Bunkley, "Fat Profits Put 2-Tier Pay on AUW agenda," *Automotive News*, February 17, 2014, at http://www.autonews.com/article/20140217/OEM01/302179958/fat-profits-put-2-tier-pay-on-uaw-agenda.

5. Mary M. Chapman, "This Time, Fiat Chrysler Workers Approve Contract," *New York Times*, October 22, 2015.
6. Catherine Ruckelshaus and Sarah Leberstein, "Manufacturing Low Pay: Declining Wages in the Jobs That Built America's Middle Class," National Employment Law Project, November 2014, at http://nelp.org/content/uploads/2015/03/Manufacturing-Low-Pay-Declining-Wages-Jobs-Built-Middle-Class.pdf.
7. U.S. Department of Labor, Bureau of Labor Statistics, "Reflections: 100 Years of U.S. Consumer Spending," May 2006, at http://www.bls.gov/opub/uscs/report991.pdf.
8. U.S. Department of Labor, Bureau of Labor Statistics, "Current Employment Statistics, Table B-1 Historical: Employees on Nonfarm Payrolls by Industry Sector and Selected Industry Detail," accessed September 2014.
9. Janelle Jones and John Schmitt, "Slow Progress for Fast-Food Workers," Center for Economic and Policy Research, August 6, 2013, at http://www.cepr.net/index.php/blogs/cepr-blog/slow-progress-for-fast-food-workers.
10. Ibid.
11. "The Demographics of the Retail Work Force," Demos, November, 18, 2012, at http://www.demos.org/sites/default/files/data_bytes/demographics.png.
12. Tom W. Smith, "Job Satisfaction in America," NORC/University of Chicago, April 17, 2007 at http://www-news.uchicago.edu/releases/07/pdf/070417.jobs.pdf; CareerBliss survey available online at http://www.careerbliss.com/facts-and-figures/careerbliss-happiest-and-unhappiest-jobs-in-america-2015/.
13. U.S. Department of Labor, Bureau of Labor Statistics, "Data Tables for Overview of May 2012 Occupational Employment and Wages," March 29, 2013, at http://www.bls.gov/oes/2012/may/featured_data.htm#largest.
14. Independent analysis of U.S. Census 2012 and 2011 American Community Survey. Data retrieved from IPUMS-USA: Steven Ruggles et al., *Integrated Public Use Microdata Series: Version 5.0* [machine-readable database] (Minneapolis: University of Minnesota, 2010).
15. Bureau of Labor Statistics, "Data Tables for Overview of May 2012 Occupational Employment and Wages."
16. Coca-Cola's brand was worth $83.8 billion in 2015 according to Statista, making it fourth on *Forbes*'s annual list of the most valuable brands.
17. U.S. Department of Labor, Bureau of Labor Statistics, *Occupational Outlook Handbook, 2014–15*, Tellers, at http://www.bls.gov/ooh/office-and-administrative-support/tellers.htm.
18. Sylvia Allegretto et al., "The Public Cost of Low-Wage Jobs in the Banking Industry," UC Berkeley Center for Labor Research and Education,

October 2014, at http://laborcenter.berkeley.edu/the-public-cost-of-low-wage-jobs-in-the-banking-industry/.

19. Justin Miller, "Banking on More than $15," *American Prospect*, August 13, 2015, at http://prospect.org/article/banking-more-15.
20. "Big Banks and the Dismantling of the Middle Class," Center for Popular Democracy, April 2015, at http://populardemocracy.org/news/big-banks-and-dismantling-middle-class.
21. Morningstar, Toronto-Dominion Bank, at http://insiders.morningstar.com/trading/executive-compensation.action?t=TD.
22. Evelyn Nakano Glenn, "From Servitude to Service Work: Historical Continuities in the Racial Division of Paid Reproductive Labor," *Signs* 18, no. 1 (Autumn 1992): 1–43.
23. Ibid.
24. Juan F. Perea, "The Echoes of Slavery: Recognizing the Racist Origins of the Agricultural and Domestic Worker Exclusion from the National Labor Relations Act," *Ohio State Law Journal* 72, no. 1 (2011): 95–138.
25. U.S. Department of Labor, Wage and Hour Division, "Final Rules on Home Care Work," 2014, at http://www.dol.gov/whd/homecare/final_rule.pdf.
26. Video recording, "Myrla Baldonado's Caregiver Testimony," National Domestic Workers' Alliance third National Congress, Washington, D.C., May 19, 2011, at https://www.youtube.com/watch?v=i5GHQ7tm2cA.
27. Linda Burnham and Nik Theodore, "Home Economics: The Invisible and Unregulated World of Domestic Work," National Domestic Workers Alliance, Center for Urban Economic Development and University of Illinois at Chicago Data Center, 2012, at http://www.domesticworkers.org/sites/default/files/HomeEconomicsEnglish.pdf.
28. David Bornstein, "A Living Wage for Care Workers," *New York Times*, July 10, 2015, at http://opinionator.blogs.nytimes.com/2015/07/10/organizing-for-the-right-to-care/.
29. Independent analysis of BLS *Current Population Survey Annual Social and Economic Supplement*. Data retrieved from IPUMS-CPS: Ruggles et al., *Integrated Public Use Microdata Series: Version 5.0*.
30. Independent analysis of BLS *Current Population Monthly Basic Data Public Use Microdata*. Files retrieved from Data Ferrett for 1990 through 2013. Data for 1970 and 1980 reflect survey responses for March of the survey year, rather than annual averages, and were retrieved from IPUMS CPS at Miriam King et al., *Integrated Public Use Microdata Series, Current Population Survey: Version 3.0* [machine-readable database] (Minneapolis: University of Minnesota, 2010).
31. Elizabeth Barber, "Who Gets Food Stamps? More Are College Grads; Half Are Working Age," *Christian Science Monitor*, January 27, 2014, at http://www.csmonitor.com/USA/USA-Update/2014/0127/Who-gets-food-stamps-More-are-college-grads-half-are-working-age.-video.

32. U.S. Department of Agriculture, Food and Nutrition Service, "Summary of Annual Data FY 2010–2014," Excel file accessible at http://www.fns.usda.gov/pd/overview.
33. U.S. Department of Agriculture, Food and Nutrition Service, "Characteristics of Supplemental Nutrition Assistance Program Households: Fiscal Year 2012," February 2014, at http://www.fns.usda.gov/sites/default/files/2012Characteristics.pdf.
34. Sylvia Allegretto et al., "Fast Food, Poverty Wages: The Public Cost of Low-Wage Jobs in the Fast-Food Industry," University of California, Berkeley, Center for Labor Research and Education, October 15, 2013, at http://laborcenter.berkeley.edu/pdf/2013/fast_food_poverty_wages.pdf.
35. Catherine Ruetschlin, "Fast-Food Failure: How CEO-to-Worker Pay Disparity Undermines the Industry and Overall Economy," *Demos*, April 22, 2014, at http://www.demos.org/sites/default/files/publications/demos-fastfoodfailure.pdf.
36. Americans for Tax Fairness, "Walmart on Tax Day: How Taxpayers Subsidize America's Biggest Employer and Richest Family," April 2014, at http://www.americansfortaxfairness.org/files/Walmart-on-Tax-Day-Americans-for-Tax-Fairness-1.pdf.
37. Democratic Staff of U.S. Committee on Education and the Workforce, "The Low-Wage Drag on Our Economy: Walmart's Low Wages and Their Effect on Taxpayers and Economic Growth," U.S. Committee on Education and the Workforce, May 2013, at http://democrats.edworkforce.house.gov/sites/democrats.edworkforce.house.gov/files/documents/WalMartReport-May2013.pdf.
38. Catherine Ruetschlin and Amy Traub, "A Higher Wage Is Possible at Walmart," *Demos*, June 4, 2014, at http://www.demos.org/sites/default/files/publications/AHigherWageIsPossible.pdf.
39. "Walmart Strategy Drives Growth and Sustainable Returns, Plans $20 Billion Share Repurchase Program over Two Years," Walmart statement, available at http://news.walmart.com/news-archive/2015/10/14/walmart-strategy-drives-growth-and-sustainable-returns-plans-20-billion-share-repurchase-program-over-two-years.
40. Barbara Ehrenreich, *Nickel and Dimed: On (Not) Getting By in America* (New York: Metropolitan, 2001), p. 193.
41. U.S. Department of Labor, Bureau of Labor Statistics, *Occupational Outlook Handbook, 2014–15*, Food and Beverage Serving and Related Workers, at http://www.bls.gov/ooh/food-preparation-and-serving/food-and-beverage-serving-and-related-workers.htm#tab-1.

Chapter Two: The New Indignity of Work

1. Annalyn Kurtz, "Subway Leads Fast Food in Under-Paying Workers," *CNN Money*, May 1, 2014, at http://money.cnn.com/2014/05/01/news/economy/subway-labor-violations/; http://www.nelp.org/page

/-/Justice/2014/Whos-the-Boss-Restoring-Accountability-Labor-Standards-Outsourced-Work-Report.pdf?nocdn=1.

2. Author's analysis of Department of Labor's "Wage and Hour Compliance Action Database," at http://ogesdw.dol.gov/views/data_summary.php.
3. Hart Research Memorandum, "Key Findings for Survey of Fast Food Workers, April 1, 2014," at http://big.assets.huffingtonpost.com/NationalWageTheftPollMemo.pdf; Tiffany Hsu, "Nearly 90% of Fast-Food Workers Allege Wage Theft, Survey Finds," *Los Angeles Times*, April 1, 2014, at http://articles.latimes.com/2014/apr/01/business/la-fi-mo-wage-theft-survey-fast-food-20140331.
4. U.S. Department of Labor, Wage and Hour Division, "Fiscal Year Statistics for WHD, FY 1997-FY2014," at http://www.dol.gov/whd/statistics/statstables.htm#flsa.
5. Kurtz, "Subway Leads Fast Food Industry."
6. Annalyn Kurtz, "10 Big Overtime Pay Violators," *CNN Money*, August 5, 2014, at http://money.cnn.com/gallery/news/economy/2014/03/13/overtime-violations/?iid=EL.
7. Ibid.
8. Ross Eisenbrey, "Improving the Quality of Jobs Through Better Labor Standards," *Full Employment*, April 2, 2014, at http://www.pathtofullemployment.org/wp-content/uploads/2014/04/eisenbrey.pdf.
9. Brady Meixell and Ross Eisenbrey, "An Epidemic of Wage Theft Is Costing Workers Hundreds of Millions of Dollars a Year," Economic Policy Institute, September 11, 2014, at https://docs.google.com/viewer?url=http://www.epi.org/files/2014/wage-theft.pdf&hl=en_US&embedded=true.
10. Annette Bernhardt, et al., "Broken Laws, Unprotected Workers: Violations of Employment and Labor Laws in America's Cities," Center for Urban Economic Development, National Employment Law Project, and UCLA Institute for Research on Labor and Employment, September 2009, at http://www.nelp.org/content/uploads/2015/03/BrokenLawsReport2009.pdf?nocdn=1.
11. U.S. Department of Labor, Wage and Hour Division, "U.S. Department of Labor Recovers $4.83 Million in Back Wages, Damages for More than $4,500 Wal-Mart Workers," May 1, 2012, at http://www.dol.gov/opa/media/press/whd/WHD20120801.htm.
12. U.S. Department of Labor, Occupational Safety and Health Administration, "Introduction to OSHA: Citations and Penalties," at https://www.osha.gov/dte/outreach/intro_osha/intro_to_osha_english/slide36.html.
13. Alexandra Berzon and Paul Ziobro, "Dollar Tree Racks Up Safety Violations," *Wall Street Journal*, October 1, 2014, at http://online.wsj.com/articles/dollar-tree-racks-up-safety-violations-1413432063.
14. MorningStar, "Dollar Tree Stores Inc, 2014 Executive Compensa-

tion," at http://insiders.morningstar.com/trading/executive-compensation.action?t=DLTR.

15. Heidi Schwartz, "Kansas Cell Tower Collapse Causes Two Fatalities—OSHA Violations Issued," *Facility Executive*, September 29, 2014, at http://todaysfacilitymanager.com/2014/09/kansas-cell-tower-collapse-causes-two-fatalities-osha-violations-issued.
16. David Weil, "Improving Workplace Conditions Through Strategic Enforcement," Boston University, April 2014, at https://www.dol.gov/whd/resources/strategicEnforcement.pdf.
17. FairWarning, "Fear Stifles Complaints of Wage Abuse," May 13, 2014, at http://www.fairwarning.org/2014/05/fear-stifles-complaints-wage-abuse/.
18. Worksafe, "California Workplace Fatality Rates Up, with Sharp Rise Among Latino Workers," September 11, 2014, at http://www.worksafe.org/2014/09/2013_fatality_numbers.html.
19. David Weil, *The Fissured Workplace: Why Work Became So Bad for So Many and What Can Be Done to Improve It* (Cambridge: Harvard University Press, 2014), p. 114.
20. Julia Preston, "Foreign Students in Work Visa Program Stage Protest, *New York Times*, August 17, 2011, at http://www.nytimes.com/2011/08/18/us/18immig.html.
21. 23 Weil, *The Fissured Workplace*, p. 117.
22. Julia Preston, "Hershey's Packer Is Fined Over Its Plant Violations," *New York Times*, February 21, 2012, at http://www.nytimes.com/2012/02/22/us/hersheys-packer-fined-by-labor-department-for-safety-violations.html.
23. Sarah Leberstein, "Independent Contractor Misclassification Imposes Huge Costs on Workers and Federal and State Treasuries," National Employment Law Project, August 2012, at http://www.nelp.org/page/-/Justice/IndependentContractorCosts.pdf?nocdn=1.
24. U.S. Treasury Department, Internal Revenue Service, "Independent Contractor Defined," August 5, 2015, at http://www.irs.gov/Businesses/Small-Businesses-&-Self-Employed/Independent-Contractor-Defined.
25. Weil, *The Fissured Workplace*, p. 124.
26. Ibid., p. 131.
27. Steven Greenhouse, "McDonald's Ruling Could Open Door for Unions," *New York Times*, July 29, 2014, at http://www.nytimes.com/2014/07/30/business/nlrb-holds-mcdonalds-not-just-franchisees-liable-for-worker-treatment.html?_r=0.
28. McDonald's Corporation, "McDonald's Statement on NLRB Ruling," December 19, 2014, at http://news.mcdonalds.com/Corporate/Media-Statements/McDonald's-Statement-on-NLRB-Actions.
29. Sruthi Ramakrishnan, "Walmart to Raise Wages for 100,000 U.S. Workers in Some Departments," Reuters, June 2, 2015, at http://

www.reuters.com/article/2015/06/02/us-wal-mart-stores-wages-idUSKBN0OI1EW20150602.

30. Jodi Kantor, "Working Anything but 9–5," *New York Times*, August 13, 2014, at http://www.nytimes.com/interactive/2014/08/13/us/starbucks-workers-scheduling-hours.html?_r=0.
31. Jodi Kantor, "Starbucks to Revise Policies to End Irregular Schedules for its 130,000 Baristas," *New York Times*, August 14, 2014, at http://www.nytimes.com/2014/08/15/us/starbucks-to-revise-work-scheduling-policies.html.

Chapter Three: Meet the New Populists

1. Robert P. Jones and Daniel Cox, "Beyond Guns and God: Understanding the Complexities of the White Working Class in America," Public Religion Research Institute, findings from the 2012 Race, Class and Culture Survey, September 20, 2012, at http://publicreligion.org/site/wp-content/uploads/2012/09/WWC-Report-For-Web-Final.pdf.
2. Pew Research Center, "The Politics of Financial Insecurity: A Democratic Tilt, Undercut by Low Participation," January 8, 2015, at http://www.people-press.org/files/2015/01/1-8-15-Financial-security-release.pdf.
3. Ife Floyd and Liz Schott, "TANF Cash Benefits Have Fallen by More than 20 Percent in Most States and Continue to Erode," Center on Budget and Policy Priorities, October 30, 2014, at http://www.cbpp.org/research/tanf-cash-benefits-have-fallen-by-more-than-20-percent-in-most-states-and-continue-to-erode.
4. Thom File, "The Diversifying Electorate—Voting Rates by Race and Hispanic Origin in 2012 (and Other Recent Elections)," U.S. Census Bureau, Washington, D.C., May 2013, at https://www.census.gov/prod/2013pubs/p20-568.pdf; Thom File, "Who Votes? Congressional Elections and the American Electorate: 1978–2014," U.S. Census Bureau, Washington, D.C., July 2015, at https://www.census.gov/content/dam/Census/library/publications/2015/demo/p20-577.pdf.
5. Jan E. Leighley and Jonathan Nagler, *Who Votes Now?* (Princeton, N.J.: Princeton University Press, 2014), pp. 129–41.
6. Ibid., pp. 158–66.
7. Lane Kenworthy and Jonas Pontusson, "Rising Inequality and the Politics of Redistribution in Affluent Countries," LIS Working Paper Series, No. 400, 2005, at http://www.econstor.eu/bitstream/10419/95499/1/483132640.pdf.
8. Eileen Fumagalli and Gaia Narciso, "Political Institutions, Voter Turnout, and Policy Outcomes," *European Journal of Political Economy* 28 (2012): 162–73, available at http://www.tcd.ie/Economics/staff/narcisog/docs/FN2012.pdf.

9. Thomas Lopez, "Shelby County: One Year Later," Brennan Center for Justice, June 24, 2014, at http://www.brennancenter.org/sites/default/files/analysis/Shelby_County_One_Year_Later.pdf.
10. Chrystia Freeland, *Plutocrats: The Rise of the Global Super-Rich and the Fall of Everyone Else* (New York: Penguin, 2014); Joseph Stiglitz, *The Price of Inequality: How Today's Divided Society Endangers Our Future* (New York: Norton, 2013).
11. Blair Bowie and Adam Lioz, "Billion-Dollar Democracy: The Unprecedented Role of Money in the 2012 Elections," *Demos*, January 17, 2013, at http://www.demos.org/sites/default/files/publications/billion.pdf.
12. Ibid.
13. Ibid.
14. Ibid.
15. Ibid.
16. Center for Responsive Politics, "2016 Super PACs: How Many Donors Give?" available at https://www.opensecrets.org/outsidespending/donor_stats.php.
17. Martin Gilens, *Affluence and Influence: Economic Inequality and Political Power in America* (Princeton, N.J.: Princeton University Press, 2012); Henry E. Brady, Kay Lehman Scholzman, and Sidney Verba, *The Unheavenly Chorus: Unequal Political Voice and the Broken Promise of American Democracy* (Princeton, N.J.: Princeton University Press, 2012); Larry M. Bartels, *Unequal Democracy: The Political Economy of the New Gilded Age* (Princeton, N.J.: Princeton University Press, 2008).
18. Gilens, *Affluence and Influence*, p. 1.
19. Ibid., p. 101.
20. Ibid., p. 117.
21. Daren Blomquist, "Slideshow: 2012 Foreclosure Market Outlook," *RealtyTrac*, February 13, 2012, at http://www.realtytrac.com/content/news-and-opinion/slideshow-2012-foreclosure-market-outlook-7021.
22. Jim Puzzanghera, "Economy Has Recovered 8.7 Million Jobs Lost in Great Recession," *Los Angeles Times*, June 6, 2014, at http://www.latimes.com/business/la-fi-jobs-20140607-story.html.
23. Paul Krugman, "The Stimulus Tragedy," *New York Times*, February 20, 2014, at http://www.nytimes.com/2014/02/21/opinion/krugman-the-stimulus-tragedy.html.
24. Benjamin I. Page, Larry M. Bartels, and Jason Seawright, "Democracy and the Policy Preferences of Wealthy Americans," *Perspectives on Politics*, 11, no. 1 (March 2013): 51–73, at http://faculty.wcas.northwestern.edu/~jnd260/cab/CAB2012%20-%20Page1.pdf.
25. Bartels, *Unequal Democracy*, p. 28.
26. Ian Haney López, *Dog Whistle Politics: How Coded Racial Appeals Have Reinvented Racism and Wrecked the Middle Class* (New York: Oxford University Press, 2014).

27. Ibid., p. 57.
28. Ibid., p. 61.

Chapter Four: The Great Power Shift

1. Barry Hirsch and David Macpherson, "Union Membership and Coverage Database from the Current Population Survey," updated annually at www.unionstats.com.
2. Harold Meyerson, "Under Obama, Labor Should Have Made More Progress." *Washington Post*, February 10, 2010, at http://www.washingtonpost.com/wp-dyn/content/article/2010/02/09/AR2010020902465.html.
3. Ken Silverstein, "Labor's Last Stand: The Corporate Campaign to Kill the Employee Free Choice Act," *Harper's Magazine*, July 2009, at http://harpers.org/archive/2009/07/labors-last-stand/.
4. Ibid, p. 43.
5. Meyerson, "Under Obama."
6. Chris Isidore, "America's Lost Trillions," *CNN Money*, June 9, 2011, at http://money.cnn.com/2011/06/09/news/economy/household_wealth/.
7. Neil Litchenstein, *State of the Union: A Century of American Labor* (Princeton, N.J.: Princeton University Press, 2002), pp. 36–37.
8. Ibid., p. 39.
9. Ibid., pp. 50–53.
10. Ibid., p. 101.
11. Gerald Mayer, "Union Membership Trends in the United States, Washington, D.C.: Congressional Research Service, August 31, 2004, at http://digitalcommons.ilr.cornell.edu/cgi/viewcontent.cgi?article=1176&context=key_workplace.
12. Litchenstein, *State of the Union*, p. 117.
13. Philip Dray, *There Is Power in a Union: The Epic Story of Labor in America* (New York: Random House, 2010), pp. 497–98.
14. Litchenstein, *State of the Union*, p. 107.
15. National Conference of State Legislatures, "Right-to-Work Resources," at http://www.ncsl.org/research/labor-and-employment/right-to-work-laws-and-bills.aspx#chart.
16. Economic Policy Institute, *State of Working America*, 12th ed, November 2012, "Average family income, by income group, 1947–2010 (2011 dollars)," Table 2.1, at http://www.stateofworkingamerica.org/chart/swa-income-table-2-1-average-family-income/.
17. Judith Stein, *Pivotal Decade: How the United States Traded Factories for Finance in the Seventies* (New Haven: Yale University Press: 2011), p. 1.
18. Stein, *Pivotal Decade*, 2.
19. Ibid., p. 15.
20. Tracy Roof, *American Labor, Congress, and the Welfare State 1935–2010* (Baltimore: Johns Hopkins University Press, 2011), p. 89.

21. Ibid.
22. Jake Rosenfeld, *What Unions No Longer Do* (Cambridge, Mass.: Harvard University Press, 2014), p. 160.
23. Roof, *American Labor,* p. 115.
24. Ibid., p. 117.
25. Henry E. Brady, Kay Lehman Scholzman, and Sidney Verba, *The Unheavenly Chorus: Unequal Political Voice and the Broken Promise of American Democracy* (Princeton, N.J.: Princeton University Press, 2012), p. 361.
26. Kim Phillips-Fein, *Invisible Hands: The Businessmen's Crusade Against the New Deal* (New York: W. W. Norton & Company, 2010), p. 153.
27. Ibid., pp. 151–56.
28. Lewis Powell, "Attack on American Free Enterprise System," August 23, 1971. The Washington and Lee University School of Law, which Lewis Powell attended, maintains an archive of his writing and work. The complete text of the Powell Memorandum is available on the website http://law2.wlu.edu/powellarchives/page.asp?pageid=1251, and from many other sources on the Internet.
29. Phillips-Fein, *Invisible Hands,* p. 154.
30. Jacob S. Hacker and Paul Pierson, *Winner-Take-All-Politics: How Washington Made the Rich Richer and Turned Its Back on the Middle Class* (New York: Simon and Schuster, 2010), p. 116.
31. Powell, "Attack on American Free Enterprise System."
32. Phillips-Fein, *Invisible Hands,* pp. 166–70.
33. Ibid., p. 188.
34. Hacker and Pierson, *Winner-Take-All-Politics,* p. 117.
35. Ibid., p. 119.
36. Ibid.
37. Ibid., p. 121.
38. Phillips-Fein, *Invisible Hands,* p. 187.
39. Alyssa Katz, *The Influence Machine: The U.S. Chamber of Commerce and the Corporate Capture of American Life* (New York: Spiegel & Grau, 2015), p. 15.
40. Lee Drutman, *The Business of America Is Lobbying: How Corporations Became Politicized and Politics Became More Corporate* (New York: Oxford University Press, 2015), pp. 8–9.
41. John Logan, "The Union Avoidance Industry in the USA," *British Journal of International Relations* (December 2006): p. 653.
42. The activist hackers Anonymous have leaked anti-union PowerPoint presentations and a video produced by Walmart used for managerial trainings and staff orientation. The links are available online in Stephen Greenhouse, "How Walmart Persuades Its Workers Not to Unionize," *The Atlantic,* June 8, 2015, at http://www.theatlantic.com/business/archive/2015/06/how-walmart-convinces-its-employees-not-to-unionize/395051/.
43. Logan, "The Union Avoidance Industry," p. 669.
44. Ibid., p. 656.

45. The recording of the taped captive-audience meeting is available at https://soundcloud.com/organizega/mckesson-labor-relations-director-holds-captive-audience-meeting-in-atlanta.

Chapter Five: The Legacy of Exclusion

1. Nancy MacLean, *Freedom Is Not Enough: The Opening of the American Workplace* (Cambridge, Mass.: Harvard University Press, 2008), pp. 159–61.
2. Ibid.
3. Ibid., p. 93.
4. Professor Enobong Hannah Branch, *Opportunity Denied: Limiting Black Women to Devalued Work* (New Brunswick, N.J.: Rutgers University Press 2011), p. 127; Patterson, *Freedom Is Not Enough*, p. 21.
5. "The Negro Drive for Jobs," *Business Week,* August 17, 1963.
6. MacLean, *Freedom Is Not Enough*, p. 54.
7. Ibid.
8. Dorothy Sue Cobble, *The Other Women's Movement: Workplace Justice and Social Rights in Modern America* (Princeton, N.J.: Princeton University Press, 2004), pp. 175–77.
9. Alice Kessler-Harris, *In Pursuit of Equity: Women, Men, and the Quest for Economic Citizenship in Twentieth-Century America* (New York: Oxford University Press, 2001), pp. 248–49.
10. Kevin Stainback and Donald Tomaskovic-Devey, *Documenting Desegregation: Racial and Gender Segregation in Private-Sector Employment Since the Civil Rights Act* (New York: Russell Sage Foundation, 2012), p. 115.
11. Cobble, *The Other Women's Movement*, p. 219.
12. MacLean, *Freedom Is Not Enough*, p. 105.
13. John Nichols, "A. Philip Randolph Was Right: 'We Will Need to Continue Demonstrations,'" *The Nation*, April 15, 2014, at http://www.thenation.com/article/philip-randolph-was-right-we-will-need-continue-demonstrations/.
14. Stainback and Tomaskovic-Devey, *Documenting Desegregation,* p. 98.
15. Ibid., p. 115.
16. Ibid., p. 140.
17. Ibid., p. 158.
18. Ibid.
19. Branch, *Opportunity Denied*, p. 22.
20. Stainback and Tomaskovic-Devey, *Documenting Desegregation*, p. 299.
21. Ariane Hegewisch and Stephanie Keller, "The Gender Wage Gap by Occupation 2013 and by Race and Ethnicity," Institute for Women's Policy Research, Washington, D.C., April 2014, at http://www.iwpr.org/publications/pubs/the-gender-wage-gap-by-occupation-and-by-race-and-ethnicity-2013.
22. Ariane Hegewisch and Heidi Hartmann, "Occupation Segregation and the Gender Wage Gap: A Job Half Done," Institute for Women's Policy Research, Washington, D.C., January 2014, at http://www.iwpr

.org/publications/pubs/occupational-segregation-and-the-gender-wage-gap-a-job-half-done.

23. Algernon Austin, William Darity Jr., and Darrick Hamilton, "Whiter Jobs, Higher Wages: Occupational Segregation and Lower Wages of Black Men," *Economic Policy Institute*, Washington, D.C., February 28, 2011, at http://s1.epi.org/files/page/-/BriefingPaper288.pdf.
24. U.S. Department of Labor, Bureau of Labor Statistics, Labor Force Statistics from the Current Population Survey, Table 11: Employed Persons by Detailed Occupation, Sex, Race, and Hispanic or Latino Ethnicity, February 12, 2015, at http://www.bls.gov/cps/cpsaat11.htm.
25. "Build a Better Texas: Construction Working Conditions in the Lone Star State," Workers Defense Project, Austin, Tex., January 2013, at http://www.workersdefense.org/Build%20a%20Better%20Texas_FINAL.pdf.
26. Author's analysis of U.S. Department of Labor, Bureau of Labor Statistics, *Current Population Survey Annual Social and Economic Supplement.* Data retrieved from IPUMS-CPS: Steven Ruggles et al., *Integrated Public Use Microdata Series: Version 5.0* [machine-readable database]. Minneapolis: University of Minnesota, 2010.
27. Devah Pager, Bruce Western, and Bart Bonikowski, "Discrimination in a Low-Wage Labor Market: A Field Experiment," *American Sociological Review* 74 (October 2009): pp. 777–99.
28. Marianne Bertrand and Sendhil Mullainathan, "Are Emily and Brendan More Employable than Lakisha and Jamal? A Field Experiment on Labor Discrimination," *American Economic Review*, September 2004, pp. 991–1013.
29. Shelley J. Correll, Stephen Benard, and In Paik, "Is There a Motherhood Penalty?" *American Sociological Review*, 112:5 (March 2007): pp. 1297–1339.
30. Hegewisch and Keller, "The Gender Wage Gap."
31. Ellen Galinsky, "The Economic Benefits of High-Quality Early Childhood Programs: What Makes the Difference," Committee for Economic Development, February 15, 2006, at https://www.ced.org/pdf/The-Economic-Benefits-of-High-Quality-Early-Childhood-Programs.pdf; "The Economics of Early Childhood Investments," Executive Office of the President of the United States, December 10, 2014, at https://www.whitehouse.gov/sites/default/files/docs/early_childhood_report1.pdf.
32. Ai-jen Poo, *The Age of Dignity: Preparing for the Elder Boom in a Changing America* (New York: New Press, 2015), p. 24.
33. Eileen Boris and Jennifer Klein, *Caring for America: Home Health Workers in the Shadow of the Welfare State* (New York: Oxford University Press: 2012), p. 7.
34. Ibid., p. 15.
35. Steven Greenhouse, "Justice to Hear Case on Wages of Home Aides," *New York Times*, March 25, 2007.
36. Boris and Klein, *Caring for America*, p. 200.

37. David Zaffrann, "Home Care Workers Announce Victory in Historic Union Election," *SEIU Healthcare Minnesota*, August 26, 2014, at http://www.seiuhealthcaremn.org/2014/08/26/home-care-workers-announce-victory-in-historic-union-election/.
38. Lydia Wheeler, "Court Backs Obama on Minimum Wage, Overtime Pay for Home Health Aides," *The Hill*, August 21, 2015, available at http://thehill.com/regulation/court-battles/251649-labor-department-wins-dispute-over-wage-rights-for-home-health-aids.
39. Rebecca Beitsch, "Some States Consider Better Pay and Benefits for Home Care Workers," *Governing*, June 5, 2015, at http://www.governing.com/topics/mgmt/some-states-consider-better-pay-and-benefits-for-home-care-workers.html.
40. U.S. Department of Labor, Bureau of Labor Statistics, "Table 1.4. Occupations with the Most Job Growth, 2012 and Projected 2022," December 19, 2013, at http://www.bls.gov/emp/ep_table_104.htm.
41. Kris Maher, "Unions Target Home Workers," *Wall Street Journal*, June 19, 2013.
42. John Fensterwald, "Friedrich's v. CTA: What You Need to Know About the Challenge to Union Dues," *EdSource*, October 20, 2015, at http://edsource.org/2015/what-you-need-to-know-about-friedrichs-v-cta-before-supreme-court-on-fair-share-fees/89260.
43. John Kasarda, "Urban Industrial Transition and the Underclass," *Annals of the American Academy of Political and Social Science*, 501, no.1 (1990): pp. 26–47.
44. Ibid.
45. Ibid.
46. Mary D. Edsall and Thomas B. Edsall, *Chain Reaction*: *The Impact of Race, Rights, and Taxes on American Politics* (New York: Norton, 1992), pp. 12–13.
47. Michelle Alexander, *The New Jim Crow: Mass Incarceration in the Age of Color Blindness* (New York: New Press, 2012), p. 52.
48. Ibid., p. 49.
49. Alexander, *The New Jim Crow,* pp. 49–50. During Reagan's first term, FBI antidrug funding rose from $8 million to $95 million. Between 1981 and 1991, Department of Defense antidrug funding surged from $33 million to over $1 billion in 1991, and the Drug Enforcement Administration's antidrug spending grew from $86 million to $1 billion—all while drug-treatment funding at federal agencies was cut by more than three-quarters.
50. The Sentencing Project, "Trends in U.S. Corrections," April 2015, at http://sentencingproject.org/doc/publications/inc_Trends_in_Corrections_Fact_sheet.pdf.
51. Christopher Uggen, Sarah Shannon, and Jeff Manza, *"State-Level Estimates of Felon Disenfranchisement in the United States, 2010,"* The Sentencing Project, July 2012, at http://sentencingproject.org/doc/publications/fd_State_Level_Estimates_of_Felon_Disen_2010.pdf.

52. Justin Wolfers et al., "1.5 Million Missing Black Men," *New York Times*, April 20, 2015.
53. Ken Jacobs, "Americans Are Spending $153 Billion a Year to Subsidize McDonald's and Wal-Mart's Low-Wage Workers," *Washington Post*, April 1, 2015.
54. Steven Fraser, *The Age of Acquiescence: The Life and Death of American Resistance to Organized Wealth and Power* (New York: Little, Brown, 2015), pp. 141–42.
55. Litchenstein, *State of the Union*, p. 74.
56. Juan Gonzalez, *Harvest of Empire: A History of Latinos in America* (New York: Penguin Books, 2011), p. 223.
57. Ibid.
58. Ibid., p. 130.
59. Ibid., p. xv.
60. Ibid., p. 269.
61. Robert Scott, Carolos Salas, and Bruce Campbell, "Revisiting NAFTA: Still Not Working for North America's Workers," Economic Policy Institute Briefing Paper No. 173, September 28, 2006, at http://www.epi.org/files/page/-/old/briefingpapers/173/bp173.pdf.

Chapter Six: The Privilege of Visibility

1. Lars Willnat and David H. Weaver, "The American Journalist in the Digital Age: Key Findings" (Bloomington: School of Journalism, Indiana University, 2014), at http://news.indiana.edu/releases/iu/2014/05/2013-american-journalist-key-findings.pdf.
2. Dean Praetorius, "Congressional Staffers: Who Are the People Behind the Scenes in Washington?" *Huffington Post*, June 17, 2011.
3. Jens Manuel Krogstad, "114th Congress Is Most Diverse Ever," Pew Research Center, January 12, 2015, at http://www.pewresearch.org/fact-tank/2015/01/12/114th-congress-is-most-diverse-ever/.
4. Ronald Brownstein, "Are College Degrees Inherited?" *The Atlantic*, April 11, 2014, at http://www.theatlantic.com/education/archive/2014/04/are-college-degrees-inherited/360532/.
5. Neil deMause, "The Recession and the 'Deserving Poor,'" *FAIR*, February 1, 2009, at http://fair.org/extra-online-articles/the-recession-and-the-deserving-poor.
6. Ibid.
7. Anne Hull, "Squeaking By on $300,000," *Washington Post*, August 16, 2009, at http://www.washingtonpost.com/wp-dyn/content/article/2009/08/15/AR2009081502957.html.
8. Pew Research Center, "Covering the Great Recession," Project for Excellence in Journalism, October 5, 2009, at http://www.journalism.org/files/legacy/Covering%20the%20Great%20Recession.pdf.
9. Jodi Kantor, "Working Anything but 9–5," *New York Times*, August 13, 2014.

10. Jodi Kantor, "Starbucks to Revise Policies to End Irregular Schedules for Its 130,000 Baristas," *New York Times*, August 14, 2014.
11. Patrick Sharkey, "Neighborhoods and the Black-White Mobility Gap," Pew Charitable Trusts Economic Mobility Project, July 2009, at http://www.pewtrusts.org/~/media/legacy/uploadedfiles/wwwpewtrusts org/reports/economic_mobility/pewsharkeyv12pdf.pdf; John R. Logan, "Separate and Unequal: The Neighborhood Gap for Blacks, Hispanics and Asians in Metropolitan America," U.S. 2010 Project of the Russell Sage Foundation and Brown University, at http://www.s4.brown.edu/us2010/Data/Report/report0727.pdf; Robert D. Putnam, *Our Kids: The American Dream in Crisis* (New York: Simon & Schuster, 2015), pp. 38–42.
12. Lawrence Mishel, "The United States Leads in Low-Wage Work and the Lowest Wages for Low-Wage Workers," Economic Policy Institute, September, 4, 2014, at http://www.epi.org/blog/united-states-leads-wage-work-lowest-wages/.
13. Timothy Egan, "Good Poor, Bad Poor," *New York Times*, December 19, 2013.
14. Gabe Wildau, "O'Reilly: [I]rresponsible and Lazy . . . That's What Poverty Is," Media Matters for America, June 16, 2004, at http://mediamatters.org/research/2004/06/16/oreilly-irresponsible-and-lazy-thats-what-pover/131278.
15. Media Matters for America, "Bill O'Reilly Names the 'True Causes of Poverty': 'Poor Education, Addiction, Irresponsible Behavior, and Laziness,'" February 2, 2012, at http://mediamatters.org/video/2012/02/02/bill-oreilly-names-true-causes-of-poverty-poor/184685.
16. Katie Palvich, "Bill O'Reilly: True Poverty Is Being Driven by Personal Behavior," *Townhall*, January 10, 2014, at http://townhall.com/tipsheet/katiepavlich/2014/01/10/bill-oreilly-true-poverty-is-being-driven-by-personal-behavior-n1777105.
17. Matt Bruenig, "The Poverty Capitalism Creates," *Policy Shop Blog, Demos*, May 1, 2015, at http://www.demos.org/blog/5/1/15/poverty-capitalism-creates.
18. Daniel Patrick Moynihan, "The Negro Family: The Case for National Action," Office of Policy Planning and Research, United States Department of Labor, March 1965, at http://www.dol.gov/oasam/programs/history/webid-meynihan.htm.
19. Ta-Nehisi Coates, "Revisiting the Moynihan Report, cont.," *The Atlantic*, June 18, 2013.
20. David Brooks, "The Cost of Relativism," *New York Times*, March 10, 2015.
21. Bryce Covert and Josh Israel, "What 7 States Discovered After Spending More than $1 Million Drug-Testing Welfare Recipients," Center for American Progress Action Fund, February 26, 2015, at http://

thinkprogress.org/economy/2015/02/26/3624447/tanf-drug-testing-states/; Jason Stein, "Scott Walker's Light-on-Details Drug-Testing Plan a Hit on the Stump," *Milwaukee-Wisconsin Journal Sentinel*, March 17, 2015, at http://www.jsonline.com/news/statepolitics/scott-walkers-light-on-details-drug-testing-plan-a-hit-on-the-stump-b99461974z1-296580231.html.

22. Tamara Draut, "New Opportunities? Public Opinion on Poverty, Income Inequality and Public Policy: 1996–2002," Demos, 2002, at http://www.demos.org/sites/default/files/publications/New_Opportunities.pdf.
23. Covert and Israel, "What 7 States Discovered."
24. Adam Taylor, "Chart: The World's Most Generous Countries," *Washington Post*, November 19, 2014.
25. Eduardo Bonilla-Silva, *Racism Without Racists: Color-Blind Racism and the Persistence of Racial Inequality in America* (Lanham, Md.: Roman and Littlefield, 2006), p. 8.
26. John Powell, *Racing to Justice: Transforming Our Conceptions of Self and Other to Create an Inclusive Society* (Bloomington: Indiana University Press, 2012), pp. 14–15.
27. Ira Katznelson, *When Affirmative Action Was White: An Untold History of Racial Inequality in Twentieth-Century America* (New York: Norton, 2005), p. 115.
28. Arthur Levein and Jana Nidiffer, *Beating the Odds: How the Poor Get to College* (San Francisco: Jossey-Bass, 1996), p. 35.
29. Sylvia Allegretto and Steven Pitts, "The State of Black Workers Before the Great Recession," UC Berkeley Labor Center, University of California, Berkeley, 2010, at http://laborcenter.berkeley.edu/pdf/2010/blackworkers_prerecession10.pdf.
30. Patricia Cohen, "Public-Sector Jobs Vanish, Hitting Blacks Hard," *New York Times*, May 24, 2015.
31. Noam Scheiber, "Pension Cuts Exempt Police and Firefighters," *New York Times*, March 19, 2015; Alyssa Battistoni, "The Dirty Secret of Public-Sector Union Busting," *Salon*, February 24, 2011.
32. Alberto Alesina and Edward L. Glaeser, "Why Are Welfare States in the U.S. and Europe So Different?" *Horizons Stratégiques*, February 2006, at http://www.cairn.info/zen.php?ID_ARTICLE=HORI_002_0051.
33. Ibid.
34. Bonilla-Silva, *Racism Without Racists*, pp. 25–61.

Chapter Seven: The Sleeping Giant Stirs

1. Workers Defense Project, "Build a Better Texas: Construction Conditions in the Lone Star State," January 2013, at http://www.workersdefense.org/Build%20a%20Better%20Texas_FINAL.pdf.
2. Ibid.
3. "Throwback Thursday: Casa Latina Keeps Growing," *Casa Latina*,

May 15, 2015, at http://casa-latina.org/news/throwback-thursday-casa-latina-keeps-growing.

4. "The Rise of Work Centers and the Fight for a Fair Economy," United Workers Congress, Briefing Paper #1, April 2014, at http://www.unitedworkerscongress.org/uploads/2/4/6/6/24662736/__uwc_rise_of_worker_centers-_sm.pdf.
5. Ai-jen Poo, *The Age of Dignity: Preparing for the Elder Boom in a Changing America* (New York: New Press, 2015), p. 114.
6. National Domestic Workers Alliance, "Daniela's Story," at http://www.domesticworkers.org/daniela-s-story.
7. Steven Greenhouse and Jana Kasperkevic, "Fight for $15 Swells into Largest Protest by Low-Wage Workers in U.S. History," *Guardian*, April 15, 2015.
8. Ibid.
9. Elephrame, "At Least 1065 Black Lives Matter Demonstrations Have Been Held in the Past 464 Days," as of October 24, 2015, at https://elephrame.com/textbook/protests.
10. Michelle Chen, "Phillip Agnew, Dream Defender," *In These Times*, January 19, 2015.
11. Steven Greenhouse, "Volkswagen Vote Is Defeat for Labor in South," *New York Times*, February 14, 2014.
12. Ibid.; Dominic Rush, "United Auto Workers Union Drops Lost Vote Appeal at VW Tennessee Plant," *Guardian*, April 21, 2014.
13. Rush, "United Auto Workers Union Drops Lost Vote Appeal."
14. Greenhouse, "Volkswagen Vote Is Defeat."

Chapter Eight: A Better Deal

1. Emmanuel Saez and Gabriel Zucman, "Wealth Inequality in the United States Since 1913: Evidence from Capitalized Income Tax Data," Working Paper 20625, National Bureau of Economic Research, October 2014.

Index

About the Author

TAMARA DRAUT is the vice president of policy and research at Demos, a national think tank headquartered in New York City, and is the author of *Strapped: Why America's 20- and 30-Somethings Can't Get Ahead.* Draut's research and writing at Demos have garnered extensive media coverage, including several columns written by Bob Herbert in the *New York Times.* The author's research, including quotes by Draut, have appeared in the *Wall Street Journal, USA Today, Newsweek,* the *Chicago Sun-Times,* the *Baltimore Sun,* the *Des Moines Register, The Atlantic,* the *Christian Science Monitor,* and dozens of others. Draut is a regular commentator on working- and middle-class issues and has appeared on *The Colbert Report, The Today Show,* network evening news programs, and several programs on Fox, including *The O'Reilly Factor;* CNN, including *Your Money;* and MSNBC, including *UP* with Chris Hayes, *The Cycle,* and *The Melissa Harris-Perry Show.* She lives with her husband and daughter in Brooklyn, New York.